Stock Market in India

Working and Reforms

Stock Market in India

Working and Reforms

Saloni Gupta
Associate Professor,
Department of Commerce,
Bharati College, University of Delhi.

NEW NC CENTURY
New Century Publications
New Delhi, India

NEW CENTURY PUBLICATIONS
4800/24, Bharat Ram Road,
Ansari Road, Daryaganj,
New Delhi – 110 002 (India)

Tel.: 011-2324 7798, 4358 7398, 6539 6605
Fax: 011-4101 7798
E-mail: indiatax@vsnl.com • info@newcenturypublications.com
www.newcenturypublications.com

Editorial office:
LG–7, Aakarshan Bhawan,
4754-57/23, Ansari Road, Daryaganj,
New Delhi – 110 002

Tel.: 011-4356 0919

First Published: **July 2010**

ISBN: **978-81-7708-241-8**

Published by New Century Publications and printed at Salasar Imaging Systems, New Delhi.

Designs: Patch Creative Unit, New Delhi.

PRINTED IN INDIA

About the Book

A stock (or share) market deals mainly in corporate securities. The securities are chiefly in the form of equity shares and debentures. The function of the stock market is two-fold: (a) to arrange for the raising of new capital [primary market function] and (b) to provide liquidity to existing securities [secondary market function].

There are 24 recognised stock exchanges in India, including the Over the Counter Exchange of India (OTCEI) for small and new companies, the old established Bombay Stock Exchange (BSE) and the National Stock Exchange (NSE) that was set up as a model exchange to provide nation-wide services to investors. As at end-March 2010, 4977 companies were listed on the BSE, which is the largest exchange in the country. The number of securities available for trading under the equities segment at NSE as on April 30, 2010 was 1872.

Associated with the NSE are the National Securities Depository Ltd. (NSDL) and the National Securities Clearing Corporation Ltd. (NSCCL). The NSDL acts as a registrar for dematerialized securities and NSCCL as a clearing house.

This book provides a comprehensive account of the working of stock market in India, focusing on reforms introduced during the post-liberalisation (1991 onwards) period. Besides, it traces recent trends in the secondary market and offers empirical evidence of level of efficiency and degree of volatility in the Indian stock market.

Author's Profile

Dr. Saloni Gupta is presently Associate Professor in the Department of Commerce, Bharati College, University of Delhi. She completed her Post-graduation, M.Phil. and Ph.D. from Delhi School of Economics, University of Delhi. She has 20 years of teaching experience. Specialising in finance, she has published a number of research papers in national and international journals of repute, including *Decision* published from IIM, Calcutta.

Contents

Preface

A stock (or share) market deals mainly in corporate securities. The securities are chiefly in the form of equity shares and debentures. The purpose of these securities is to raise long-term funds for companies engaged in production. The function of the stock market is two-fold: (a) to arrange for the raising of new capital (primary market function) and (b) to provide liquidity to existing securities (secondary market function).

There are 24 recognised stock exchanges in India, including the Over the Counter Exchange of India (OTCEI) for small and new companies, the old established Bombay Stock Exchange (BSE) and the newer National Stock Exchange (NSE) that was set up as a model exchange to provide nation-wide services to investors.

As at end-March 2010, 4977 companies were listed on the BSE, which is the largest exchange in the country. The number of securities available for trading under the equities segment at NSE as on April 30, 2010 was 1872.

BSE—one of the oldest exchanges in the world—accounts for the largest number of listed companies and has also started a screen-based trading system with the introduction of the Bombay On-Line Trading system. NSE—which in the recent past has accounted for the largest trading volumes—has a fully automated screen-based system that operates in the wholesale debt market segment as well as the capital market segment.

Associated with the NSE are the National Securities Depository Ltd. (NSDL) and the National Securities Clearing Corporation Ltd (NSCCL). The NSDL acts as a registrar for what are now predominantly dematerialized securities and the NSCCL as a clearing house.

The setting up of the NSE as an electronic trading platform set a benchmark of operating efficiency for other stock exchanges in the country. The establishment of NSDL in 1996 and Central Depository Services (India) Ltd. (CSDL) in 1999 has enabled paperless trading in the exchanges. This has also facilitated instantaneous electronic transfer of securities and eliminated the risks to the investors arising from bad deliveries in the market, delays in share transfer, fake and forged shares and loss of scrips. The electronic fund transfer (EFT) facility combined with dematerialisation of shares has created a conducive environment for reducing the settlement cycle in stock markets.

Stock exchanges all over the world have been traditionally formed as *mutual* organisations. The trading members not only provide broking services, but also own, control and manage such exchanges for their mutual benefit. In India, NSE was set up as a demutualised corporate body, where ownership, management and trading rights are in the hands of three different sets of groups from its inception. The Stock Exchange, Mumbai—one of the two premier exchanges in the country—has since been corporatised and demutualised and renamed as the Bombay Stock Exchange Ltd (BSE).

Corporate governance has emerged as an important tool for protection of shareholders. The corporate governance framework in India has evolved over a period of time since the setting up of the Kumar Mangalam Birla Committee by SEBI. India has a reasonably well-designed regulatory framework for the issuance and trading of securities, and disclosures by the issuers with strong focus on corporate governance standards.

To enhance the level of continuous disclosure by the listed companies, SEBI amended the listing agreement to incorporate segment reporting, related party disclosures, consolidated financial results and consolidated financial statements. The listing agreement between the stock exchanges and the companies has been strengthened from time to time to enhance corporate governance standards.

I take this opportunity to place on record my deep sense of gratitude to Professor A.K. Seth of the Department of Commerce, Delhi School of Economics, University of Delhi for his constant support and guidance. Thanks are also due to

Professor T.P. Madhusoodanan of the Institute for Financial Management and Research, Chennai, Professor S.K. Jain, Head of the Department of Commerce, University of Delhi and Mrs. Pramodini Verma, Principal, Bharati College, University of Delhi for their co-operation and moral support to complete this work.

My husband Rajesh—critic and friend—and our sons Rijul and Shrey stood me in good stead at every stage of the completion of this tedious work. Many thanks to them!

New Delhi
May 12, 2010

Saloni Gupta

List of Abbreviations

ADF	Augmented Dickey-Fuller (Test)
ARCH	Auto-Regressive Conditional Heteroscedasticity
ARMA	Auto-Regressive Moving Average
BL	Box Ljung (Statistic)
BSE	Bombay Stock Exchange
CAPM	Capital Asset Pricing Model
CRSP	Centre for Research in Security Prices
DJIA	Dow Jones Industrial Average
EMH	Efficient Market Hypothesis
FIIs	Foreign Institutional Investors
GARCH	Generalised Auto-Regressive Conditional Heteroscedasticity
IID	Independent Identical Distribution
Nifty	National Index of Fifty Shares (of the NSE)
NSE	National Stock Exchange
NYSE	New York Stock Exchange
PP	Phillip-Perron (Test)
RWH	Random Walk Hypothesis
S&P 500	Standard and Poor's Index of 500 Stocks
Sensex	Sensitive Index of Thirty Shares (of the BSE)
VR	Variances Ratio

1

Stock Market: Theoretical Framework

1.1 Efficient Stock Market

Structurally, the stock market consists of the stock exchanges, listed companies and stockholders; its function is to facilitate share trading. Intrinsically, the stock market creates channels to connect different market participants. Through these channels, the stock market performs the critical role of capital resource allocator. Observing the practices of stock markets, we find that sometimes, the stock markets allocate capital resources inefficiently and in such situation, the rate of expansion of the economy suffers. An allocationally efficient stock market should allocate capital resources into the most productive sectors as soon as possible. Allocation efficiency of a stock market should consist of both internal efficiency and external efficiency, in other words, operational efficiency and informational efficiency.

A stock market is said to be operationally efficient when it possess liquidity, orderliness and sound organisation (Juttner 1990). The liquidity of a stock market refers to the fact that the stocks can be bought and sold in a short span of time, and at representative market prices. Informational efficiency requires that stock prices reflect all available information at all times (Fama 1970), which includes historical information, public information and private information. It is only when the stock prices reflect this information, that they can provide correct signals for efficient capital allocation. On the contrary, if there does exist a monopoly or slow embedding of information in the market, someone would exploit this inefficiency to reap abnormally high returns. In this case, the stock prices may be distorted and provide an inappropriate signal for capital allocation.

Operational, informational and allocational efficiency are inherently related to each other. An operationally inefficient stock market may inhibit the spread of information, which would undoubtedly block capital movements into the most productive channels. Empirical studies, particularly statistical tests on the efficiency of stock markets, are usually undertaken to study the informational efficiency. Such statistical tests have been widely applied in the body of literature known as Efficient Market Theory. This is so because the data of stock prices and benchmark index values is readily available and is suitable for the tests of informational efficiency of stock markets. Highly organized and elaborate information dissemination machinery facilitates an enquiry into the behaviour of the market in response to arrival of information affecting share prices. The findings and conclusions pertaining to informational efficiency can then throw reasonable light on the state of operational efficiency and allocational efficiency. For this reason, test of market efficiency in its informational connotation is the centrepiece of financial studies.

1.2 Efficient Market Hypothesis (EMH)

The expected price of a security at the end of one period from today, given today's set of information, is equal to today's price compounded at some desired return commensurate with the risk level of the security. This might alternatively be stated as "today's price is the best estimate of tomorrow's price, after present-valuing tomorrow's price at the appropriate rate of return." Or to express it by the means of a mathematical equation and a diagram, if all the current information is labelled as ϕ_t and E (R_{t+1}) is the expected return to compensate for risk during one time period, the efficient market might be thought of as:

Next Expected Price with our Information = Current Price +Return for Risk

$$E[P_{t+1} / \phi_t] = P_t [1 + E(R_{t+1} / \phi_t)]$$

1.3 Information Sets and Classification of Market Efficiency

The efficiency of the market depends on the information available in the market. Roberts (1967) initially distinguished three levels of market efficiency by considering three sets of information reflected in the prices. Later, Fama (1970) reconstructed the framework by creating the famous Efficient Market Hypothesis (EMH). Firstly: weak form efficiency, which implies that the information contained in the past prices of stocks is fully reflected in the current prices of stocks. Secondly: semi-strong form efficiency, which implies that all publicly available information is fully reflected in the current prices of stocks. Thirdly: strong form efficiency, which implies that all information, including historical, public and private information, is fully reflected in the current market prices of stocks. The information of each successive set is nested in prices cumulatively. Thus, the second set of information includes all the historical information and all the current public available information. The third set of information includes all the historical information, all the current public information and all privately held information. Thus, if the market is semi-strong form efficient, it is also likely to be weak form efficient. Furthermore, if the market is strong form efficient, it is also likely to be weak form efficient and semi-strong form efficient. The graphical association of the three sets of information and three classifications of market efficiency are illustrated in Figure 1.1.

From the trace of market efficient curve (ME), it can be seen that a market is a weak form efficient market only when all historical information is available in the market. When all historical and current public information is available in the market, the efficiency of the market crosses into the second level, viz. semi-strong form efficiency. The third level, i.e., the strong form efficient market occurs when all the information such as historical, current public and private information, are available in the market. Conversely, if a market is not weak form efficient, it is likely to be neither semi-strong form nor strong form efficient, due to the relevant set of information not being fully available to the market.

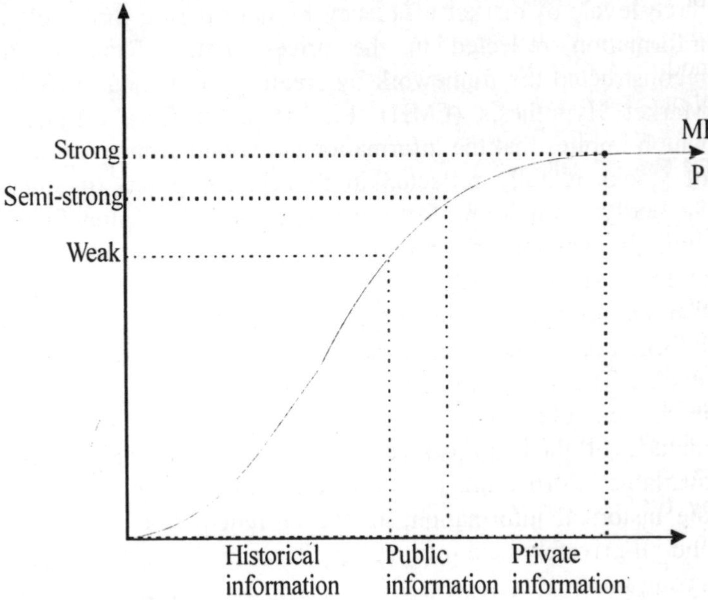

Figure 1.1 The Classifications of Market Efficiency in EMH

Such a hypothesis assumes that these are:

- A large number of rational, profit maximizing investors in competition with each other, to predict stock prices.
- An availability of the all-important current information to almost all investors at an almost free price.

Although the first tests of market efficiency were reported as long ago as 1900, the classification of efficiency into three levels did not emerge until 1959 since it was not until the fifties that research in the area systematically developed. Earlier classifications of efficient market literature tended to be dominated by the names of the models that were used to describe share price behaviour and formulated to endow the concept of market efficiency with testable implications.

The most general of these models was the 'fair game' model that expresses efficiency in terms of the opportunities for speculators to earn excess returns. The 'submartingale' and 'random walk' models were two special cases of the fair game model, and are more specifically concerned with the sequence of price changes over time.

1.4 Fair Game Model

The definition statement that in an efficient market price "fully reflect" available information is so general that it has no empirically testable implications. To make the statement testable, the process of price formation must be specified in terms of some model. Therefore, there is a need to define more exactly what is meant by the term "fully reflect". The fair game model is based on the assumptions that: (a) the conditions of market equilibrium can be stated in terms of expected returns, and (b) the information set Φ_t is fully utilized by the market in forming equilibrium expected returns and thus current prices. Symbolically, the fair game model states:

$$x_{j,t+1} = p_{j,t+1} - E(p_{j,t+1}/ \Phi_t)$$

where, $x_{j,t+1}$ is the excess market value of security j at time t+1 i.e. it is the difference between the observed price and the expected value of the price that was projected on the basis of information Φ_t. and

$$E\ (\tilde{x}_{j,t+1}/ \Phi_t) = 0$$

(as per the definition of fair game model, the expected excess market value is zero).

Similarly,

$$Z_{j,t+1} = r_{j,t+1} - E(\tilde{r}_{j,t+1}/ \Phi_t) \text{ and } E\ (\tilde{Z}_{j,t+1}/ \Phi_t) = 0$$

where, $\tilde{Z}_{j,t+1}$ is the return at t+1 in excess of the equilibrium expected return. The fair game model asserts that the expected excess returns, given the information set Φ_t are zero. This implies that the information occurring randomly is incorporated in the prices immediately and that the past price trends cannot be used to make future forecasts i.e. the future price movements are random and cannot be predicted. The role of "fair game" models in the theory of efficient markets was first recognized and studied rigorously by Samuelson (1965) and Mandelbrot (1966).

1.5 Submartingale and Martingale Models

When a sequence of prices is such that the expected value of the price in one period is equal to or greater than the price in the previous period, it is said to follow a stochastic process known as a submartingale. In such a process, the expected value of future price changes is independent of past price changes. Symbolically, the sequence of prices follow the submartingale process when,

$$E(\tilde{p}_{j,t+1}/\Phi_t) \geq p_{j,t} \text{ or } E(\tilde{r}_{j,t+1}/\Phi_t) \geq 0.$$

where, the $\tilde{p}_{j,t+1}$ and $\tilde{r}_{j,t+1}$ are random price and return variables of security j at time t+1. On the other hand, when the expected returns and price changes are zero, the price sequence follows a martingale process. The relationship that is stated above implies that expected returns conditional on Φ_t are non-negative and therefore, the trading rules based only on the information in Φ_t cannot have greater expected profits than a policy of always buying-and-holding the securities during the future period in question. Tests of such rules are an important part of the empirical evidence on the efficient markets model.

The effect of these joint conditions—efficient markets and random adjustments to information—suggests that successive price changes

- will not be systematically related to past price movements or other past information, and
- will occur in a random pattern around some intrinsic value based on economic fundamentals.

Accordingly, many researchers have suggested the hypothesis that stock prices behave similar to a 'random walk' —a series in which successive values are independent of previous values. In regard to stock prices, the *random walk hypothesis* says that stock price changes "have no memories", or stated differently, that the past history of stock prices cannot be used in any meaningful way to predict future prices.

1.6 Random Walk Model

In the early treatments of the efficient markets model, the statement that the current price of a security "fully reflects" available information was assumed to imply that successive price changes (or more usually, successive one-period returns) are independent. In addition, it was usually assumed that successive changes (or returns) are identically distributed. Together the two hypotheses constitute the random walk model. Formally, the model says

$$f(r_{j,t+1} / \Phi_t) = f(r_{j,t+1})$$

which is the usual statement that the conditional and marginal probability distributions of an independent random variable are identical. In addition, the density function f must be the same for all t.

The stock market is a complex mechanism and therefore it may be naïve to represent it by a pure random walk process. The question is: How much dependence or independence is there between past and future events? Though successive price changes may not be strictly independent, the actual amount of dependence may be so small that profitable trading rules cannot be formulated. Certainly, the dependence would have to be great enough to allow a profit in excess of the transactions cost (commissions, transfer taxes, etc.) associated with buying and selling. Certainly, while the market might not be a perfectly efficient capital market, it might be an economically efficient capital market – that is, the dependence might not be large enough to allow abnormal profits after all transactions costs. Also, even if dependence exists, it is necessary to show that this will help predict future prices, that is, that the dependence will occur in the future at a specified time. However, if our stock markets are relatively efficient, it appears doubtful that such predictive patterns wouldn't be fully reflected already in the current price.

Of course, the mere statement that stock price movements may approximate a random walk would hardly be convincing without some empirical testing. As would be detailed in chapter-3, various researchers have conducted two main types of empirical research from time to time in order to test the RWH:

- Study of stock price patterns and cycles.
- Tests of technical trading rules.

The goal of the first type of research has been to determine if stock price movements are independent over time and how the price changes are distributed. Accordingly, stock price changes have been studied over a number of time periods (daily, weekly, monthly, and seasonally). Also, the changes have been related to the effect of volume, new listings, new issues, and so forth. The goal of the second type of research has been to test whether either mechanical or technical trading rules could be used to produce a significantly better profit than a simple buy-and-hold strategy. Rules for filters (buy when the price rises x percent; sell when it falls x percent), moving averages, relative strength and insider trading have also been tested.

1.7 Is Informational Efficiency Possible?

Efficiency refers to two aspects of adjustment of share price to new information, the speed and quality (direction and magnitude) of the adjustment. Sometimes it is suggested that the efficient market researchers refer only to the speed aspect. This is quite incorrect. It would be clearly an odd interpretation of efficiency if a doubling of the price of a share were regarded as an efficient reaction to new information, simply because the movement was instantaneous, if the information in fact warranted a substantial reduction in the price. Both aspects of the price reaction are equally important. The main effect of efficiency should be that it precludes most, if not all, investors from being able to systematically outperform the market.

The market, as we know it in practice, does not have a reputation of being an efficient and reliable price-setter, and that it frequently, and sometimes significantly, misinterprets the economic signals it receives. The investment process, therefore, is popularly represented as consisting of the discovery and purchase of securities which are undervalued and of holding these until they cease to be 'good value'. Successful identification of mis-priced securities is generally assumed to be possible by personal study of relevant available information, or by seeking out expert advice from various sources.

It has been well documented that the investment strategies appropriate for an efficient market would be significantly different from the strategies appropriate for an inefficient market. Can the market be beaten or is the conventional investor in search of mis-priced securities largely a victim of self-deception? The answer to this question can facilitate informed decision making, as evidence on either side can lead to a framework of practical guidelines, not only for investors, but also for investment advisers, corporate managers, market regulators etc. Though various kinds of investment intermediaries make all possible efforts to persuade investors that their performance is superior to that of others, and that it is a simple matter to beat the averages; but as a matter of fact the proportion of 'smart people' who try this and fail is surprisingly large. Ben Graham (the father of security analysis) understood the risk inherent in above-average return, as well as the fact that most people don't "beat the averages."

Thus, it can be said that the market's reputation as a price-setter is derived from two main sources

- The 'official' body of research literature, which by and large applies rigorous statistical research methodology.
- The 'unofficial' word of mouth impressions and personal experiences that pass from one investor or market practitioner to another.

If the unofficial or conventional view held by practitioners implies that the market is inefficient, a variety of analysis may become fruitful. In this context, the *chartist* seeks to predict future movements by seeking to interpret past patterns on the assumption that 'history tends to repeat itself'. The *fundamental* analyst studies corporate financial reports and other relevant available information to try to gain an insight into the 'real worth' of shares in the hope of identifying those that the market has mis-priced. The *inside/expert dealer* seeks to acquire/process information not yet publicly available for the purposes of exploiting it before it is transmitted to the market.

The conventional view, therefore, may be described as the Inefficient Market Hypothesis, since it is obvious that, if it is to be worthwhile for investors to engage in any of the above activities, one must assume that the market is, in fact, inefficient. The implication of efficiency, on the other hand, is that share prices always reflect their intrinsic worth and can be taken at their face value.

It is generally accepted that a very high proportion of those who accept the general substance of EMH are academicians/researchers and a very high proportion of those who accept the general substance of EMH are market participants/practitioners. It is also more or less agreed that the stock market is more likely than other markets (like markets for property, art or antiques etc) to be efficient in generating prices that fully reflect the worth of the assets being traded because of homogeneity of the product, its independence from investors' tastes, its location independence and the market's extensive information support. It is for these reasons that researchers have been continuously testing the efficiency of the stock markets the world over, despite conclusive findings eluding them.

1.8 Empirical Evolution of Testing

How well do past returns predict future returns? How quickly do security prices adjust to and reflect public information announcements? And do any investors have private, 'beat the market' information that is not fully reflected in security prices? These are the questions that have been the subject matter of lot of empirical research works in the interesting and ever-growing field of market efficiency.

Bachelier (1900) worked on asset pricing and developed many mathematical properties of Brownian motion and martingales, which were the earlier mathematical expression of market efficiency. In most of the pre-1970 literature, the common equilibrium pricing model in tests of stock market efficiency was the hypothesis that 'expected returns are constant through time'. Market efficiency then implied that 'returns are unpredictable from past returns or other past variables, as prices follow a random walk'.

Kendall (1953), Roberts (1959), Granger and Morgenstern (1963), Samuelson (1965) and Mandelbrot (1966) found support for the random walk hypothesis.

Alexander (1961) developed the filter rule methodology and initially found that stock price changes were dependent and allowed abnormal profits to be made, but in a later paper, with the correction for bias he concluded that the filters only rarely compared favourably with buy-and-hold and supported the independence assumption of the random walk model.

Fama (1965) observed that any dependence that might exist in stock price series was not strong enough to be capable of being used to increase the expected profits of the trader. Despite finding some strength in the argument that the distribution of price changes in a speculative series deviates from the normal distribution, Fama's study presented strong and voluminous evidence in favour of efficient market hypothesis.

Many other studies, broadly similar to Fama's, that examined the short horizon returns, like Fisher (1966), Lo and MacKinlay (1988), and Conrad and Kaul (1988) found suggestive evidence that daily, weekly, and monthly returns are predictable from past returns. However, at least for individual securities, the variations in expected returns were not substantial enough to significantly dent the efficiency hypothesis.

Shiller (1984) and Summers (1986) created a momentum for a debate on the reliability of the 'close to zero(0) autocorrelations of short horizon returns' which were the basic evidence in favour of efficiency till then. They argued that the tests missed the inefficiency and gave spurious and unreliable conclusions in favour of efficiency. Lot of studies then gave both sides of evidence on this issue.

De Bondt and Thaler (1985), Poterba and Summers (1988), Jagadeesh and Titman (1993), T.P. Madhusoodanan (1995,1998), and many others gave psychological descriptions of irrational bubbles, over and under reaction, contrarian strategies, return reversal v/s return persistence, and mean reversion possibilities-which would go against, or at least dilute the efficiency hypothesis.

Many others; like R.W. Banz (1981), Reinganum (1981), Keim (1982), Ariel (1987), Keim and Stambaugh (1984) etc pointed out the empirically observed anomalies like size effect, seasonal effects, return volatility, dividend payout anomaly, price earning anomaly etc; which are left unexplained by the assumption of efficiency.

At the same time Fama and French (1988b), Barberis, Shleifer and Vishny (1996), Daniel, Hirshleifer and Subrahmanyam (1997) and many others argued that Market Efficiency has, by and large, survived the challenge from the literature on experimental psychology and long-term return anomalies. They argue that these anomalies can be explained within the broader framework of efficiency; with some fine-tunings in the models and the data.

In one of the first significant studies conducted in India O.P. Gupta (1985) used runs test and serial correlation test to find support for the independence assumption of the random walk model.

J.C. Sharma (2002) rejected the assumption of normality in both the pre and post liberalisation return series in the Indian Stock Markets. His study also revealed a very strong predictive power of negative autocorrelations for future return, as indicated by the mean reverting tendencies, particularly for the pre liberalisation period.

Event studies have produced useful evidence on how stock prices respond to information contained in an event relating to a particular scrip. Many studies focused on returns in a short window (a few days) around a clearly dated event.

Event studies are the cleanest evidence we have on efficiency and Keith B. Johnson (1966); Fama, Fisher, Jensen and Roll (FFJR 1969); Jinho Byun and Michael Rozeff (2003) have demonstrated ample evidence in support i.e., quick adjustment, consistent with efficiency is noted by them; using largely the stock split announcement events.

Asquith and Mullins (1983, 1986), Masulis and Korwar (1986), Dodd (1980), Asquith (1983) etc have given event study evidence on efficiency by studying a variety of events like earnings announcements, fresh offerings of equities, corporate actions like mergers etc.

However, some studies like the ones by S. Basu (1977), Aswath Damodaran (1993), Chowdhury, Sadique and Akhter (2002) found slow/lagged or incomplete adjustment for information becoming available, thus indicating inefficiency in the market. On the strong form of efficiency, the utility of private or special information possessed by certain individuals has been examined.

Michael C. Jansen (1968) found that mutual funds were on average not able to predict security prices well enough to outperform a buy-and-hold policy, and that there was very little evidence that any individual fund was able to do significantly better than what could be expected from mere random chance.

Jaffrey F. Jaffe (1974) and M.M. Goyal (1992) found that recommendations and special information of even a good investment magazine failed to decisively beat the market.

However, Joseph E. Finnerty (1976) found that insiders, probably because of their access to privileged information, can outperform the market in their stock selections. This finding tended to refute the strong form of the EMH.

Similar conclusions were given by Dan Givoly and Dan Palmon (1985) and N.S. Malik (2006). However, the more sensible version of the efficiency hypothesis would say that, since cost of information is an important factor, prices reflect information to a point where the marginal benefits of acting on the information (i.e. the profits to be made) do not exceed the marginal costs.

Thus, it is seen from a review of literature that the market efficiency issue is yet to be definitely settled. There are ever-growing dimensions of further research in this field and more coherent explanations need to be developed about various aspects of share price behaviour and return predictability. Continued testing is imperative before definite conclusions can be drawn on either side of efficiency. The present study is also an attempt in this direction. The perennially significant and interesting question of whether or not the major stock markets are 'efficient' in pricing the securities that are traded there is going to be examined for the Indian Stock Market, taking a variety of data series and using a comprehensive gamut of testing tools, as elaborated in the following sections.

1.9 Database of the Present Study

The study uses the market index data as well as the individual share price data. To facilitate the comparison of pre-liberalization and post-liberalization period, the data covers a fairly long period of time. The dates of observations, however, vary from series to series according to the data availability.

As a proxy for the market portfolio, the study uses the BSE-Sensex and NSE-S&P CNX Nifty price indices. Studying market indices is very important because a market index acts as a barometer of any stock market. The BSE Sensex is a scientifically designed index, based on globally accepted construction and review methodology. First compiled in 1986, Sensex is a basket of 30 constituent stocks representing a sample of large, liquid and representative companies. The base year of Sensex is 1978-79 and the base value is 100. As the oldest index in the country, it provides the time series data over a fairly long period of time (From 1980 onwards). The index initially used to be computed based on the "*Full Market Capitalization*" methodology, but was shifted to the Free-Float Methodology with effect from September 1, 2003. The *Free-Float Market Capitalization*" methodology of index construction is regarded as an industry best practice globally.

The Sensex price data under study consists of daily market-close prices, weekly market- close prices (i.e. week-end) and monthly market-close prices (i.e. last Friday of the month) from January 1, 1980 to October 20, 2005. The relevant data is collected from the different issues of The Stock Exchange Review, Bombay Stock Exchange, Mumbai and from the web site of BSE (www.bseindia.com). However, weekly data is self-developed with the help of daily data, as it was not available in any of these sources. Further the data is divided into two sub-periods viz. Sub-period I (1980-1990) and Sub-period II (1991-2005). All the tests are conducted for these two Sub-periods as well as on the full sample period to observe as to whether Indian stock market confirms to the belief that it has become more efficient in the post-liberalization period. The rational for using 1991 as the cut off year was that starting this year major policy initiatives were taken by the Government of India towards economic liberalization.

The second index used in the study is S&P CNX Nifty. It is one of the most scientific constructed indices in India. It comprises of 50 blue chip, large cap, liquid and highly traded stocks representing over 23 sectors of the economy. S&P stands for Standard & Poor, an investment advisory service that maintains one of the most widely followed benchmarks of stock market performance, the S&P 500 index. The CNX stands for CRISIL National Stock Exchange Index, after the two companies that came together to form the index. Again Daily, Weekly and Monthly closing values are taken for the period from July 5, 1990 to October 7, 2005. The data is available on the web site of NSE (www.nseindia.com). However, these series are not divided into any sub-periods and only full sample period is studied.

Besides the index data, the individual share data is also employed in the study. All the fifty-seven individual scripts that have been chosen for the study have remained the part of BSE-SENSEX for three years or more. The composition of BSE-SENSEX keeps on changing and therefore, over the long period covered under the study many companies kept moving in-and-out of the Sensex. Therefore, to have a balanced representation of different industries over the entire period of the study, and to study the most significant individual scrips, this criterion of three years' inclusion in the Sensex is adopted for selecting the scrips. Thus, most of the scripts are from 'A' group.

The list of the companies and the period for which the data is analysed is given in Table 1.1. For individual shares also, daily, weekly and monthly closing prices are considered and all the tests are conducted for two sub-periods (wherever data permits) as well as on the full sample periods. Moreover, we have ignored the days with no trading and have used return data only for the trading days. There are two reasons for doing that. Firstly, non-trading is not a common feature for the scrips we have selected as they all are actively traded scrips. Secondly, revisions of expectations, which take place during non-trading days, automatically get reflected in the opening price of the next trading day.

Data relating to the individual scrips could not be found before 1988 and for some of the scrips the data was not available even from 1988. For scrips whose data is available since January 1988 the period of study has been divided into two sub periods, i.e. Sub period I (up to December 1990) and Sub Period II (January 1991 till the end).

As it is well known, share prices change abruptly when a company splits its existing shares or issues bonus shares or right shares.

Table 1.1: List of Companies and the Study Periods

S. No.	Company name	Data analysis period
1.	A.C.C	04/01/88 to 17/02/06
2.	Asian Cable	01/01/90 to 28/11/97
3.	Bajaj Auto	04/01/88 to 17/02/06
4.	Balarpur Industries	01/01/90 to 17/02/06
5.	Bharti Tele	18/02/02 to 17/02/06
6.	BHEL	12/10/92 to 17/02/06
7.	Bombay Burmah	01/01/90 to 17/02/06
8.	Bombay Dyeing	04/01/88 to 17/02/06
9.	Castrol	04/01/88 to 17/02/06
10.	Ceat Ltd	04/01/88 to 17/02/06
11.	Century Textiles	04/01/88 to 17/02/06
12.	Cipla Ltd	01/01/90 to 17/02/06
13.	Colgate Palmolive (India)	09/01/88 to 17/02/06
14.	Crompton Greaves	02/01/90 to 17/02/06
15.	Cummins (India)	04/01/88 to 17/02/06
16.	G.E.Shipping	04/01/88 to 17/02/06
17.	Glaxo Smithkline	04/01/88 to 17/02/06
18.	Grasim Industries	09/01/88 to 17/02/06
19.	Gujarat State Fertilisers	04/01/88 to 17/02/06
20.	Gujarat Ambuja Cement	04/01/88 to 17/02/06
21.	HDFC	02/01/90 to 17/02/06
22.	Hero Honda	04/01/88 to 17/02/06
23.	Hindalco	04/01/88 to 17/02/06
24.	Hindustan Motors	04/01/88 to 17/02/06
25.	Hindustan Lever	04/01/88 to 17/02/06
26.	Hindustan Petroleum	11/09/92 to 17/02/06
27.	ICICI Bank	24/09/97 to 17/02/06
28.	ICICI Ltd	03/01/90 to 30/05/02
29.	IDBI Ltd	20/09/95 to 17/02/06
30.	Indian Hotel	04/01/88 to 17/02/06
31.	Infosys Technologies	14/06/93 to 17/02/06
32.	IPCL	20/11/92 to 17/02/06
33.	ITC Ltd	04/01/88 to 17/02/06
34.	Larsen & Toubro	04/01/88 to 17/02/06

Contd...

35.	Mahindra & Mahindra	04/01/88 to 17/02/06
36.	Mukand Ltd	04/01/88 to 17/02/06
37.	Nestle (India)	04/01/88 to 17/02/06
38.	NIIT Ltd	24/05/93 to 17/02/06
39.	Novartis	04/01/88 to 17/02/06
40.	ONGC Corporation	01/08/95 to 17/02/06
41.	Philips (India)	04/01/88 to 29/08/03
42	Premier Auto	04/01/88 to 17/02/06
43.	Ranbaxy Lab	04/01/88 to 17/02/06
44.	Dr. Reddy's Lab	01/01/90 to 17/02/06
45.	Reliance Industries Ltd	04/01/88 to 17/02/06
46.	Reliance Energy	01/01/90 to 17/02/06
47.	Steel Authority of India Ltd	01/10/92 to 17/02/06
48.	Satyam Comuters	26/11/92 to 17/02/06
49.	State Bank	04/03/94 to 17/02/06
50.	Siemens Ltd	04/01/88 to 17/02/06
51.	Tata Chemicals	04/01/88 to 17/02/06
52.	Tata Motors	04/01/88 to 17/02/06
53.	Tata Power	04/01/88 to 17/02/06
54.	Voltas Ltd	04/01/88 to 17/02/06
55.	Wipro	25/01/91 to 17/02/06
56.	Zee Tele	25/11/93 to 17/02/06
57.	Zenith Birla	04/01/88 to 17/02/06

Therefore the individual share prices have been adjusted for stock splits, right issues and bonus issues, wherever applicable, to make them comparable and to be able to draw meaningful conclusions.

In short, the study uses the following data sets to evaluate RWH:

1. Daily pre-liberalisation, daily post-liberalisation, daily overall period, weekly pre-liberalisation, weekly post liberalisation, weekly overall period, monthly pre liberalisation, monthly post liberalisation, monthly overall period data-sets of BSE-SENSEX (for the period 1.1.1980 to 20.10.2005, i.e., nearly 25 years' BSE data of closing index values).
2. Daily, weekly, monthly data-sets for NSE-S&P CNX Nifty

(for the period 5.7.1990 to 7.10.2005, i.e., nearly 15 years' NSE data of closing index values).

3. Daily pre liberalisation, daily post liberalisation, daily overall period, weekly pre liberalisation, weekly post liberalisation, weekly overall period, monthly pre liberalisation, monthly post liberalisation, monthly overall period data-sets of 57 individual scrips that have been part of the BSE Sensex (the period of study varies, according to the availability of data for each individual scrip).

On all these datasets a comprehensive gamut of testing tools, as enumerated and elaborated below, has been applied in order to facilitate the assimilation of the true and complete picture of the behaviour of the market.

1.10 Methodological Issues

Over the decades various techniques have been used for the transformation of the data and for judging the statistical properties of the data series. Box-Cox transformation, Natural logarithm transformation are commonly used transformation techniques whereas ARMA, ADF, ARCH, Jarque-Bera test, chi-square test are applied for observing the characteristics of the data series under study.

Under the study each price series (index as well as individual) is transformed into its natural logarithm price series. In view of the inherent heteroscedasticity of price changes it is considered advisable to transform it into log price changes. Log transformation is likely to render the price changes to be homoscedastic and thereby make the series stationary. To smooth the price changes this transformation is done as it depicts the rate of change rather than actual change. The first differences of log prices are referred log returns that are used throughout the study. The simple return is frequently found in the literature before 1980, and the log return has been popularly employed in the literature after 1980. The logarithmic return will be applied in all the empirical tests in this study. Unless otherwise specified, the returns used from now are logarithmic returns.

The return (r) is measured as:

$r_t = \log_e (p_t / p_{t-1})$, t = 1,2-----,n

$r_t = \log_e (p_t) - \log_e (p_{t-1})$

where r_t is the rate of return for the period t, and p_{t-1} and p_t are the prices for two successive periods t-1 and t and $\log_e$ is the natural logarithm to the base e.

Given the fact that the presence of a stochastic trend or deterministic trend in a financial time series or its non-stationarity or stationarity in levels is a prerequisite for conducting any tests of random walk hypothesis or efficient market hypothesis, the study begins with testing of stock market return series for a unit root using Augmented Dickey Fuller (ADF) (1979) and Phillips–Perron (PP)(1989) tests. The tests are applied on BSE-index return and NSE- index return at the significance level of 5 percent. A stationary time series is one for which: the mean and variance are constant over time; they depend only on the distance or lag between the two time periods, and not on the actual time at which they are computed. However, the prices of stocks are generally non-stationary and log stock prices are stationary. The absence of a unit root in the series confirms stationarity or a deterministic trend. On the contrary, the presence of a unit root indicates that the given series has become unstable or non-stationary; showing an uneven growth. Thus, Table 1.2 shows the results of these tests:

We see that the hypothesis of a unit root is rejected by both the tests at the 5 percent level, indicating both the series are stationary (i.e. a deterministic trend). It appears that there exists strong component of non-randomness in our index return of BSE-Sensex and NSE-Nifty. Moreover, the non-random component is stronger in Sub-period II that representing the post-liberalisation period.

The existence of deterministic or non-random component is a necessary but not a sufficient condition for stock market to be inefficient because it does not necessarily imply that stock returns are predictable. Therefore, some more powerful tests are conducted in the study.

Table 1.2: Unit Root Tests Applied on Return of Two Market Indices

BSE-Sensex	ADF	PP
Daily Returns		
Sub-Period I	-32.9792	-42.6589
Sub-Period II	-40.8329	-53.6748
Overall Period	-52.5224	-68.5924
Weekly Returns		
Sub-Period I	-14.5778	-23.4042
Sub-Period II	-18.4571	-25.3576
Overall Period	-23.7145	-34.6775
Monthly Returns		
Sub-Period I	-8.4569	-10.4532
Sub-Period II	-8.2416	-12.0665
Overall Period	-11.6759	-15.8765
NSE-Nifty		
Daily Returns	-42.3362	-53.5280
Weekly Returns	-18.4711	-25.2450
Monthly Returns	-8.8775	-11.8911

Note: This table reports unit-root tests for daily, weekly and monthly returns series constructed from BSE-Sensex and NSE-Nifty index. The 5 percent critical values for ADF & PP is –2.86 percent when intercept is included in the regression

Stock price behaviour following a random walk is the area of concern of the weak form market efficiency. To test the RWH Runs tests, Serial correlation, Filter Rule and its variations, Spectral analysis, Variance ratio are some of the most commonly used tests. It is beneficial to compare this study with previous similar studies on different markets; therefore the serial correlation coefficient test, the runs test and the variance ratio test are employed here. All these tests are tests of weak form of market efficiency, therefore, deal with historical data with respect to past price information.

Professor Eugene F. Fama of the University of Chicago did one of the first comprehensive studies into the dependence, or independence, property of stock prices. As an initial examination of dependence, the linear relationship of one price change (let's call it $\pm P_t$) to the next price change (say $\pm P_{t+1}$) was investigated. It was hypothesized that if a relationship did exist, there would be a statistically significant correlation coefficient indicating this relationship. Since this correlation coefficient indicates the relationship between two successive events within the same time series, it is called a serial correlation coefficient. If the relationship exists, the coefficient would be near either +1 or -1; if no strong relationship is evident, the coefficient would be near to 0.

The model of the serial correlation coefficient is

$$\rho(k) = \frac{Cov(r_t, r_{t-k})}{\sqrt{Var(r_t)}\sqrt{Var(r_{t-k})}}$$

$$= \frac{Cov[r_t, r_{t-k}]}{Var[r_t]}$$

where ρ (k) is the serial correlation coefficient of the time series r_t, with r_t being the return of an index or an individual stock at time t; k is the lag of the period. In the present research the lags are selected as one through ten. The standard deviation of ρ (k), given a large sample, can be estimated as:

$$\sigma(\hat{\rho}(k)) = \sqrt{\frac{1}{n-k}}$$

where n is the number of observations. But when k is relatively small compared to the sample size n, the standard normal statistics x can be written as:

$$x = \hat{\rho}(k)\frac{n}{\sqrt{n-k}}$$

H_O: ρ (k) = 0, the null hypothesis states that the serial correlation coefficient, ρ (k), is not significantly different from zero. H_a: ρ (k) $\neq 0$, the alternative hypothesis implies that the subsequent changes of observations in the time series are serial correlated. The tests are carried out at significance levels of $\alpha = 0.05$ and $\alpha = 0.01$. When the absolute value of x is less than the critical value 1.96 or 2.576, we accept the null hypothesis at the 5 percent or 1 percent significance level respectively, and the market can be concluded to be weak form efficient. Otherwise, we reject the null hypothesis, in which case we are quite sure that market is not weak form efficient.

Alternatively, when the absolute value of $\rho(k)$ is less than twice the standard error, we accept the null hypothesis.

To test the joint hypothesis that all the serial correlation coefficient, $\rho(k)$ are simultaneously equal to zero, the Box-Ljung (1978) statistic is applied.

$$BL = n(n+2)\sum_{k=1}^{m}\frac{\hat{\rho}^2(k)}{n-k}$$

By summing the squared serial correlations, the BL-statistic is designed to detect departure from zero serial correlation in either direction and at any leads and lags. If the BL-statistic is larger than 18.31 or 23.21, the joint null hypothesis is rejected at the 5 percent or 1 percent significance level respectively.

As a parametric test, the serial correlation coefficient could be adversely affected by outlying observations. The non-parametric tests provide a useful analysis of asymmetrically distributed data. The run test is a non-parametric statistic designed to determine whether the changes between observations are correlated or random. A run is a sub-sequence of 'like observations' with the first and the last observation of the run being preceded and followed, respectively, by an unlike observation. Of course, when the first (last) observation of the run is the first (last) observation of the entire sequence, it cannot be preceded (followed) by an unlike symbol. e.g. + + + + +,0 0 0 0, –,–,0,+ indicates five(5) runs. The sign '+' stands for a positive return, "– "stands for a negative return; '0' means zero return. The run test assumes that if the price changes are random, the actual number of runs (r) should be close to the expected number of the runs (μ_r). For large sample, r is approximately normally distributed, with median as centre value. When n_1 is cases less than the median value and n_2 is cases more than and equal to median value, then

$$\mu_r = \frac{2n_1n_2}{n_1+n_2} + 1$$

And standard error of runs, σ_r would be as follows

$$\sigma_r = \sqrt{\frac{2n_1n_2(2n_1n_2 - n_1 - n_2)}{(n_1+n_2)^2\,(n_1+n_2-1)}}$$

We can then employ the standard normal test-statistics, Z with

$$Z = \frac{r-\mu_r}{\sigma_r}$$

We set up the null hypothesis Ho: r = μ_r, and the alternative hypothesis H_a: r $\neq \mu_r$. The test will be performed at significance levels of $\alpha = 0.05$ and $\alpha = 0.01$. When the absolute value of Z is less than the critical value1.96 or 2.58, we accept the null hypothesis at the 5 percent significance level or at the 1 percent significance level respectfully as the case may be. The actual numbers of runs are equal to the expected number of runs and the market is considered to be an efficient market. Too many or too few actual runs are inconsistent with randomness. Thus, when trends in stock price dominate the series, the actual runs are less than the expected runs and negative Z-statistic is founa. Conversely, when there is a preponderance of stock price reversals, the actual runs are greater than the expected runs and positive Z-statistic is found.

The Variance Ratio (VR) methodology was developed by Lo and Mackinlay (1988) to test the random walk theory is based on the assumption that the variance of the random walk increments is linear in the sampling interval. Specifically, the variance estimated from the q-period returns should be q times as large as the variance estimated from one-period returns. To understand this proposition we use the following methodology.

Let X_t denote stochastic process satisfying the following recursive relation:

$X_t = \mu + X_{t-1} + \epsilon_t$, $E[\epsilon_t] = 0$, for all t,........................(1)

where μ is an arbitrary drift parameter and the random disturbance term ϵ_t has a zero mean and a zero auto covariance, $E[\epsilon_t, \epsilon_{t-k}] = 0$, for any non zero k. Under the random walk hypothesis, the variance of X_t increments must grow linearly with the size of the interval. That is, consider a qth lag difference of X_t, where q is any integer greater than one. The ratio of the $(1/q)^{th}$ of the variance of $(X_t - X_{t-q})$ to the variance of $(X_t - X_{t-1})$ is equal to one. As long as the increments are uncorrelated this relationship holds asymptotically even in the presence of heteroscedasticity.

Suppose that one obtains nq+1 sample observation, $(X_o, X_1, \ldots, X_{nq})$of the log of the stock prices. The variance ratio of q observations, VR (q) is defined as,

$$VR(q) = \frac{Var(r_t^q)}{Var(r_t)} \quad \ldots\ldots(2)$$

where $Var(r_t^q)$ is an unbiased estimator of 1/q of the variance of the q –period return and $Var(r_t)$ is an unbiased estimator of the variance of one –period returns. More specifically,

$$Var(r_t^q) = \frac{1}{m}\sum_{t=q}^{nq}(x_t - x_{t-q} - q\mu)^2 \quad \ldots\ldots(3)$$

$$Var(r_t) = \frac{1}{nq-1}\sum_{t=1}^{nq}(x_t - x_{t-1} - \mu)^2 \quad \ldots\ldots(4)$$

where $m = q(nq-q-1)(1-(q/nq))$ with $\mu = (1/nq)(X_{nq} - X_0)$ and $(Er_t^q) = \mu q$

Cochrane (1988) shows that this variance ratio is asymptotically equivalent to a weighted sum of serial autocorrelation coefficient estimator such that:

$$VR(q) = 1 + 2\sum_{k=1}^{q-1}(1 - \frac{k}{q})\,\rho(k) \quad \ldots\ldots(5)$$

where ρ (k) is the estimator of kth autocorrelation coefficient.

It is apparent in (5), that when the returns of the security are uncorrelated the serial correlation coefficient in lag one to q should be simultaneously near zero and the VR (q) should be 1.

Therefore, we set up the null hypothesis as H_0: VR (q)=1, and the alternative hypothesis H_a: VR(q)≠1. The test will be carried out at significance level of α=0.05 and α=0.01. If the absolute value of test–statistics is less than the critical value, 1.96 or 2.576, we accept the null hypothesis at the 5 percent significance level or at the 1 percent significance level, which states that the returns are uncorrelated. Otherwise, we reject the null hypothesis, which means that the returns are serially correlated.

The standard normal test statistics for the variance ratio test under the assumption of homoscedasticity Z(q) and heteroscedasticity Z*(q) were constructed by Lo and MacKinlay (1988). As data under study is not heteroscedastic, therefore, the test statistics under the assumption of heteroscedasticity are not calculated.

The standard Z test statistics for testing the equality of VR (q) to be unity is :

$$Z(q) = \frac{\sqrt{nq}\,[VR(q)-1]}{\phi(q)^{1/2}} \approx N(0,1) \quad\text{......................(6)}$$

where ϕ (q)=[2(2q-1)(q-1)]/3q, which is the asymptotic variance of the variance ratio under the assumption of homoscedasticity. In order to facilitate comparison of this study with previous researches (Lo and MacKinlay 1988 and Shiguang Ma 2004) on other markets, the q is selected as 2,4,8 and 16.

Most researches estimate the variance ratio and the test statistics under the two alternate assumptions of heteroscedasticity and homoscedasticity. But in the present research the assumption of heteroscedasticity has been dropped since it has been established that the data under analysis is not heteroscedastic. Spearman's rank correlation test is used to detect the heteroscedasticity of the data. For that, first we fit a regression to the data and obtain the residuals.

The regression is given by

$X_t = \alpha + \beta X_{t-1} + \mu_t$

where α is intercept,β is slope and μ_t is the error term .The series (X_t) which is used represent logarithm of the stock prices. After ranking both $|X_{t-1}|$ and $|\mu_t|$ according to an ascending or descending order, we compute the Spearman's rank correlation coefficient between the two. We find that the calculated values are less than the critical values and hence the correlations are not statistically important. This test proves that our data is not heteroscedastic and therefore the test statistics (z*(q)) are not estimated under the assumptions of heteroscedasticity.

Variance ratio test is much more powerful and reliable than the usual tests of random walk models. A variance ratio of less than one implies that the returns of short intervals tend toward mean reversion over a long interval. On the other hand a variance ratio of exceeding one implies that the returns of short interval are inclined to trend over a longer interval.

There is a systematic relationship between the serial correlation coefficient, the runs test and the variance ratio test. The significant positive serial correlation of return leads to actual runs of the returns being less than the expected runs, and the relevant variance ratio being larger than one, therefore, implies that a trend exists in a time series of security prices. Whereas a significant negative serial correlation coefficient leads to actual runs of the return being more than the expected runs, and the relevant variance ratio being less than one, therefore, indicates the existence of reversal in price movement.

1.10.1 Test of Volatility: Using the BSE-Sensex as proxy for the market, we have characterised the behaviour of stock market volatility for the period 1980 to 2003. Standard deviations of daily returns and monthly returns are calculated to gauge the size of volatility. Control Charts are made to get an idea of highly volatile years, months and days. These unusual years, months and days are examined in detail to explain volatility.

For the sake of simplicity we use daily data to construct sample standard deviations, without imposing any parametric model. Multivariate models are unnecessarily complicated and difficult to estimate. Furthermore, although the choice of a parametric model may be essential for volatility forecasting, it is less important for describing historical movements in volatility.

The standard deviation of return (r) from a sample of n observations is the square root of the average squared deviation of returns from the average in the sample.

The logarithmic standard deviation is expressed in percentage terms after multiplying it by 100.

In short, the study uses manifold tests, as listed below, in order to test the RWH, including the evaluation of the data characteristics as a precursor to testing efficiency.

- Unit Root Test (Augmented Dicky Fuller & Phillips-Perron Tests)
- Runs Test
- Serial Correlation Test
- Box-Ljung Statistic
- Variance Ratio Test
- Test of Volatility

This kind of a multi-fold empirical testing is expected to lead to a more comprehensive analysis and more multi-directional scrutiny of stock market efficiency so that a true and complete picture of the behaviour of the market can emerge. In fact the results of the study, discussed in chapter-4 and 5 and interpreted in chapter-6, demonstrate that a comprehensive analysis does not suffer from a distorted view that may occur when only one test/model is used on just one particular type of data. The results from a variety of tests on a variety of data-sets make possible a better synthesis of and a dynamic insight into the often confusing behaviour of the markets.

2

Review of Theoretical and Empirical Studies on Stock Market

2.1 Introduction

This chapter reviews the theoretical and empirical literature on the efficient market model as it has evolved. A periodic review of research done in any field is of significance to both researchers and policy makers. While researchers can use the review to identify research gaps and gather reference bibliographic material; decision makers and policy formulators can understand and appreciate the progression of the developments, to use the research findings to shape their decisions or policies suitably. Also, the new entrants to a field can get a bird's eye view of the state of research in that field through such a review. The objective of this chapter, therefore, is to provide to these interest groups a comprehensive commentary on the nature of research done on the stock market efficiency, with particular reference to India, in recent years and findings thereof.

However, a review of this kind invariably presents considerable difficulties. What comprises research? What should be the period of review? What should be the objectives of a review? How does one ensure that the coverage is comprehensive? It is clear that questions outlined above are capable of generating varied responses. Hence, we begin by briefly outlining the basis on which the review has been done in this section. At the onset, work done in India and US from 1965 till date has been reviewed, though we have included some other important studies too. The literature is now so large that a full review is impossible, and is not attempted here. Instead, we discuss the work that was found most significant and interesting. Views on what we have learnt from the research on market efficiency in its various dimensions and implications are discussed. The objective is to provide an outline of the various studies including their objective, data source, methodology and important findings, along with a synthesis of important findings with others as they emerged. Despite best efforts, abstracts of all works could not be obtained or prepared. In such cases, the works have merely been listed in the bibliography for further ready reference.

All the empirical research on the theory of efficient markets has been concerned with whether prices "fully reflect" particular subset of available information. The initial studies were concerned with what we call weak-form tests in which the information subset of interest is just past price (or return) histories. Most of the results here come from the random walk literature. When extensive tests seemed to support the efficiency hypothesis at this level, attention was turned to semi-strong form tests in which the concern is the speed of price adjustment to other publicly available information (e.g., announcements of stock splits, annual reports, new security issues, etc.) Finally, of more recent origin are the strong form tests in which the concern is the market's ability to adjust and reflect, in security prices, even the special or private information.

As more and more researches were conducted in more and more dimensions of the related aspects of efficiency, the need was felt for a more broad-based terminological categorisation, which would provide a wider umbrella for understanding and synthesizing these diverse but inter related dimensions. Instead of weak-form tests, which are only concerned with the forecast power of past returns, the first category now covers the more general area of *tests for return predictability*, which also includes the voluminous work on forecasting returns with variables like dividends yields and interest rates. Since market efficiency and equilibrium-pricing issues are inseparable the discussion also includes tests of asset-pricing models and anomalies like seasonality, size effect, volatility, weekday effect etc. For second and third categories the now popular names are event studies and tests for private information respectively. The review follows this new classification and seeks to capture the essence of empirical research in more or less this historical sequence.

2.2 Tests for Return Predictability

At the very outset it needs to be noted that to a large extent the empirical work in this field preceded the development of the theory. Research on security prices did not begin with the development of a theory of price formation, which would be then subjected to empirical tests. Rather, the impetus for the development of a theory came from the accumulation of empirical evidence in the mid to late 1950s and early 1960s that the behaviour of common stock prices could be well approximated by a random walk. Faced with the evidence, economists felt compelled to offer some explanation and rationalization. What resulted was a theory of efficient market stated in terms of random walks, within the broad parameters of the more general "fair game" model.

The first empirical work on random walk hypothesis was conducted by Bachelier (1900), a French mathematician, in the form of study of assets pricing. He studied French government bonds and concluded that the price of the bonds follows a random walk, although he did not *per se* use this term in his paper. Basically he worked on asset pricing and developed many mathematical properties of Brownian motion and martingales, which were the earlier mathematical expression of market efficiency. His work is considered the origin and the justification for the development of the random walk theory. Thereafter a number of studies for the refinement of the theory followed.

Kendall (1953) examined the correlation of weekly price changes in 19 British securities and the spot trading prices of cotton and wheat. Kendall found that the time series are random and each price looks like a random number drawn from a symmetrical population of fixed dispersion. Roberts

(1959) applied a simulation study to the pattern of weekly changes in the Dow Jones Industrial Average (DJIA). He tested whether the familiar stock price pattern could be replicated using the assumption that the price follows a random walk. He stated that the weekly change of the index has the same appearance as a time series generated from a sequence of random numbers.

Alexander (1961) developed the filter rule methodology and applied it in the analysis of the random walk. He examined both the DJIA from1897 to 1929 and Standard and Poor's index of 500 stocks (S&P 500) from 1929 to 1959. The filter sizes he designed in his analysis ranged from 5 to 30 percent of price changes. He found that, generally, filters of different sizes have, for various time periods, generated higher returns than those obtained from a simple buy-and-hold strategy. This meant that stock price changes were dependent and allowed abnormal profits to be made. Thus, weak form efficiency was rejected in Alexander's study. In a later paper, however, Alexander derived a bias factor and used it to correct his earlier work. With the correction for bias it turned out that the filters only rarely compared favourably with buy-and-hold, even though the higher broker's commissions incurred under the filter rule were ignored. Alexander's new filter results tended to support the independence assumption of the random walk model.

Granger and Morgenstern (1963) introduced spectral analysis (an approach originally developed in physical science) into the study of independence of successive security price changes. The spectrum of a time series is a frequency-domain representation of the autocorrelation function of that series, so that the spectrum analysis can give a relatively complete picture of the autocorrelation in any stationary stochastic process with finite variance. The evidence from their study showed that monthly and seasonal cycles might have been caused by mean changes over time. Thus their result supports the random walk hypothesis. The role of ''fair game" models in the theory of efficient markets was first recognized and studied rigorously by Samuelson (1965) and Mandelbrot (1966). I now give a more detailed commentary on some of the most prominent and trend-setting works in India and abroad.

Eugene F. Fama (1965) conducted a study which went on to become the reference point for the entire research on stock market efficiency, so much so that he came to be known as the father of the theory of Random walk. Although a lot of field work had already been done in this regard but his was the first comprehensive work on EMH. This study examined two separate hypotheses related to the theory of random walk, viz.

- Successive price changes are independent and
- The price changes conform to normal probability distribution.

According to him, intrinsic values for individual securities were not inconsistent with the random walk hypothesis. He argued that the process of price determination in an intrinsic value-random walk market proved the independence of price changes. Further, if successive bits of new information arise independently across time, and if noise or uncertainty concerning intrinsic values does not tend to follow any consistent pattern, then successive price changes in a common stock will be independent. One more argument in its favour was that with vagueness or uncertainty surrounding new information, "instantaneous adjustment" really has two implications. First, actual prices will initially over-adjust to the new intrinsic value as often as they will under-adjust. Second, the lag in the complete adjustment of actual prices to successive new intrinsic value will itself be an independent random variable. Sometimes preceding the new information, which is the basis of the change (i.e. when the market anticipates the information before it actually appears) and some times following it. It was argued that in this case successive price changes in individual securities will be independent random variables.

He also argued that one of the forces that help to produce

independence of successive price changes might be the existence of sophisticated traders. They were either superior chart leaders or superior intrinsic value analysts. The comparative advantage of the superior analyst over his less talented competitors lies in his ability to predict consistently the appearance of new information and evaluate its impact on intrinsic values. If there were sufficient superior analysts, their existence would be sufficient to ensure that actual market prices were, on the basis of all available information, best estimates of intrinsic values. In this way, of course, the superior analysts rendered intrinsic value analysis a useless tool for both the average analysts and the average investor; and perhaps even well-informed and well-endowed specialist in each security was sufficient for this to happen. Empirical testing of the EMH was done using serial correlation model, theory of runs and the filter technique.

The data used throughout his research consisted of daily prices for each of the thirty stocks of the Dow-Zones Industrial Average. The time period varied from stock to stock but usually ran from about the end of 1957 to September 26, 1962. Thus there were thirty samples with about 1,200-1,700 observations per sample. Using the data, the sample serial correlation coefficient for daily, four, nine and sixteen day logarithm price changes were computed for each stock. The evidence produced by his model using different time lags indicated that dependence in successive price changes was either extremely slight or completely non-existent. This conclusion was further examined by the runs test. The approach to run testing in his study was three-dimensional. The differences between expected and actual numbers of runs were analysed by totals, then by sign and finally by length. The results of various run tests were consistent with the results of serial correlation.

As far as these tests were concerned, Fama observed that any dependence that existed in these series was not strong enough to be capable of being used to increase the expected profits of the trader. However, there were situations in which they did not provide an adequate test of either practical or statistical dependence. To overcome this problem, Alexander's filter technique was used on the same data and it was found that the evidence didn't go against the RWH. Therefore, none of the tests in this study gave evidence of any significant dependence in the first differences of the logarithms of stock prices. That is, the past history of the series cannot be used to increase the investor's expected profits.

Having examined the first hypothesis i.e. independence of price changes, he addressed the second assumption i.e. the price changes conform to normal probability distribution. The form of the distribution of price changes is important information to anyone who wishes to do empirical work in this area. The power of a statistical tool is usually closely related to the type of distribution to which it is applied. Prior to the work of Mandelbrot the usual assumption, called the Gaussian hypothesis, was that the distribution of price changes in a speculative series is approximately Gaussian or normal. In the best known expositions of the Gaussian hypothesis.

Bachelier (1900) and Osborne(1959) used arguments based on central-limit theorem to support the assumption of normality. They argued that price changes from transaction to transaction in an individual security are independent, identically distributed, random variables with finite variance, and if transactions are fairly uniformly spaced through time, the central limit theorem would lead us to believe that the daily, weekly, and monthly price changes will each have normal or Gaussian distribution since they are the simple sums of the changes from transaction to transaction. Benoit Mandelbrot (1962) questioned Gaussian hypothesis. Mandelbrot's main assertion was that, in the past, academic research has too readily neglected the implications of the leptokurtosis usually observed in empirical distributions of price changes. If the empirical distributions were long-tailed, they would contain many more observations in their extreme tail areas than would be expected under a hypothesis of normality. Fama analysed the daily first difference differences of log prices of each of the thirty individual stocks in the Dow-Jones Industrial Average. The results showed some degree of leptokurtosis for every stock. In every case the empirical distributions were more peaked in the centre and had longer tails than the normal distribution.

Fama found that the Mandelbrot hypothesis seemed to fit the data better than the Gaussian hypothesis. However, having said that, Fama observed that the acceptability of Mandelbrot's stable Paretian hypothesis instead of the Gaussian hypothesis would require further empirical documentation and broad-based testing on other speculative series. Moreover, some of the graphs could be considered acceptable within a hypothesis of "approximate" normality. Thus despite finding some strength in the argument that the distribution of price changes in a speculative series deviates from the normal distribution, Fama's study presented strong and voluminous evidence in favour of the random-walk hypothesis.

Pao L. Chang and M. King Deets (1970) investigated the independence condition to examine whether the prices did follow a random walk. They compared the theoretical portfolio return under the naïve buy-and-hold strategy (henceforth BH) with the theoretical portfolio return under the rebalancing strategy (henceforth RB). They argued that "If the returns to the individual securities are to be usefully classified as being independent, at least four conclusions must be apparent from the actual data. First, the BH strategy should generally be superior to the RB strategy. Second, as the frequency of rebalancing is intensified, the rebalancing return should decrease, thus making the BH strategy progressively more superiors. Third, as more securities are added to the portfolio, the superiority of BH should begin to diminish.

Finally, as the decision horizon is lengthened, the superiority of BH should increase." Weekly price relatives for the 30 stocks comprising the Dow Jones Industrial Average were used as a basis for testing the hypothesis. The period covered was from December 31, 1937 to February 21, 1969, a span of 31 years. There were 1625 weekly observations on the 30 stocks totalling 48,750 weekly price relatives. The return under the two strategies were compared by changing different variables viz. number of securities, frequency of rebalancing strategy, and length of decision-horizons.

The evidence was on the whole contrary to predictions. First, buy-and-hold was inferior, not superior. Second, rebalancing return was indeed a function of the frequency of rebalancing but resulted in greater, rather than lesser, superiority under increased frequency. Third, increasing the number of securities in the portfolio as predicted did increase the return of the rebalancing strategy in the sample for short rebalancing periods but not for longer ones. Fourth, increasing the length of the decision horizon tended to increase, not decrease the superiority of the rebalancing strategy. The cumulative effect of persistent negative serial correlation results was a function of the rebalancing period. This allowed the trader to earn an economic profit through frequent portfolio rebalancing, involving selling off some portion of those securities that have historically experienced a relatively superior return and replacing them in the portfolio with securities that have experienced a relatively inferior return. In short, the fact that rebalancing yields a greater return than buy-and-hold indicated security prices were not independent.

N. Krishan Rao and K. Mukherjee (1971) examined the validity of the R-W hypothesis for the Indian Aluminium Company's weekly average share prices for the sixteen year period from 1955 to 1970 by employing spectral methods. Considering that a price is composed of a long term trend component (permanent) and a short term or transitory component; the study was confined to the transitory component only. The permanent components represent the true or intrinsic value, functionally related to company's fundamentals; and the transitory components represent various psychological forces, fads etc. This analysis tried to find the existence of departures from fundamentals, if any, and to explain them. An analysis of the data revealed that the R-W hypothesis, found to be true for many American and British market share prices, was valid for the Indian Aluminium Company's weekly average share prices for the study period. They suggested that the study could be extended to other individual stocks, to draw more generalised conclusions.

J.L. Sharma and Robert E. Kennedy (1977) sought to test the applicability of the random walk hypothesis to the stock market in a less developed country (LDC), namely, India, and to compare this behaviour to that of stock markets in advanced, industrialised countries, namely the United States and England. For this purpose, the price behaviour of a broadly reflective stock market indices of common stocks of three international markets viz. (a) Bombay Variable Dividend Industrial Share Index (BVDISI or Bombay Stock Index); (b) London Financial Times Actuaries 500 Stock Index (FT-A500) of the London Stock Exchange; and (c) New York Standard & Poor's 425 stock Exchange (S&P 425) of the New York Stock Exchange were examined. The data covered a period of 11 years consisting of 132 monthly observations (as on the last Friday of each month), for the 11-year period 1963-73. The log price series were examined using a non-parametric test (runs test) and a parametric test for independence (analysis of spectral densities of the data for any cyclical components).

Although there were slight differences in the characteristics of the first difference series of the three indices, the characteristics of the first differences of the log indices were essentially the same. A comparison of the three indices revealed that the observed numbers of runs closely follow each other. The observed frequencies of lengths of runs closely fitted a binomial distribution with probability of 0.5 for either rise or fall. The chi-square (X^2) values were small, and therefore, the null hypothesis that the price changes were independent and the probability of rise or fall in price was equal could not be rejected. The result obtained in this study that the probability of rise or fall was equal to 0.5 was inconsistent with the results obtained by Alexander. The spectrum of the log first difference for all the three stock indices was also flat. The spectrum showed power both at low frequencies and at relatively higher frequencies, at periods 18 months, at 3.3 months, and 2.5 months. The spectrum as a whole was flat, confirming the random-walk hypothesis. Based on these tests, it was concluded that stocks on the Bombay Stock Exchange obeyed a random walk and behaved similar to the stock prices in the markets of advanced industrial countries examined in this study. D. Ray (1976) used almost a similar methodology involving serial correlation, runs test and spectral analysis on 31 scrips and got non conclusive results on applicability of the RWH.

Rosenberg and Rudd (1982) took the next logical step towards examining the RWH. Having observed the lack of serial correlation in the total returns of securities, the researchers tested for serial correlation with respect to each of the major components of a security's return. A security's total return is generally recognized to be composed of two major elements, the return that is common to all securities and the return that is specific to the individual security. The study found a positive serial correlation for the common component and a corresponding negative correlation for the specific component, resulting in an increased predictability of the total returns. Although the findings suggested a violation of the weak form of efficiency, the study ignored the impact of transaction costs, and there was no evidence that the results amounted to an exploitable inefficiency.

O.P. Gupta (1985) employed weekend (Friday) closing prices of 39 shares listed on the four principal stock exchange of India viz. Bombay, Calcutta, Delhi and Ahmedabad for the period January 1971 to March 1976. The size of the sample companies was comparatively large under Indian conditions and consisted of only the most active scrip. Following the promulgation of Companies (Temporary Restrictions on Dividends) Ordinance (later replaced by Act) on July 6, 1974 which restricted the distribution of dividends by companies, the stock exchanges remained closed during the major part of July 1974. Thereafter, listless and gloomy conditions prevailed in the market and prices of almost all the shares registered a severe fall. In view of the prevalence of this extraordinary situation, it was considered necessary to truncate all the share price series on July 5, 1974 and to analyse them separately for two time periods—one before and the other after the enactment of the said Act with a view to investigate whether the "post-dividend restriction period" share price behaviour displayed a different pattern in comparison to that of "pre-dividend restriction period". During the period covered by the study, some companies had issued bonus and right shares. Therefore, in those cases the ex-bonus or ex-right prices were adjusted to make them comparable with the cum-bonus or cum-right quotations. However, no adjustment was made for cash dividend. The RWH was tested by means of (a) a parametric test for independence viz. serial correlation coefficient for lags extending from 1 to 30 and (b) a non-parametric test for randomness viz. runs test. Log Random Walk model had been used to make the series stationary. Both the tests generally supported the independence assumption of the random walk model.

Yalaguresh B. Yalawar (1985) attempted to examine the rates of return on equities obtainable in the stock market and the weak form efficiency of the Bombay Stock Exchange in pricing the equities traded on its floor. Using a sample of 122 frequently traded common stocks and monthly closing transaction price data over a 20 year period, 1963-82, the study performed the Spearman Rank Correlation Coefficient test for lags from one to ten months and runs test on stock by stock basis. In the case of one month and 10 month lagged return, there were respectively 21 and 17 correlation coefficients that were statistically significant at 0.05 level. While majority of significant correlation for one month's lag was negative, those for 10-month lag were positive. Nevertheless these significant correlations were so small that it would have been difficult to profit from any trading rule based on this linear dependence. Hence, it was argued that the results supported the random walk hypothesis and that the BSE was efficient in the weak form at least in pricing the actively traded common stocks.

Lauren J. Feinstone (1987) proposed to extend the study of the efficiency of asset markets and processes to the intra-day data, envisioning a floor trader or an individual who follows the market during the day. The data set contained all price movements during the day, plus explicit information about the times of trades. The data set used throughout this study consisted of intra-daily futures prices on the Deutsche Mark (DM) as traded at the International Monetary Market (IMM) during July 1977 for maturity in September 1977. He performed an improved version of the filter rule test, in addition to autocorrelation tests at intervals as short as 30 seconds. The results indicated that the future market in foreign exchange functions almost instantaneously to absorb new information. Both autocorrelation tests and trigger rule tests (improved version of filter rule test) indicated that a chartist would have a difficult time making a profit from this market, and even a floor trader may not be able to profit.

Yakov Amihud and Haim Mandelson (1987) offered to resolve a crucial issue pertaining to efficiency that is whether the opening price contains all the information available in the sequence of opening prices, which preceded it, and whether the closing price reflects all the information contained in the sequence of preceding closing prices. The above form of the market efficiency hypothesis implies that the serial correlation of both open-to-open and close-to-close returns should be equal to zero. On the other hand, if different trading mechanisms give rise to different price adjustment processes, we may observe a different serial autocorrelation pattern for the open-to-open and close-to-close returns. This study offered to resolve this issue by comparing the price behaviour of New York Stock Exchange Stocks in the opening transactions with the price behaviour of the same stocks, traded at the same exchange during the same period, in the closing transactions. The opening transactions represented the outcome of a call trading procedure, whereas trading at the close was carried out at prices that were set or affected by the exchange's market makers.

Comparison of price behaviour under the two trading mechanisms used the daily opening and closing prices of the 30 NYSE stocks, which constituted the Dow Jones Industrial list during the period February 8, 1982 to February 18, 1983. To test the above hypothesis, they first replicated Fama's tests of first-order autocorrelation using both close-to-close and open-to-open returns and then, as a further test of the random-walk, they estimated the standard auto regressive moving-average (ARMA) for their opening and closing return series. Both series showed deviations from normality though the opening return distribution exhibited greater peakedness and fatter tails than that of the closing returns. The residual variance of the open-to-open returns was greater than that of the close-to-close returns, reflecting less noise in the dealership market (i.e. closing transaction) than in the clearinghouse (i.e. opening transaction). The pattern of first-order serial correlation was generally negative in the opening and positive in the closing series. Even the positive correlations were more significantly different from zero as compared to Fama's findings. Moreover, the study suggested that simple autocorrelation tests might have been insufficient to detect market inefficiencies, since they disguise the pattern. For opening returns, the results of the ARMA model indicated more significant deviations from the random-walk form of the market efficiency hypothesis than those obtained under serial correlation tests. Taken as a whole, the evidence suggested that trading at the opening exposed traders to a greater variance than in the close, reflecting the difference between the trading mechanisms.

Lo and MacKinlay (1988) proposed the variance ratio test for the random walk hypothesis. They suggested that the variance ratio test is more powerful than the well known Dickey-Fuller unit root or the Box-Pierce Q tests. They applied the test on weekly returns on portfolios of New York Stock Exchange stocks, grouped according to size and found some evidence to reject the random walk model for the sample period of 1962 to 1985. They found positive autocorrelation, which was stronger for portfolios of smaller stocks. Almost similar conclusion were drawn by Conrad and Kaul (1988), who found that the weekly returns were positively correlated, and more so for portfolios of small stocks. However, the possibility of spurious autocorrelation in portfolio returns, induced by non-synchronous trading for securities in the portfolio was not ruled out and such possibility was greater for portfolios tilted towards small stocks. Moreover, the results indicated that because of the variance reduction obtained from diversification, portfolios produce stronger indications of time variations in weekly expected returns than individual stocks. Thus, even these new results tended to confirm that, at least for individual stocks, the variations in expected returns is only a small part of the variance of returns, and as such efficiency hypothesis could not be rejected. Moreover, the reliability of any conclusions based on price movements of small stocks were often seen with suspicion as the pricing and value fundamentals of small stocks were relatively unclearly understood.

Eugene F. Fama and Kenneth R. French (1988a) examined autocorrelation of stock return for increasing holding period i.e. a period from 1926 to 1985. They examined the results for industry portfolios and for portfolios formed on the basis of size to see if the returns followed a random walk or were they predictable based on some time-varying pattern. Early tests of market efficiency examined autocorrelation of daily and weekly stock returns. Sample size for such short return horizons were typically large, and reliable evidence of close to zero auto-correlation was common. Therefore, it was largely concluded that the stock market was efficient. Some recent researchers challenge this interpretation. They argue that autocorrelations of short-horizon returns can given the impression that such mean-reverting components of prices are of no consequence when in fact they account for a substantial fraction of the variation of returns.

This study assumed that a stock price was a sum of a random walk and a stationary price component. The random-walk price component produced white noise in returns and the stationary price component caused negative autocorrelation in returns. Simple regression analysis was used for this purpose. First order autocorrelation of industry and decile portfolio returns for the period 1926-85 formed a U-shaped pattern across increasing return horizons. The U-shaped pattern is consistent with the hypothesis that stock prices also have random walk components that eventually dominate long-horizon returns.

The autocorrelation became negative for 2-year returns, reached minimum values for 3-5 year returns, and then moved back towards 0.0 for longer return horizons. The negative autocorrelation of return generated by a slowly decaying component of prices was weak at the short return horizons, but it became stronger as the return horizon increases. Eventually, however, random-walk price components began to dominate the variation of returns, and long-horizon autocorrelation moved back towards zero.

Autocorrelation may reflect market inefficiency, but sub period results suggested that the strong negative autocorrelation of the period 1926-85 might have been largely due to the first 15 years. Autocorrelations for periods after 1940 (i.e. after the end of the great depression, an extraordinary period) were closer to zero and they did not show the U-shaped patterns of the overall period. Stationary price components might be less important after 1940, or perhaps prices no longer had temporary components. Authors suggested that this issue would require more powerful statistical techniques.

Grant Mcqueen and Steven Thorley (1991) used a Markov chain model to test the random walk hypothesis for stock prices. Given a time series of returns, a Markov chain is defined by letting one state represent high returns and the other represent low returns. The random walk hypothesis restricts the transition probabilities in the Markov chain to be equal irrespective of the prior years.

The transition probability estimates for annual returns were calculated and used to form likelihood ratio tests of equal transition probability constraints imposed by the random walk hypothesis. Tests for negative serial dependence in annual returns were performed on both real and excess continually compounded returns for equally as well as value-weighted portfolios of all NYSE stocks for the calendar years 1947 to 1987.

The Markov chain tests also confirmed the findings of Lo and MacKinlay (1988), with below average weekly returns often following below average returns and above average weekly returns often following above average returns. Small stocks were shown to exhibit more positive weekly serial correlation than large stocks, and large stocks were shown to follow a random walk over the last decade under the study.

S.K. Chaudhuri (1991) used daily price quotations of 93 actively traded shares for the period January 1988 to April 1990 to examine the serial independence of share price changes in Indian market. He found positive correlation but the magnitude of correlation coefficient was small. The results were similar to those of Fama (1965) and Fisher (1966). From the viewpoint of an investor, serial dependence of such a low order can hardly be used for predicting future course of price changes in any meaningful manner.

M. Ranganatham and V. Subramaniam (1993) tested empirically the weak form of EMH using the frequency domain approach of spectral analysis. It used the financial time series of the Economic Times (ET-All Industries/All India) Index (base year 1984-85) collected for a period of seven years (1984-90) on a daily basis. The first difference log series having 1557 observations in total was subjected to spectral analysis. The number of lags considered was 155. Estimation using this method produced a point estimate of power at different frequencies. The interval estimates, i.e. the upper and the lower confidence intervals could be obtained by using the chi-square approximation with the appropriate Equivalent Degree of Freedom (EDF). The upper confidence interval and the lower confidence interval at each frequency were connected by lines to construct the Upper Confidence Band (UCB) and the Lower Confidence Band (LCB). These bands were plotted along with the power spectrum on an arithmetic scale. A visual examination of the plot of power spectrum against frequency for the E.T. Series showed that there were prominent spikes at lower frequency range.

The largest periodic component reported in his paper was corresponding to a cycle of 123 days. There was evidence of the presence of periodic cycles in the movement of share prices, which is against the assertion of the weak form of EMH. But compared to the lower frequency ranges, the spectrum at the higher frequency ranges was almost flat. The use of index series may have given a completely false impression of the extent of price fluctuation in individual price series. For a better understanding of the structure of price movements in the Indian Stock Market, the use of this technique on a large sample of individual share price series is called for.

R. Vaidyanathan and Kanti Kr. Gali (1994) tested the weak form of efficiency using three tests, namely the runs tests, serial correlation test and the filter rule test using daily data. For the runs test, they covered four different time periods, namely the years 1980, 1985, 1989 and 1990. In each year the period from April to November was covered so that at least 120 daily data points were available for each company. In addition, data for the period April 1989 to November 1990 (20 months) was used for performing an analysis for ten individual scrips and three market indices. The extended period was used to see whether using more data would affect the result. In each period closing share prices were collected over a period of eight months. The results of runs test as well as of serial correlation test suggested that the market was efficient at weak level throughout the period under study. However, part of the randomness could have resulted from the fact that two out of three indices comprised of very actively traded stocks only. The third test namely the "Filter Rules Test" was performed with the assumptions that short-sales were not allowed and transaction cost was zero. It was observed that while operators with zero transaction costs might be able to make profits from using the filter rule trading strategy, general investors cannot hope to make profits from such a strategy. The average excess return for all the filters was substantially negative. However, the filter for which the rule was profitable was different for different scrips. Thus, for the operators to gain from the rule, they should know in advance which filter level is profitable. Therefore, it was concluded that all the three tests supported EMH.

R.P. Mahapatra (1995) took twenty-six equity stocks listed and actively traded in the Bombay Stock Exchange during January 1989 to December 1992 for the study. The monthly price data was used and a test of 'Relative Strength Theory (RST)' in the Indian Stock Market was carried out as a measure to test Capital Market Efficiency. The RST holds that stocks which had out-performed the market in the past should continue to out-perform the market in the future conversely, stocks that have done poorly, should continue to perform poorly. If the theory of relative strength is correct, it is possible to derive useful information from past prices for predicting future prices. This situation will occur only when the market is not efficient in the weak form. The rank correlation analysis was used to examine whether the performance of a stock in one period relates to its performance in the following period. The results disclosed that the Indian Stock Market seemed to be less efficient in the short run but more efficient in the longer run, thereby rejecting RST in the long run. A.S. Santhappearaj & R.S. Reddy (2000) conducted a similar study and found evidence for validity of relative strength theory in the Indian financial market in the short-run but not in long run. A.S. Ramasastri (2001) tested the weak form of market efficiency in Indian stock market during 1996-98, the post-liberalisation period. The daily closing values of sensex for three years from January 1, 1996 to December 31, 1998 were used to find returns for 724 days. A more powerful tool spectral analysis was also used and the results were enough to conclude in favour of EMH.

G.P. Samanta (2002) examined the changing weak-form informational efficiency of Indian stock market in recent years. The data covered daily information on BSE-100 index for a period of nine years from January 4, 1993 to December 31, 2001. In order to assess the evolving weak-form efficiency over time, entire data period was partitioned into 18 sub-periods and spectral shape tests were carried out separately in each sub-period. Based on empirical results it was seen that the extent of informational efficiency (weak-form) of Indian stock market fluctuated substantially from sub-period to sub-period. The market was considerably inefficient during each sub-period till June 1996, achieved high level of efficiency during 1996 to December 1999 and showed efficiency at relatively lower level thereafter except a little aberration during 2000.

J.C. Sharma (2002) sought to examine whether Indian stock market became relatively more efficient in the wake of financial sector reforms, especially in the capital market, implemented with an objective to improve its efficiency. The time series data of excess and real returns on RBI's ordinary share prices for two-sub period, 1948-49 to1984-85 and 1985-86 to 1998-99 were used for this purpose.

Firstly, to shed some light on the behaviour of the Indian stock market, the fundamental statistics of the two return series (i.e. real stock returns and excess returns) were calculated. The mean in each series was higher for the post liberalisation period as compared to the pre liberalisation period. Both the series depicted leptokurtic distribution of returns throughout the sample period as well as in both the sub-periods.

Secondly, the Jarque-Bera test was conducted to test the null hypothesis of the normality of the distribution. It revealed the rejection of the assumption of normality in both the return series. Besides these properties, the phenomenon of 'auto-regressive conditional hetroscedaticity' (ARCH) was also investigated for both the series. The presence of ARCH phenomenon requires the use of a "hetroscedasticity consistent test statistic", to measure the efficiency of stock market to circumvent the bias caused from using the conventional test statistics. It was observed that ARCH phenomenon was much stronger in the pre-liberalised phase as compared to the post-liberalisation period.

Thirdly, the presence of a stochastic trend in a financial time series, which is a pre-requisite for conducting any tests of random walk hypothesis, was also tested. For the purpose the 'Augmented Dickey-Fuller (ADF) test was applied. Based on ADF test null hypothesis could not be rejected and thus it appeared that there existed strong stochastic trend component or random walk component in excess and real stock return.

Fourthly, to detect that the short-term fluctuations dominate the stochastic trend components, Variance Ratio approach was used. The Variance Ratio (VR) methodology developed to test the random walk theory was based on the assumption that the variance of the random walk increments was linear in the sampling intervals. It was evident from the empirical application of VR approach on Indian stock returns that they did not follow the random walk in the first sub period and also for the full sample period. During the second sub period, which had also witnessed the major reforms in financial sector, a tendency in VR statistic to move towards unity was generally observed but due to limited size of the sample it was difficult to predict with confidence whether stochastic trend dominated the movements of stock market prices or returns.

Lastly, French and Fama's (1988a) test of autocorrelation of multi-period returns to test mean reverting behaviour of stock prices was also used under this study. It revealed a very strong predictive power of negative autocorrelations for future return which was reflected by high values of correlation coefficients between the actual and predicted values particularly for the first sub period. This also proved the fact that stationary component accounts for a significant variation in stock returns and thus, dominates the variations for a sufficiently long horizon. Although the predictive powers had relatively weakened for the second sub period, it was still on a very high side pointing to the fact that stationary component explains more than half of the expected variations in stock return even after financial liberalisation process was already in full swing. Thus the market remained largely inefficient even after the liberalisation as per the empirical findings of this study. This would also point to the need for further enlarging the scope of economic reform agenda in general and financial reforms in particular.

Michael Cooper, Roberto C. Gutierrez and Bill Marcum (2005) examined whether cross-sectional patterns in stock were evident in "real time" without the benefit of hindsight. Since researchers had already documented an abundance of evidence that stock returns are predictable ex-post facto, this appeared a logical consequential enquiry. They developed a recursive out-of-sample method to assess the ex-ante predictability of stock returns using three premier forecasters: book-to-market equity, firm size, and one year lagged return. The study addressed whether an investor would have chosen to implement them. Would an investor, in real-time, have found these market-beating strategies amid the plethora of alternatives, or was the market beatable only after the clarity and benefit of hindsight? They used all NYSE, AMEX, and NASDAQ non-financial firms listed on the CRPS monthly stock return files and the Compustat annual industrial files from 1963 through 1997. They found that the market was difficult to beat despite being given three of four variables that are the ex-post premier cross-sectional variables. Thus the conclusions supported the EMH. At a minimum, the findings soften the debate on inefficiency, given that the level of predictability is markedly lower than previously believed.

2.2.1 Point and Counter-Point: Anomalies Challenging EMH and Alternative Explanation/Defence against them: In the recent years, as reviewed in the ensuing section, evidence to the contrary has also surfaced in the finance literature, which is labelled as 'anomaly'. The documented anomalous price behaviour included apparent under reaction, apparent over reaction and puzzling variation of prices with day-of-the-week effect, size effect, dividend yield anomaly, earning yield anomaly etc. While some anomalies, such as those explained in relation to Dividend Yield, Market Capitalization, Price Earnings etc might be rightly said to be pointing at the inappropriateness of CAPM, the observance of Intra-Month, Weekend and Intra-day 'seasonals' point out a general weakness of all asset pricing models or imperfections in the trading process itself. Many of these anomalies have also been described as fads or psychological effects or irrational bubbles by various researchers; though many others don't agree to these descriptions. According to them, Market Efficiency has, by and large, survived the challenge from the literature on experimental psychology and long-term return anomalies. They argue that these anomalies can be explained within the broader framework of efficiency, with some fine-tunings in the models and the data. Some of the key researches in this context are being briefly reviewed below.

R.W. Banz (1981) was first to document the phenomenon

of 'size-effect'. Studying "The Relationship between Return and Market Value of Common Stock' during 1931-75, he found that the statistical association between returns and size was negative and significant. The differences in the returns accruing to shares of the smallest and the largest firms were found to be quite handsome in the various stock markets. The inverse relationship between the company size and common stock return is now extensively documented in the finance literature. Various attempts have been made in explaining the size effect. Roll (1981) conjectured that large abnormal returns of small firms could be due to understatement of risk (or overstatement of risk-adjusted returns) because of infrequent trading of small firms. Christie and Hertzel (1981) argued that the size effect could be due to non-stationarity of beta. A firm whose common stock price has recently declined – i.e., a firm which is becoming 'small' has effectively experienced, other things remaining constant, an increase in debt-equity ratio and therefore a concomitant increase in the risk of its equity. Thus, historical estimates of beta that assume such risk as being constant over time shall amount to understating the risk and overstating the risk adjusted returns of stocks whose market capitalisation had just fallen. Chan (1983) made an adjustment for this bias, as a result of which the size effect was reduced to a magnitude whose economic significance was debatable. Brown, Kleidon and Marsh (1983) found that when averaged over all months, the size effect reverses itself for sustained period; in many periods there is a consistent premium for small size, in fewer other periods there is a discount.

Reinganum (1981) found that approximately 50 percent of the return difference between small and large firm stocks found by was concentrated in January. He further reported that 50 percent of the January effect was concentrated in the first five trading days of the year. This turn-of-the-year return behaviour was also found by Roll (1983) who notes that small firms have abnormally large returns on the last trading day in December. Cooke and Rozeff (1984) document that P/E, P/B and price effects too are more pronounced in January. Keim (1982) found that the size effect is concentrated in January. The January effect is stated to be caused by year-end-tax induced trading, which depresses stock prices temporarily at the end of the fiscal year. Once selling pressure abates, prices rebound to their normal level. The rebound is what is considered as the turn-of-the-year effect. Popularly called as Tax Loss Selling Hypothesis (TLS), the hypothesis maintains that tax laws influence investors' portfolio decisions by encouraging the sale of securities that have experienced recent price declines so that short-term capital loss can be offset against taxable income. TLS argument relies on the assumption that investors wait until the tax-year-end to sell their common stock losers. The heavy selling pressure during this period supposedly depresses the price of shares. After the tax-year-end, the selling pressure disappears and prices rebound to their equilibrium levels. Therefore, TLS predicts abnormal returns in the months immediately following the tax-year-end. The study by De Bondt and Thaler (1985) provided some support for the tax-loss selling hypothesis. (over/under reaction & later reversal linked to "month of the year" effect.) However, TLS is seen primarily in terms of the explanation for small firm effect, for small firm stocks are more likely candidates for tax-loss selling since these stocks typically have higher variances of price changes, and therefore, larger probabilities of large price declines.

Ariel (1987) examined the intra-month seasonals and showed that for the period 1963 to 1981 the average returns for US common stocks, using CRSP index returns as proxy for the returns, are positive only for the last day of the month and for days during the first half of the month; during the latter half of the month, returns are indistinguishable from zero. He concluded that during his sample period all of the market's cumulative advance occurred around the first half of the months, the second half contributed nothing to the cumulative increase. Research on "week-end effects" has shown that average stock returns tend to be higher on Fridays and negative on Mondays. Cross documented this as early as in 1973 and French in 1980.

Keim and Stambaugh (1984) found consistently negative Monday returns for Standard and Poor's (S&P) Composite Index, for stocks traded on NYSE, AMEX and also for stocks traded on OTC. The 'week-end' effect can even be decomposed into the 'intra-day' stock return patterns. A striking difference was found by Lawrence Harris (1988) between Monday and other week days in the first 45 minutes of trading. The mean return in this interval for the NYSE portfolio was negative on Monday (-0.13 percent) while on other days it was positive (0.09, 0.14, 0.12 and 0.10 percent respectively). In general too, there is an anomalous tendency for large returns to occur at the beginning and at the end of the trading day. Whole of the beginning-of-day returns accrue over several transactions, the large positive end-of-day returns accrue only on the last transaction of the day. Ray Ball (1989) attributed these 'seasonals' to the absence of consideration of supply factors in financial asset pricing theory. He argued that all modern financial models address to the implications of pure exchange only, i.e. supply is assumed to be determined exogenously. He felt that when supply factors are considered, these anomalies won't be found startling: In a competitive world market returns should equal the marginal efficiency of investment (MEI). Though there is no theory of how the MEI varies over time, casual observation does suggest that MEI on weekends is lower than on week days. Mondays are said to have higher work absenteeism than other weekdays, with possibly lower MEI. Nights presumably are less productive than days. All this illustrates the feasibility of any seasonal pattern in the absence of consideration of supply parameters of asset pricing.

Warner De Bondt and Richard Thaler (1985) propounded one of the most important long-term return anomalies' theories. They suggested that, most people tend to "overreact" to unexpected and dramatic news events. Over-reaction is a relative term in comparison of some correct reaction and Bayes' rule prescribes correct reaction to new information. They concentrated on an empirical test of the over-reaction hypothesis. Specifically, two hypotheses were suggested: (a) Extreme movements in stock prices will be followed by subsequent price movements in the opposite direction; (b) The more extreme the initial price movement, the greater will be the subsequent adjustment. Both hypotheses would imply a violation of weak-form of market efficiency.

So their goal was to test whether the over-reaction hypothesis is predictive. Monthly return data for New York Stock Exchange (NYSE) common stocks, as compiled by the Centre for Research in Security Prices (CRSP) of the University of Chicago, were used for the period between January 1926 and December 1982. An equally weighted arithmetic average rate of return on all CRSP listed securities served as the market index. They focused on stocks that had experienced either extreme capital gains or extreme losses over periods up to five years. In other words "Winner" (W) and "loser" portfolios (L) were formed, conditional upon past success returns. For every stock j, the market-adjusted excess returns residuals were calculated i.e. $\mu_{jt} = R_{jt} - R_{mt}$. For any period t, the same constant market returns R_{mt} were subtracted from all R_{jt}'s. Then they calculated cumulative excess returns for the entire period. The cumulative excess returns were ranked from low to high and portfolios were formed. Firms in the top 35 stocks were assigned to the winner portfolio "W", and firms in the bottom 35 stocks to the loser portfolio L. Thus, the portfolios were formed conditional upon excess return behaviour prior to t=0, (formation date) and same procedure was adopted for period subsequent to t=0. They then computed the cumulative average residual returns for all securities in the portfolio prior and subsequent to t=0 and compared these values. Results consistent with the over-reaction hypothesis, evidence against weak-form market efficiency was found. Portfolios of prior "loses" were found to out perform prior "winners". Thirty-six months after portfolio formation, the losing stocks had earned about 25 percent more than the winners, even though the latter were significantly more risky.

Lawrence H. Summers (1986) questioned the power of common tests of market efficiency. The central message of the huge literature on market efficiency was the supreme difficulty of earning abnormal returns making use only of publicly available information. This paper had not disputed this conclusion. Rather, it had taken issue with the corollary implication of the efficient market view that market price represented rational assessment of fundamental values. It suggested caution in treating stock prices or changes therein as rational reflections of fundamental values. The study suggested that certain types of inefficiency in market valuations were not likely to be detected using standard methods. This point is important for both corporate financial policy and for event study research. This means the evidence found in many studies that the hypothesis of efficiency couldn't be rejected should not lead us to conclude that market prices represent rational assessments of fundamentals valuations. Rather, we must face the fact that most of our tests had relatively little power against certain types of market inefficiency.

These were exactly the sort of errors in valuation one would expect to see if market valuations involved inflation illusion or were moved by fads as some experts suggested. The study also suggested that valuation errors, if present, would be difficult to detect by looking at observed returns. However, both theoretical and empirical considerations suggested the likelihood that market valuations differ frequently and substantially from fundamental values. Indirect empirical evidence suggested the importance of valuation errors. This analysis suggested that a more catholic approach should be taken to explaining the behaviour of speculative prices. The inefficiency entertained was one in which the deviation of the price from the rational market fundamental was persistent and potentially large. This deviation was similar to a speculative bubble, which could induce "excess" volatility and negative autocorrelation in returns. The major contribution of this paper lies in the observation that, while the pricing error can contribute substantially to the variance of returns, the negative autocorrelation can be too small to detect inefficiency using common techniques. Thus, he argued that most tests of market efficiency have had little power to reject market efficiency against this alternative version of inefficiency.

Eugene F. Fama and Kenneth R. French (1988b) examined the issue of 'Dividend Yields and Expected Stock returns'. This followed the anomaly evidence demonstrated by Rozeff (1984) and Shiller (1984) that dividend yields (D/P) can forecast short horizon stock returns. Similar arguments were also advanced by Campbell and Shiller (1988) who found that the E/P ratios have reliable forecast power, which also increases with the return horizon i.e, as the period increases, the forecast power also increases. Fama and French noted that though there was much evidence that stock returns were predictable, the predictable component of returns is a small fraction (usually less than 3 percent) of the return variance. Even where the existing researches had suggested strong predictability they could not reject the hypothesis that stock prices are random walks. Fama and French confirmed the existing evidence that the predictable (expected) component of returns is a small fraction of short-horizon return variances. Regressions of returns on yields typically explain less than 5 percent of monthly or quarterly variances.

They further offered evidence that the forecast power of the dividend yields (D/P) increases with the return horizon. The explanation offered is two fold: firstly that the high autocorrelation causes the variance of expected return to grow faster than the return horizon; and secondly the cumulative price effect of the expected return shock and the associated opposite price shock is roughly zero. This happens because the growth of variance of the unexpected returns with the return horizon is attenuated by a discount-rate effect. Thus the shocks to the expected return generate opposite shocks to the current prices. As a result it was concluded that, on an average, the future price increases implied by the higher expected returns are just offset by the decline in the current prices and time-varying expected returns generate only mean reverting or temporary component of prices.

James M. Poterba and Lawrence H. Summers (1988) investigated transitory components in stock prices. Using data from the United States and 17 other countries they showed that, statistically, tests had little power to detect persistent deviations between market prices and fundamental values. That is there may be significant departures from fundamentals, yet the statistical tests may not capture them and from test result statistics it may appear that prices are random. They also investigated whether prices were indeed mean reverting, by using variance-ratio tests and regression analysis. They analyzed monthly returns on both the value-weighted and equal-weighted NYSE indices from the CRSP database for the period 1926-1985. The study considered excess returns, with the risk-free rate measured as the treasury bill yield, as well as real returns measured using the Consumer Price Index (CPI) inflation rate. Though mean reversion was more pronounced for the equal-weighted than for the value-weighted returns, but the variance ratios at long horizons were well below unity for both, raising question marks over EMH. Their results also suggested that stock returns show positive serial correlation over short periods and negative correlation over longer intervals. The conclusions emerging from this data were corroborated by data from other nations and time periods. Although individual data sets did not consistently permit rejection of the random-walk hypothesis at high significance levels, the various data sets together strengthened the case against its validity.

I.M. Pande and Ramesh Bhat (1988) wanted to assess the

extent to which the users and prepares of accounting information in India were aware of the efficient market hypothesis (EMH) and accepted the empirical findings on EMH in the Indian context. In spite of some empirical evidence in favour of the capital market efficiency in weak form and mildly in favour of semi-strong form, the experts as well as the capital markets participants in India allege that the market is excessively speculative and inefficient. This study used the methodology developed by Mayer-Somes and sent questionnaires to (1) the chief financial executives; (2) academicians; (3) Chartered Accountants; and (4) cross-section of investors and brokers. The first three groups fell in the category of accounting information preparers and the last group belonged to the user category. Fifteen percent of investors exhibited no understanding of EMH in any of its forms. 55 percent of investors understood the EMH in all three of its forms.

The results also indicated that the respondents who understood EMH did not necessarily accept it in reality. Majority of the respondents in each category thought that the fundamental and technical analysis could be used to out-perform the market. Index comparison was considered to be less useful than the technical and fundamental analysis. On the various information sources, 82 percent of the Chartered Accountants and Company respondents considered the audited financial statements to be useful, 76 percent of company respondents considered other publicly available information to be useful. 87 percent of the accounting academicians thought inside information to be useful in out-performing the market. Thus there was suggestive evidence that anomalies and inefficiencies prevailed in the market as per the belief of key players.

Narasimhan Jagadeesh and Sheridan Titman (1993) presented an alternative to the view suggested by De Bondt and Thaler (1985) that stock prices overreact to information, leading to success of contrarian strategies which bought past losers and sold past winners. This study argued that trading strategies which buy stocks that have performed well in the past and sell stocks that have performed poorly in the past, viz relative strength strategies, could also generate significant positive returns. This study investigated the efficiency of the stock market by examining the profitability of a number of trading strategies. The strategies they considered would select stocks based on their returns over the past 1, 2, 3 and 4 quarters. They also considered holding periods that varied from 1 to 4 quarters. This gave a total of 16 strategies. In addition, they examined a second set of 16 strategies that would skip a week between the portfolio formation period and the holding period. To increase the power of their tests, the strategies they examined included portfolios with overlapping holding periods. The period of the study was 1965 to 1989, of NYSE and AMEX stocks. The profits of the above strategies were calculated for both a series of buy and hold portfolios and a series of portfolios that were rebalanced monthly to maintain equal weights. Trading strategies that bought past winners and sold past losers realised significantly abnormal returns over the period of study. The strategy they examined in most detail, which would select stocks based on their past 6-month returns and would hold them for 6 months, realised a compounded excess return of 12.01 percent per year on average.

The evidence was, thus, consistent with delayed price reaction to firm-specific information, rather than overreaction as DeBondt and Thaler had suggested. The long term performances of past winners and losers revealed that half of their excess returns in the year following the portfolio formation date dissipated within the following 2 years. The returns of the stocks in the winners and losers portfolios around their earnings announcements in the 36 months following the formation period were also examined and a similar pattern was found. Specifically, stocks in the winner portfolio realised significantly higher returns than the stocks in the losers' portfolios few months following the formation date.

However, the announcement date returns in the 8 to 20 months following the formation date were significantly higher for the stocks in the losers' portfolio than for the stocks in the winner portfolios. The evidence of initial positive and later negative relative strength returns suggested that common interpretations of return reversals as evidence of over-reaction and return persistence (i.e. past winners achieving positive returns in future) as evidence of under-reaction were probably overly simplistic. A more sophisticated model of investor behaviour is needed to explain the observed pattern of returns. It is possible that the market under-reacts to information about the short-term prospects of firms but over-reacts to information about their long-term prospects.

T.P. Madhusoodanan (1995) tested the over-reaction hypothesis, using the winner-loser effect suggested by De Bondt and Thaler for the first time in India. According to the study, the strategy of purchasing loser shares and short selling winner shares would be able to generate an excellent arbitrage return in the Indian case. He used weekly data on average stock prices, which were adjusted for bonus and right issues. The data pertained to the share prices of 186 companies, which covered the period from April 1989 to March 1995. The rate of return was calculated from this data. The returns were calculated as the continuously compounded ones. From the return series, the excess returns over the market were calculated. Market return was calculated from the RBI weekly index of share price for all industries. After calculating weekly excess returns over a 52 weeks period, cumulative excess return (CER) was estimated. Those CERs were then ranked from high to low and portfolios were formed. Shares ranked as top 10 formed a winner portfolio and shares ranked as bottom 10 formed a loser portfolio. The process was repeated for the five years viz. 1989-90, 1990-91, 1991-92, 1992-93 and 1993-94. In addition to the RBI index, he took the BSE Sensex and BSE National to check whether any significant differences existed. The performance of these winner and loser portfolios was tested in the next year. In order to account for risk, an equation was used which simultaneously estimated beta (a measure of risk) and the abnormal return.

He found that the returns in Indian stock market also showed winner-loser effect and hence supported the over-reaction hypothesis. However, when the market witnessed an artificial boom, the strategy of over-reaction had not received the punishment it deserved, while during the recession period as well as normal periods, over-reaction based strategy did pay well. On the basis of this analysis, it can be said that the current winner alone should not lure investors, because the current losers may have the potential of giving better returns in the next period. Therefore, fundamentals were more important than impressive over-reaction. If the investors resist from overreacting and take decisions based on the fundamentals it will also be conducive for injecting efficiency in the market, so essential for maintaining good investment climate.

The study by Barberis, Shleifer and Vishny (1996) was motivated by evidence from cognitive psychology of two judgement biases: (a) the representative's bias: people give too much weight to recent patterns in the data and too little to the properties of the population that generates the data: (b) conservatism. In the model of stock prices, proposed by BSV to capture the two judgement biases, earnings were a random walk, but investors falsely perceived that there were two possible earning regimes. In regime A, which investors assume is more likely, a stock's price under-reacts to a change in earnings because investors mistakenly think the change is likely to be temporary. When later earnings do not confirm this expectation (i.e. when earnings don't turn out to be temporary), stock prices show a delayed response to earlier earnings. In regime B, which investors think is less likely, a run of earning changes of the same sign leads investors to perceive that a firm's earnings are trending. Once investors are convinced that the trending regime B holds, they incorrectly extrapolate the trend and the stock price over-reacts. Because earnings are a random walk the over-reaction is exposed by future earnings, leading to reversal of long-term returns. Regime A in the BSV model was motivated by the evidence of short term momentum in stock returns and the evidence of delayed short term response of stock prices to earnings announcements.

Regime B was meant to explain the long-term return reversals of De Bondt and Thaler (1985). The prediction of regime B was reversal of long-term abnormal returns. Specifically, persistent long-term pre-event returns were evidence of market over-reaction, which should eventually be corrected, in post-event returns. In short, not surprisingly, the BSV model did well on the anomalies it was designed to explain. Viewed as a whole, the long-term return literature seems more consistent with the market efficiency prediction that long-term return continuation and long-term return reversal are equally likely chance results.

Daniel, Hirshleifer and Subrahmanyam (1997) adopted different behavioural foundations than the BSV model. In DHS there were informed and uninformed investors. The uninformed ones were not subject to judgement biases. But stock prices were determined by the informed investors, and they were subject to two biases, 'over-confidence' and 'biased self-attribution'. Over confidence led them to exaggerate the precision of their private information about a stock's value. Biased self-attribution caused them to down-weight pubic information about value, especially when the public information contradicted their private information. Over-reaction to private information and under-reaction to public information tended to produce short-term continuation of stock returns, but long-term reversals.

Thus, though based on different behavioural premises, the DHS predictions were close to those of BSV, and the DHS model shared the empirical successes and failures of the BSV model. DHS made a special prediction about what they call selective events. These were events that occurred to take advantage of the mis-pricing of a firm's stock. For example, managers announce a new stock issue when a firm's stock price is too high, or they repurchase shares when the stock price is too low. These public signals produce an immediate price reaction that absorbs some of the mis-pricing. But in the DHS model, the announcement period price response was incomplete because informed investors over-weighed their prior beliefs about the stock's value. (The conservatism bias of the BSV model would produce a similar result). Eventually, the mis-pricing was fully absorbed as further public information would confirm the information implied by the event announcement. The general prediction for selective events was thus momentum; stock returns after an event announcement will tend to have the same sign as the announcement period return.

The problem is that all models for expected returns are incomplete descriptions of the systematic patterns in average returns during any sample period. As a result tests of efficiency are always contaminated by a bad-model problem. The bad-model problem is less serious in event studies that focus on short return windows. But the problem grows with the return horizon. Thus it would appear that Anomalies are chance results; apparent over-reaction to information is about as common as under-reaction, and post-event continuation of pre-event abnormal returns is about as frequent as post event reversal. Most importantly, consistent with the market efficiency prediction, those apparent anomalies can be due to methodology, most long-term return anomalies tend to disappear with reasonable changes in technique.

T.P. Madhusoodanan (1998) analysed the mean reverting tendencies of share prices in the Indian stock market. He argued that the investors tend to overreact to information about the company and market, and hence stock prices will revert back in the future. He tested it under the null hypothesis of homoscedasticity as well as hetroscedasticity. He used the technique of variance ratios to test the mean reversion behaviour. The study was carried out using aggregate level of market indices and disaggregated level of individual companies. The weekly data on 120 stocks traded on the Bombay Stock Exchange (BSE) and two market indices, BSE sensitive index of 30 stocks and BSE National Index of 100 stocks were taken for the analysis. The data pertained to the period from January 1987 to December 1995. The results showed that there were a number of auto-correlations significant at different lags, and most of them at higher lags were negative. This indicated the possibility of long-term mean reversion in the Indian Stock Market. The variance ratio tests suggested that at the aggregate level of BSE sensitive and national indices, the random walk hypothesis cannot be accepted, and the movements appeared to be persistent. From the analysis, it could be argued that hetroscedasticity did not seem to be playing an important role in the Indian stock market. At the disaggregated level of individual stocks, all of them except one showed significant auto-correlations, positive at lower lags and negative at higher lags. The variance ratios were significantly different from one (1) for a vast majority of the cases. Only 16 out of 120 stocks showed random behaviour. The persistent behaviour shown by the market indices were shown by a majority of the individual stock also.

2.3 Semi-Strong Form Tests of the Efficient Market

Event studies, introduced by Fama, Fisher, Jensen, and Roll (FFJR, 1969), produced useful evidence on how stock prices respond to information contained in an event relating to a particular scrip. Many studies focused on returns in a short window (a few days) around a clearly dated event. Each individual test of semi-strong form of efficiency is concerned with the adjustment of security prices to one kind of information generating event. Most of the studies are limited to a few major types of information generating events. The initial major work was apparently the study of stock splits by Fama, Fisher, Jensen, and Roll (FFJR), and a large number of the subsequent studies were adaptation and extensions of the techniques developed in FFJR. However, even before FFJR, some early attempts had been made to study the price changes associated with event information, mainly information regarding stock-splits.

Bellomore and Blucher (1956) selected 100 splits randomly during the period 1946-1956 to study this behaviour. They found that from eight weeks before, and up to the day after the announcement, 86 out of 100 stocks registered percentage price increase greater than those of the Standard and Poor's stock price index for the relevant industry group. From the day after to eight weeks after the announcement date, however, only 43 stocks registered percentage price increases greater than the relevant industry index and on the average during this period split shares only increased 2 percent more in price than non-split shares in the same industry. This suggested that even if one purchases as soon as the announcement is made, split shares would not in general provide higher returns than non-split shares. The same is likely to be true of all publicly available information. Therefore, it seemed to be no way to use a split to increase one's expected returns, unless, of course, inside information concerning the split or subsequent dividend behaviour is available.

Keith B. Johnson (1966) wanted to test the significance of the relationship between price change and stock-split. Although this study did not provide a direct testing of efficiency of stock market but it was an attempt to develop a model that will provide a test of whether there is a significant price change associated with the information about stock splits after controlling for fundamental factors (earnings and dividends) and for stock market trend. Stock splits included those instances in which the number of common shares outstanding was increased by a factor of 2:1 or greater. The splits occurring during calendar year 1959 among common stocks listed on the New York Stock Exchange (NYSE) were taken for the study. A period of 12 months surrounding a split was considered and since there was often visible evidence of some extraordinary price activity prior to the split date, especially around the time of the announcement of a board meeting to vote on a split, it was felt that the period prior to the split date should be somewhat longer than six months. Consequently, P_i was designed as the price seven and one-half months prior to the split date and P_f then became the price four and one-half months after the split date. The data revealed that there was a significant (< 0.05) relationship between price relative and split while controlling for the effect of earnings, dividends and market trend. In other words, there was a significant relative price change associated with a stock split, after taking into consideration the other factors included in the models.

One explanation was that the information concerning the fundamental factors that determine stock prices was simply brought to the market's attention by the split, and possibly sooner than might otherwise occur. The knowledge that, on the average, a positive relationship exists between price change and splitting would appear to be useful to investors only insofar as they can predict several months in advance that, stock split will occur. Otherwise the information implications of a split would get quickly and fully reflected in prices and therefore no gains would be possible if this information came at a stage close to the actual announcement. On the average, the holdings of investors who owned stocks about eight months prior to their split in 1959 and held them until approximately four months after they split outperformed the holdings of those investing for the same period in non-split stocks, irrespective of any dividend increase in the latter. The FFJR's Study concluded similar results later.

Fama, Fisher, Jensen and Roll (FFJR 1969) tested the speed of adjustment of price to specific kinds of new information in this paper. The prime concern of this paper was to examine the process by which common stock prices adjust to the information (if any) that is implicit in a stock split. The splits included all stock dividend of 25 percent or greater. In order to get reliable estimates, twenty-four successive months of price-dividend data around the split date were used. Hence a security must be listed on the Exchange for at least twelve-month before and twelve months after the split. From January 1927, through December 1959, 940 splits meeting these criteria occurred on the New York Stock Exchange and the same were taken for the study. Security return for this period were adjusted by isolating whatever extraordinary effects a split and its associated dividend history may have had on return. It was necessary because during this period, economic and hence general stock market conditions were far from static. A linear regression model was used for this. Least square method was used to estimate its parameters, but it was observed that expected values of the residuals (μ) were non-zero in months close to the split. However, this model assumed that the expected value of residuals will be zero. Hence in order to avoid error, months having expected values of the residuals as zero were excluded from the sample.

The final analysis concentrated on examining the behaviour of the estimated residuals of split securities in the months surrounding the splits. The data presented important evidence that on the average the market's judgements concerning the information implications of a split were fully reflected in the price of a share at least by the end of the split month but most probably almost immediately after the announcement date. Thus the results of the study lent considerable support to the conclusion that the stock market is "efficient" in the sense that stock prices adjust very rapidly to firm-specific information. Still, an import question remained unanswered; 'was the adjustment so rapid that information about splits can in no way be used to increase trading profits'? This study did not allow full examination of this question. Simple examination of the policy of buying splitting securities as soon as information concerning the possibility of a split becomes available was done. This suggested that the policy of buying splitting securities as soon as a split was formally announced did not lead to increased returns.

Myron S. Scholes (1972) provided an important insight about the period of adjustment of new information. It described the procedure of adjustment as well as duration of adjustment of new information into share prices. The event concerned for this study was the large-block sales of stock called secondary distributions. Sales rather than the purchases of shares were chosen because large-block purchases of securities often reflect attempts to acquire control of the firm rather than the more normal kind of investment demand that was his main concern here. Secondary distributions were chosen in lieu of primary distributions because new issues were often associated with important events such as expansion programmes, changes in capital structure, and the like. These events and what they mean to management's views and intentions have not always been completely anticipated and discounted by the market, so that price adjustments, sometimes of fairly substantial size, accompany the announcement of new issue by the firm. If it is possible to determine whether the seller was likely to possess information, this might permit to determine the average value of information and the market's adjustment to the value of this information.

Also, since no one was likely to sell if he had good information, he only had to worry about information effects in one direction. A complete list of all secondary distributions for listed New York Stock Exchange firm was compiled for the period January 1947–December 1965 from the Investment Dealers' Digest. Since daily price data were available from July1961 to December 1965, most of the analysis was concentrated over this time period, a period in which there were 345 secondary distributions. Monthly data on prices were available for the period 1947-65.

The longer period was used to confirm the analysis of the daily data sample. The parameters of the market model were estimated using 100 days of return data on each security in the sample around the day of the secondary but excluding the six observations prior to the secondary and seven observations including and subsequent to the day of the secondary. An estimated prediction error was computed for a period of twenty-five days prior to the secondary and for fourteen days subsequent to the distribution. This methodology provided a means of estimating the average effects of the sale of large-block distributions on security prices. The estimated prediction errors were abnormal returns, returns not accounted for by the security's normal relationship to the market as described by the market model. By taking averages of the prediction errors for each day relative to the distribution day, he was able to estimate the average abnormal return on each day associated with the sale of the large-block distributions. The abnormal performance through time of a portfolio of secondary distributions purchased at the start of the period of interest and held through the end of the period of interest. It appeared that the total adjustment to the sale of a secondary distribution took approximately six days, from day 0 to day 5.

W.H. Hausman, R.R. West and J.A. Largay (1972) questioned the earlier findings by Johnson and argued that his study contained a rather arbitrary assumption concerning the relevant time period over which stock splits and price behaviour were studied. They suspected that the substitution of different and possibly more logical time periods might significantly alter Johnson's conclusions. With the appearance of a second paper by FFJR their suspicion received considerable support. After reading the FFJR study, they were sufficiently confident about their tentative hypothesis, and wanted to use a methodology similar to Johnson's to study the relationship between splits and stock price behaviour over different time periods. Further more, they felt that by doing so they would shed additional light on several issues raised by FFJR, and would reconcile some surface differences between their results and Johnson's and in general, would provide a synthesis of the analysis of stock splits.

Their results clearly indicated that buying stock on (or after) the date on which a split had been publicly announced did not lead to systematic price appreciation greater than the appreciation that might be expected from underlying factors such as corporate earnings and the industry-by-industry outlook for stock price movements. On the basis of their findings, they would want to amend the statement of Johnson (relationship between splits and price behaviour would appear to be useful to investors only insofar as they can predict several months in advance that a stock split will occur) to read that this information was useful even if it was received as late as twenty-eight days before the announcement of the split. Although they admitted that their choice of the twenty-eight day period was arbitrary, it did prove the point that prior information about a likely split could benefit an investor.

Their empirical results suggested that much of the price change associated with a split actually occurs before rather than after the announcement becomes public. This finding implied: (1) That the impending announcement of a stock split typically "leaks" to some people in the period preceding the board meeting at which the decision is formalised; and (2) that certain very astute security analysts look at the data about a company's earning, know of an impending board meeting, and simply conclude that the time is right for a split to be declared. Neither their results nor FFJR's gave any clue as to which of these possibilities (or any other possibility) was responsible for what was observed in the data, although their own hunch was that the former hypothesis was the more likely of the two.

S. Basu (1977) made an attempt to determine empirically the relationship between investment performance of equity securities and their P/E ratios. While the efficient market hypothesis denies the possibility of earning excess returns, this price-earning ratio hypothesis asserted that P/E ratios, due to exaggerated investor expectations, might be indicators of future investment performance. The effect of P/E ratio information on share prices was studied during the period

April 1957 to March 1971. Thus this study can be considered as an event study from one perspective and an analysis of anomaly from another, as it examined the return forecast power of the P/E ratio (called the price-earning anomaly, which argues that lower the P/E ratio-higher the returns).

The general research design was employed to examine the relationship between P/E ratios and investment performance of equity securities. For any given period under consideration, two or more portfolios consisting of securities with similar P/E ratios were formed. The risk-return relationships of these portfolios were compared and their performance was then evaluated in terms of pre-specified measures. Finally, as a test of the efficient market hypothesis the returns of the low P/E portfolio were compared to those of a portfolio composed of randomly selected securities with the same overall level of risk. Data represented over 1400 industrial firms, which actually traded on the NYSE between September 1956 and August 1971.

During this period, the low P/E ratio seemed to have, on an average, earned higher absolute and risk-adjusted rate of return than the high P/E securities. This was also generally true when bias on the performance measures resulting from the effect of risk was taken into account. These results suggested a violation of the hypothesis that security price behaviour is consistent with the EMH. The result reported in this paper were consistent with the view that P/E ratio information was not "fully reflected" in security prices in as rapid a manner as postulated by the semi-strong form of the EMH. Securities trading at different multiples of earnings, on average, seemed to have been inappropriately priced vis-à-vis one another and opportunities for earning "abnormal" returns were afforded to investors. Tax exempt and tax paying investors who entered the securities market with the aim of rebalancing their portfolios annually could have taken advantage of this by acquiring low P/E stocks. From the point of view of these investors "market inefficiency" seemed to have existed. On the other hand, transactions and search costs and tax effects hindered traders or speculators from exploiting the market's reaction and from earning net 'abnormal' returns which were significantly greater than zero. Therefore, the hypothesis that capital markets were efficient in the sense that security price behaviour was consistent with the semi-strong version of the 'fair game' model could not be rejected unequivocally. In conclusion, the behaviour of security prices over the 14-year period studied was perhaps not completely described by the EMH and there was a suggestive evidence of inefficiency.

The other significant 'events' that have been studied to examine the efficiency at the semi-strong level are: dividend announcements, new issue of shares and corporate control transactions like mergers and takeovers. Charest (1978), Asquith and Mullins (1983) observed that unexpected changes in dividends are on average associated with stock-price changes of the same sign (The result is a surprise, given that the Miller-Modigliani (1961) theorem, and its refinements (Miller and Scholes (1978)), predict either that dividend policy is irrelevant or that dividends are bad news because (during the periods of the tests) dividends are taxed at a higher rate than capital gains. Asquith and Mullins (1986), Masulis and Korwar (1986) gave another surprising result that new issues of common stock are bad news for stock prices, and Dann (1981), Vermaelen (1981) found that redemptions, through tenders or open-market purchases, are good news. One might have predicted the opposite, that is, stock issues are good news because they signal that the firm's investment prospects are strong. Dodd (1980), Asquith (1983) found that mergers and tender offers on average produce large gains for the stockholders of the target firms. Proxy fights, management buyouts and other control events are also wealth-enhancing for target stockholders.

Aswath Damodaran (1993) developed a simple approach towards estimating the price adjustment coefficient for different return intervals as functions of the return variances in these intervals. This measure was derived from the description of the price process contained in Amihud Y. and Mendelson H. (1987) as a combination of an intrinsic value adjustment factor and a noise term. The approach developed here was used to estimate price adjustment coefficient for all firms listed on the CRSP daily returns tape from 1977 to 1986. The estimates were made separately for two five-year periods, the first extending from January 1977 to December 1981 and the second covering January 1982 to December 1986. Firms on the NYSE on the basis of market value were classified into five classes and price adjustment coefficient were estimated for each class and these coefficients were compared with estimates obtained for NASDAQ stocks with data available on the CRSP-NMS tape. This was an appealing way of measuring the information efficiency of a particular stock, a group of stocks or the overall market. For the formulations for the price adjustment coefficient, three critical assumptions were made. The first was that the intrinsic value process was i.i.d. and followed a random walk. The second was that the noise terms and intrinsic value processes were independent. The third was that the price adjustment coefficient approached one as the return interval was extended. A return interval of twenty days was chosen for tests but to examine the sensitivity of the results alternative intervals ranging from ten to forty days periods were also estimated.

Damodaran's Results showed evidence of lagged price adjustment for short return intervals (one to three days) in both estimation periods. The one-day price adjustment coefficients were not dramatically different for different classes. The values of coefficients were ranging from 0.61 for the smallest firm to 0.72 for the largest firms. Similarly, there were only marginal differences in co-efficient for longer return intervals. When the price adjustment coefficient for firms in the NYSE/AMEX sample were compared to those for a NASDAQ sub-sample, the result showed that the over-the-counter stocks had much lower price adjustment coefficient for return intervals up to five days. Moreover, the firms in the latter (OTC) group had higher intrinsic variance and noise components in the price process, than firms on the major exchanges.

Damodaran suggested that the approach used here to estimate price adjustment coefficient could be used to examine the price adjustment process around any "event" that satisfies the following conditions. First, the event should be hypothesised to increase or decrease the speed of price adjustment. Second, a sufficient number of firms should have experienced the event to allow the researcher to draw on the cross-sectional distribution of price adjustment coefficient, to accept or reject the hypothesis. Third, there should be sufficient return data available (500 trading days or more if daily return data is used) before and after the event available on each firm to make reasonable estimates of variances in longer return intervals. The approach developed in this paper was also used by Damodaran and Lim (1991) to examine price adjustment coefficients around option listing and to conclude that prices adjusted much more quickly to new information after the listing of options. Other events that would seem to satisfy these conditions include stock splits, first time listing on the exchange, dual listing on international exchanges, earnings and dividend announcements.

K.G. Sahadevan and M. Thiripalraju (1995) investigated into the lead/lag relationship between money supply and stock return in the Indian context. It was to test a frequent argument, mostly advanced on the basis of common sense, that movements in aggregate indices of common stock prices could be predicted from prior changes in money supply. A set of regressions of stock returns on past, current and future terms of money supply were carried out and their explanatory power across various sample periods tested. Efficient market hypothesis contradicts with the widespread conventional wisdom that money has a lagged effect on stock market and that investors can use the lag in formulating profitable trading rules. There is no disagreement on the proposition that monetary changes do affect stock return; but whether it effects with a lag or lead or contemporaneously only makes all the difference.

The study used monthly observations on Sensex, RBI Index, M_1 and M_3 for a period spanning over 14 years ending March 1994. Simple regression model was used to explain the relationship between stock return and money supply. The hypothesis that any past information whether monetary or non-monetary, does not have any lag effect on stock price was found to have no empirical support. In most cases, it was found that five months lagged money supply had significant influence on current stock returns. Stocks were found to be least responsive to changes in money balances in the Indian context. This was evidenced by the fact that only less than 5 percent of the household savings were being channelled to stock market. Since major portion of the household savings were held in the form of physical assets, bank deposits, currency and provident and pension funds, the possibility of opting stocks as a hedge against fall in return on money was the least. Finally, it was observed that in a country like India where a major chunk of unaccounted money is channelled to stock market, no empirical studies would reveal the true structural relationships between money supply and stock return.

Shah Saeed Hassan Chowdhury, M. Shibley Sadique and M. Selim Akhter (2002) focused on how the firm size affects the speediness of stock price adjustment to information. The model developed by Amihud and Mendelson (1987) and extended by Damodaran (1991, 1993) was used in this study. The indices of BSE-30, BSE-100 and BSE-200 were used as a proxy for the portfolios of different firm sizes. The data included the indices from January 5, 1992 through April 16, 1999. Further, the entire period was divided into two sub-periods: 1992-95 and 1996-99. An estimation model, which was developed by Amihud and Mendelson, was used to estimate the price adjustment coefficient. Price adjustment coefficient represented the speed of adjustment of information into prices. The observed price changes upon arrival of new information were partitioned into (i) intrinsic value changes and (ii) noise changes. The different values of price adjustment co-efficient (Suppose "g") stated that:

- g = 0 represents an extreme case of no reaction
- 0 < g < 1 represents partial adjustment
- g = 1 represents full (though noisy) price adjustments; and
- g>1 represents overreaction to information.

The results obtained confirmed that the Indian stock market had a lagged information adjustment process. It took few days before the full information was reflected in the indices. Lagged adjustment processes were found for all the three indices under study, indicating inefficiency in the market. The study also showed that the market had become more prone to partial adjustment after the regional crisis in 1997. Contrary to the hypothesis, the BSE-30 took the longest time for adjustment of new information into stock prices, suggesting slower price adjustment process for the big firms. Consequently, the BSE-100 and the BSE-200 emerged as more efficient indices than the BSE-30. The high frequency trading of big firms might have induced more price fluctuation for which the index of the BSE-30 took more time to adjust to new information. Trading of high frequency resulted in over-reaction and it took time to adjust to its true values.

Jinho Byun and Michael Rozeff (2003) measured the postsplit performance of 12,747 stock splits from 1927 to 1996 using more time periods and by applying a uniform set of up-to-date procedures. The results, based on a variety of subperiods and methodologies, indicated that buyers and sellers of splitting stocks did not, on average, earn abnormal returns that are significantly different from zero. Between 1927 and 1996, neither of the two main methods used found performance significantly different from zero for splits of 25 percent or larger. Even for some selected sub periods, some sub samples displayed positive abnormal returns using one method but negligible abnormal returns were found using the other method. Overall, they concluded that stock split evidence against market efficiency was neither pervasive nor compelling. They argued that although previous researches reached contradictory conclusions regarding long-term market efficiency with respect to stock splits, their results not only gave fresh evidence in favour of efficiency but also had implications for other studies claiming to discover market inefficiencies in long-term abnormal returns. They strongly argued that the appearance of significant abnormal returns is sensitive to time period, method of estimation, and sampling.

Their findings, although limited to stock splits, provide a message of caution and scepticism towards the claim that long-run abnormal performance pervades financial markets in response to publicly announced events. Before we abandon market efficiency in favour of long-run market under reaction (or overreaction) to various events, prudence demands several commonsense steps. These include evaluating evidence gathered over many, many years and over many kinds of markets and making efforts to evaluate the fallibilities of our methods of modelling, sampling, and measuring long-run abnormal returns. If we do conclude that long-run abnormal performance exists after a given event, prudence demands, for several reasons, that we do not rashly conclude that markets are so inefficient that prices are routinely biased by large amounts, such as 50 to 100 percent. First, if investor biases are at work, they are likely eventually to be followed by losses and learning. Second, a large amount of useful economic reasoning is based on rationality. Third, it is a fact that model errors and benchmark and sampling issues affect abnormal return measures. Fourth, even if market prices reflect the imperfections of humans as information processors, market imperfections such as arbitrage costs, default risks, and short-selling costs also may rationally limit how traders response in their attempts to profit and by their actions to affect market prices.

Event studies, introduced by Fama, Fisher, Jensen, and Roll (FFJR, 1969), produced useful evidence on how stock prices respond to information. Many studies focused on returns in a short window (a few days) around a clearly dated event. The assumption in studies that focus on short return windows is that any lag in the response of prices to an event is short-lived. When the stock price response to an event is large and concentrated in a few days, the way one estimates daily expected returns (normal returns) in calculating the abnormal returns has little effect on the inferences drawn.

As a result the event studies are the least encumbered by the 'joint-hypothesis problem' that the market efficiency must be tested jointly along with an asset-pricing model. Largely for this reason, the event studies are the cleanest evidence we have on efficiency and with very few exceptions, the evidence is supportive i.e., quick adjustment consistent with efficiency is noted.

There is, however, a developing literature that challenges this assumption, arguing instead that stock prices adjust slowly to information, so one must examine return over long horizons to get a full view of market inefficiency. It is here that the two important segments of the market efficiency research, viz, event studies and long term return anomalies meet. Does new information get rationally reflected in the price, or is there random over or under reaction to the new information? And further, does new information get fully reflected quickly, almost instantaneously, or is there a gradual and slow adjustment? If the response of prices to the information seems to occur slowly then post-announcement drift in the abnormal returns would be an inefficient anomaly.

2.4 Tests for Private Information

The strong form of the efficient market hypothesis assumes all available public and private information is fully reflected in a security's market price. The strong form, in terms of market participants, also assumes of monopolistic access to information. There are two possible ways of testing the efficiency of the strong-form. One is to determine whether insiders earn better than average profits from their market transactions. Another is to evaluate the performance of mutual funds. In studying the performance of mutual funds the major goals are to determine (a) whether in general fund managers seem to have access to special information which allows them to generate "abnormal" expected returns, and (b) whether some funds are better at uncovering such special information than others.

Michael C. Jansen (1968) evaluated the performance of mutual funds, confining his attention only to the issue of evaluating a portfolio manager's predictive ability-that is, his ability to earn returns through successful prediction of security prices which were higher than those which we could expect given the level of riskiness of his portfolio. This dimension of performance evaluation has implication for the theory of random walk in so far as it comments on the utility of private or special information. He measured the absolute performance of portfolios rather than ranking portfolios. The model for this purpose was derived from the basic asset pricing model, which implied that the expected return on any asset is equal to the risk free rate plus a risk premium given by the product of the systematic risk of the asset and the risk premium on the market portfolio.

The risk premium on the market portfolio is the difference between the expected returns on the market portfolio and the risk free rate. Assuming that the asset pricing model was empirically valid, the realised returns on any security or portfolio could be expressed as a linear function of its systematic risk, the realised returns on the market portfolio, the risk free rate and a random error, which had an expected value of zero. If the manager were a superior forecaster (because of special knowledge not available to others) he would tend to systematically select securities which realise random error e>0. Hence his portfolio would earn more than the "normal" risk premium for its level of risk. Therefore, an evaluation model was developed that incorporated and reflected the ability of the manager to forecast the market's behaviour as well as his ability to choose individual issues. The sample consisted of the returns on the portfolios of 115 open end mutual funds for which net asset and dividend information was available in Wiesenberger's Investment Companies for the ten-year period 1955-64.

The evidence on mutual fund performance indicated that not only these 115 mutual funds were on average not able to predict security prices well enough to outperform a buy-and-hold policy, but also that there was very little evidence that any individual fund was able to do significantly better than what could be expected from mere random chance. Moreover, these conclusions remained valid when they measured the fund returns gross of management expenses (that is assuming their book-keeping, research, and other expenses except brokerage commissions were obtained free). Thus on average the funds apparently were not quite successful enough in their trading activities to recoup even their brokerage expenses. The results upheld the strong level efficiency of the market.

Jaffrey F. Jaffe (1974) sought to estimate the profitability of insider trading. Researchers were interested in the amount of special information insiders possess, as well as in the profit they earned from such knowledge. The average investor seeks out useful information in the "Official Summary of Insider Trading (Washington)", the monthly report listing the transactions of corporate officials. Another objective of this paper was to test the information content of the official summary. A random sample of trading months was drawn covering 200 large firms in the period 1962-68. This was referred to as the "initial sample". The sample covered trades in approximately 1000 firms' months. Some adjustments were made in the initial sample because of certain problems concerning measurement of insider trading. All transactions from the initial sample whose value was greater than US$20,000 were assembled into a sub-sample. This sub-sample of intensive trading contained 370 trades. Since brokerage commissions were approximately 1 percent per transaction, insiders might not trade on special information that would lead only to stock price movement of the order of transaction costs.

In addition, under section 16(b) of the U.S. Securities and Exchange Act of 1933-34, an insider was prosecuted and required to return all profits from a purchase and subsequent sale (or a sale and a subsequent purchase) occurring within 6 months of each other. This law discouraged them for trading. Many insiders presumably transacted for reasons other than to profit from special information. Moreover, insiders might purposely trade without information to camouflage trading based on special information. Insider gains might also be marked by "gamesmanship". Some of these phenomena may act to camouflage the gains from trading on inside information. To minimise these effects, the study made use of additional samples limited to large trades or to months where there was an especially great preponderance of trades in a single direction. In order to estimate the profitability of insider trades, the study examined the performance of a security subsequent to specific types of insider trades in that security, which was called as trading events.

The model developed by Sharpe and Lintner was used here. This model postulated a linear relationship between the expected return on a security and the co-variance of the security's return with the return on a portfolio composed of all securities in the market (commonly called the 'market portfolio'). Since it was assumed that insiders possessed more special information concerning their own security than concerning the market as a whole, the study examined the residuals of securities subsequent to insider trading events. To estimate the profit of insiders, individual residuals and cumulative residuals were calculated. In order to calculate net profit that insiders earn, transaction costs were subtracted. The study assumed a transaction cost of 2 percent. It was concluded that insiders did possess special information. However, after adjustment for transaction cost, only the intensive trading sample with 8-months holding periods were earning statistically larger returns (a 5 percent cumulative abnormal return). Results suggested that investors could profit by prompt use of official summary's information on intensive trading companies. Official summary contained information on future stock prices, a finding inconsistent with much of the research on efficient capital market. The data suggested that the best of the trading rules based on information in the official summary involve an examination of intensive trading companies, as only those samples possessed residuals greater than the cost of transaction. The author suggested that the future research might further examine whether strategies based on intensive trading companies, as well as entirely new strategies, can consistently outperform a naïve buy-and-hold strategy.

Joseph E. Finnerty (1976) conducted a study to ascertain as to how well insiders do, relative to the market in general. In the earlier study (Jaffe), the selection of samples was based on "intensive" insider trading criteria, i.e. the samples were biased in favour of those insiders whose performance would more than likely be superior to the average insider. This bias invalidated the findings for a test of the strong form. By testing the entire population of insiders, this study evaluated the performance of the 'average' insider. The time period for this study was from January 1969 to December 1972. The data were from the S.E.C.'s official summary of stock Transactions for NYSE firms. For the total period, there were over 30,000 recorded individual transactions; 9602 buy transactions and 21,487 sell transactions. Insiders 'buy portfolio' and insider 'sell portfolios' were formed for each month of the time period. Thirty-six such buy/sell portfolios were formed, starting with January 1969 and ending with December 1971.

Portfolio returns for each of the thirty-six buy/sell portfolios were computed for the portfolio formation month and for each of the eleven subsequent months. Simple regression methodology was used assuming the linearity of the relationship between the risk-adjusted rates of return for the insider portfolio and the risk adjusted rates of market return.

The results for both the buy and sell portfolios showed the fact that insiders, probably because of their access to privileged information, can outperform the market in their stock selections (a 4.8 percent cumulative abnormal return over an 8 month period). From the monthly differential returns for the buy portfolio, most of the above average returns were realised in the first six months. The first month had the greatest amount of above average return. This might indicate either that the information on which the insiders act soon became public knowledge and was discounted by the market quite quickly or that the knowledge that the insiders had been accumulating certain stocks, prompted the public to acquire the same stocks and thereby bid up the prices. The monthly differentials for the sell portfolios presented a different picture, with most of the below average performance-taking place uniformly throughout the subsequent months. It would appear that initially as the insiders were selling, either the information, that they were selling, was not immediately released; or the market did not immediately discount the fact that insiders were selling.

In comparing the results of this study with Jaffe's work, the existence of above average insider returns was agreed upon. One difficulty in comparison was due to Jaffe's lumping together of both the buy and the sell transactions into one statistic. In addition, Jaffe's results indicated the short run nature of insiders' above average performance. By limiting his study to the two hundred target companies on the CRSP tape, he omitted from consideration smaller companies whose insiders may have had a better appreciation of the value of insider information. To sum up the findings of this study, it corroborated those of Jaffe: Insiders were able to outperform the market. Insiders could and did identify profitable as well as unprofitable situation within their corporations. This finding tended to refute the strong form of the EMH.

Stephen Figlewski (1978) developed a model of a speculative market in which the redistribution of wealth among traders with different information and ability was studied. He defined a speculative market as a market for a good demanded not (entirely) for its own sake but for resale (or potential resale) in the future. The current price in a speculative market will always have at least a component which is the market's estimate of the future price. Present price would reflect the best information about the future in the sense that the present price, plus normal profits, would be the best estimate of the future price. He defined market efficiency as a function of market participants with given set of information. Efficiency, thus, depended upon the ability of market participants i.e. ability to process the information. Throughout this paper, "efficiency" was taken to mean strong form efficiency. According to him return of informed trader was equal to return of uninformed trader. Because more return of informed trader would be accompanied by the cost of information which will offset the higher return.

In spite of ability to process information, availability of money is also very important. In the short run, efficiency is difficult to achieve since weightage are not given through information but through the availability of money (e.g. "suppose I have superior information than others but don't have money to invest in the market than my weightage will be very less although I am well informed because with small money I am not in a position to affect the prices. My informational processing ability will be under valued"). He concluded that in the short run the market tends towards increased efficiency, but in neither the short run nor the long run is full efficiency likely. The average deviation from efficiency was shown to depend on traders' characteristics such as the quality and diversity of their information and their risk aversion.

Dan Givoly and Dan Palmon (1985) examined the extent to which the abnormal return gained by insiders was realised by price changes arising from the disclosure of the trade itself or from subsequent disclosure of specific news about the company to which the insiders might be privy. A sample of 68 companies was randomly selected from the population of companies whose fiscal year ended December 31 and which were listed on the American Stock Exchange (AMEX) throughout the 3-year period from 1973-75. The AMEX sample represented relatively small companies that were thought to offer higher profit potential to insiders and therefore was likely to reflect trading on inside information. The performance measure employed was the abnormal return, where the normal rate of return was estimated from the familiar market model using daily rates of return. The market rate of return was computed as the equally weighted index of all securities listed on the American and New York Stock Exchanges. Examination of data for individual industries suggested that the phenomenon of abnormal gains to insiders was widespread although the level of the abnormal return varied among industries. The finding of excess return subsequent to insider trading was in accord with the results of previous studies (based on different samples), like Jaffe (1974) and Finnerty (1976). This study estimated the abnormal return of 8.0 percent over an 8-month holding period (compared with 5 percent in case of Jaffe and 4.8 percent in case of Finnerty). The greater abnormal returns found in this study might be due in part to the fact that the sample consisted of relatively small AMEX-listed companies while Jaffe and Finnerty's samples consisted of large companies in the NYSE. Moreover, the results also showed that a significant abnormal return was produced in the wake of the trades themselves, lending support to the conjecture that (outside) investors accept the superior knowledge and follow the footsteps of insiders.

M.M. Goyal (1992) conducted this study to discover whether the capabilities and special information of chartists and fundamentalists could enable an investor to earn above normal returns. For that, all scrips which a reported investment magazine (capital market) recommended for buying in its issue No. VI/14 dated September 30-October 13, 1991 were sampled. There were, in all, 94 such scrips across various industries. Two portfolios were made. One by making equal investment in each of these scrips and the other by making weighted investment according to the recommendations. Return on these scrips in one year's time was calculated and compared with return on market portfolio. In order to calculate the return on market portfolio, sensex was used. Results of this enquiry suggested that recommendations of even a good investment magazine failed to decisively beat the market. Although the average yield appeared to be higher for the investor who acted upon these recommendations, most of the differences could be attributed to random factors, since four out of five were not found to be significant even at 10 percent level in either of these two portfolios.

N.S. Malik (2006) attempted to investigate the performance of country funds by using the dataset of developed and emerging markets of the world. This study incorporated both the approaches followed in the world of investment management viz, active and passive management, to analyze the relative performance of country funds vis-à-vis their respective bench mark indices across the emerging and developed markets of the world. The results indicated that the country funds that followed the active portfolio management strategies proved to be dramatically different in reporting the significantly higher returns (in US Dollar terms) compared to the passive portfolio (buy-and-hold) management strategies. The study supported the claim that these strategies are highly dynamic and remunerative for all the stake holders over a longer period (greater than 80 percent of the country funds out-performed their respective bench mark indices over a period of five years). In terms of the magnitude of out-performance over a period of five years, 40.82 percent of out- performers beat the bench marks by more than 50 percent, where as, 14.29 percent over-performed the bench marks by at least 100 percent. Thus there was evidence that it is possible to beat the market by following active portfolio management strategies.

2.5 Conclusion

Thus, it is seen that the market efficiency issue is yet to be definitely settled and there exists a controversy in the finance literature as to whether or not the major stock markets of the world are 'efficient' in pricing the securities that are traded there. This controversy manifests itself not only in the classical confrontation between the stock market practitioners and the stock market theorists, but also in the research findings that have unearthed evidence both for and against efficiency.

What causes variations in expected returns, are these variations rational, and can these be predicted are the vital questions which will still be asked and to which concrete answers still need to be found out. There are ever-growing dimensions of further research in this field and more coherent explanations need to be developed about the link between the expected returns and business conditions on one hand, and between variations in expected returns and macro-economic variables like consumption, investment and saving on the other.

3

Indian Stock Market: Reforms and Refinements

3.1 Introduction

Stock market is described as the barometer of the state of health of a nation's economy. The Indian stock market has been attracting considerable attention in recent years, especially after the liberalisation of the economy. Since India started its economic reform in early 1990s, it has ensured its current position as one of the largest developing countries in the world. Meanwhile, its emerging stock market has experienced tremendous growth. It is widely anticipated that India's stock market will continue to develop swiftly in the future and will play an important role in the world market. The increasing influence of India's Stock Market at the world level has evoked widespread academic and business interest.

The financial sector in India has developed quite significantly in both size and sophistication. A major fillip to strengthen the financial system was given by the rapid expansion of the stock market, especially in the later part of the 1980s and subsequently by initiating financial sector reforms on the recommendation of the high-powered Narasimham Committee in 1992-93. Wide ranging financial reform measures were implemented since then to make the financial system more market oriented, thereby aiming at increasing its efficiency. In the capital market, for instance, some of these reforms included repealing the Capital Issues (Control) Act of 1947; setting up the Securities Exchange Board of India (SEBI) to protect investors and to enhance transparency of the capital market; freeing the companies to approach capital market after clearance by SEBI; allowing the foreign institutional investors (FIIs) an access to the domestic capital market on registration with SEBI; permitting private sector to set up mutual funds; relaxing the guidelines for investment in money market instruments; bringing UTI under the regulatory jurisdiction of SEBI; commencing the operations of Over the Counter Exchange of India (OTCEI) and National Stock Exchange of India with nationwide stock trading and electronic display, clearing and settlement facilities; permitting Indian companies an access to international capital markets through Euro equity issues and liberalisation of the investment norms for NRIs so that NRIs and overseas corporate bodies can buy shares and debentures without prior permission of RBI. The Indian capital market in general and stock market in particular has witnessed metamorphic changes, which have occurred in response to these domestic initiatives coupled with the emerging liberal and deregulated global financial environment.

3.2 Pre-Requisites of Efficient Security Market

Continuous price formation of securities is the main function of a stock exchange. The collective judgement of many people operating simultaneously in the market, resulting in the emergence of a large number of buyers and sellers at any point of time, has the effect of bringing about changes in the levels of security prices in small graduations, thereby evening out wide swings in prices. The ever-changing demand and supply conditions result in a continuous revaluation of financial assets, with today's prices being yesterday's prices-altered, corrected, and adjusted, and tomorrow's values being again today's values-altered, corrected, and adjusted. The process is an unending one. Stock market thus acts as a barometer of the state of health of the nation's economy, by constantly measuring its progress or otherwise. An investor can always have his eyes turned towards the stock exchanges to know, at any point of time, the value of the investments and plan his personal needs accordingly.

Stock markets in India have a long history. The first stock exchange was set up in Bombay in 1875. Since then, the number of stock exchanges in the country has grown to 23 including the Over the Counter Exchange of India (OTCEI) and the National Stock Exchange (NSE). Each stock exchange is managed by a governing body and for regulation and control of transactions; each stock exchange has bylaws and regulations, which are more or less uniform in all stock exchanges.

Broadly speaking an efficiently functioning security market is one that inspires confidence of both the suppliers of funds and the raisers of funds. In more specific terms the following are the pre-requisites of efficient security market system:

1. **Absence of information based gains:** The concept of perfect information is a pre-requisite for efficient financial market. It means same and free information to all. In other words it means that

- There is no insider trading
- There is no misleading information by the raiser
- There should not be any foul play by intermediaries
- There is no kerb trading

2. **Correct valuation of financial assets:** It means proper pricing and valuation of financial assets or financial instruments. Normally security prices should be based on fundamentals i.e. their valuation should be based on the underlying strengths and weaknesses and accordingly a fair return should be payable on them. However in reality this may not happen and some distortions take place due to speculation, rigging etc in secondary market.
3. **Maximization of Convenience and Minimization of transaction costs to both the supplier of funds and the raiser of funds:** An essential aspect of this quality of the efficient financial markets is the presence of Mutual Funds whose main role is maximization of convenience, minimization of transaction cost and diversification of risk (by investing in different instruments).

Thus in reality the financial system may not be efficient and thereby its contribution to the economic development is constrained by presence of all these hurdles discussed above, with the result that the savings don't get channelised towards productive investments at right time, in right quantum and at efficient costs.

3.3 Secondary Market Reforms

The all-encompassing process of liberalisation unleashed in 1991 had a wide-ranging impact on the capital market in India. Structural reforms and introduction of technology have changed the look and feel of the bourses today from what they were a couple of decades ago. Until 1988, the stock exchanges were more or less self-regulatory organizations but they have not been discharging their self-regulatory role, as a result of which malpractices had crept into trading, adversely affecting the investors' interests. Several committees examined and made recommendations to reform the organizations of the stock exchanges. To streamline the stock market functioning and to improve the stock market efficiency, many steps have been taken in a series of reforms in recent times. The SEBI was set up to monitor the functioning of the stock exchanges. The following discussion gives an insight about the notable reforms that have taken place over the years, more specifically after the initiation of the liberalisation process in 1991.

3.4 Compilation of SENSEX and Later Refinements

The Bombay Stock Exchange sensitive index number of equity prices (base 1978-79=100) comprising of 30 scrips was introduced on January 2, 1986. The index has established a place for itself amongst everyone concerned with the securities market and has been widely accepted as a fair reflector of the trend of prices on the Bombay Stock Market. Being a "Sensitive Index", it consists of practically all the market leaders. One can identify the booms and bust of the Indian equity market through SENSEX.

In order to fulfil the need of the market participants for still broader, segment-specific and sector-specific indices, the Exchange has continuously been increasing the range of its indices. It compiled more broad-based index series namely

BSE-100 (initially called BSE National Index), BSE-200 and BSE-500 in January 1989, May, 1994 and 1999 respectively. In 2001, BSE launched the BSE-PSU Index, DOLLEX-30 and the country's first free-float based index—the BSE TEC*k* Index. The Exchange shifted all its indices to a free-float methodology (except BSE PSU index) in a phased manner. Since September 2003 the SENSEX is calculated on a free-float market capitalization methodology, which is the global best practice. The Exchange launched dollar-linked version of BSE-100 index i.e. Dollex-100 on May 22, 2006.

The values of all BSE indices are updated every 15 seconds during the market hours and displayed through the BSE Online Trading (BOLT) system, BSE website and news wire agencies.

3.5 Establishment of CRISIL

Credit Rating and Information Services of India Ltd was promoted in 1987 by the Industrial Credit and Investment Corporation of India Limited (ICICI) and Unit Trust of India (UTI). Its other shareholders include Asian Development Bank, Life Insurance Corporation of India, State Bank of India, Housing Development Bank of India, HDFC etc.

The principal objective of CRISIL is to rate debt obligations of Indian companies. The ratings provide a guide to the investors as to the degree of certainty of timely payment of interest and principal on a particular debt instrument. The rating indicates CRISIL's current opinion as to the relative safety of timely payment of interest and principal on a particular debt instrument, fixed deposit programme or short term instrument. The key considerations involved in rating relate to:

- business analysis covering industry risk, market position of the company within the industry and the operating efficiency of the company;
- financial analysis covering earning protection, adequacy of cash flows;

- management evaluation covering track record of the management planning and control systems, depth of managerial talent and succession plans;
- regulatory and competitive environment covering structure and regulatory framework of the financial system, trends in regulation/deregulation and their impact on the company.

Hence, investors can get superior information at very low cost and take calculated risk in the investments. Corporate borrowers with good rating can raise funds at comparative cheaper rates in the capital market.

3.6 Establishment of SEBI

The reform of the financial services sector, especially the securities markets, has been at the very heart of the process of economic reforms, which has aimed at engendering a much larger role for the private corporate sector in the economy and allocation of capital through market channels. In this context, the need for an independent regulatory body, which would be empowered to regulate the securities markets and be responsible for fostering its development, was widely felt. Thus, the Securities and Exchange Board of India (SEBI) was set up in 1988 as an administrative arrangement. In 1992, the SEBI Act was enacted, which gave it the statutory status.

The SEBI operates within the legal framework of the SEBI Act, 1992. The statutory objectives of the SEBI as enshrined in the SEBI Act are:

- Protection of investors interests in securities market
- Promotion of the development of the securities market
- Regulation of the securities market and
- Matters connected therewith and incidental thereto

In keeping with these statutory objectives, the SEBI has set for itself strategic aims for each of the four key spheres which encompass SEBI's activities in relation to the investors, issuers, intermediaries and the regulatory regime. To the investors, the SEBI strives to assure that their rights are protected, they are enabled to make informed choices and decisions in a market which is fair in the financial dealings. To the issuers, the SEBI strives to provide a transparent and efficient market where they are enabled to raise resources at low cost, but conduct themselves in accordance with the highest standards of corporate governance and that they are conscious of and meet their regulatory obligations. To the intermediaries, the SEBI strives to render a market in which they can compete freely and operate in a manner which gives the investors and market participants the confidence that the market is efficient, orderly and fair.

With these strategic aims in view, the SEBI has been constantly reviewing and reappraising its existing policies and programmes, formulating new policies and regulations to nurture areas hitherto unregulated/inadequately regulated and to implement them in a manner to promote the growth of the market with transparency, fairness, efficiency and integrity. The SEBI has been taking measures to modernise the securities market to enhance its fairness, transparency and efficiency. The SEBI had also stepped up its efforts to protect the integrity of the market through various risk containment measures, surveillance system and enforcement actions.

Besides, the developments in the securities market have highlighted several concerns about market design and effectiveness for speedy detection and deterrent action in the case of market frauds. In the area of market design, the change of settlement cycles from account period to T+5 rolling and gradually to T+2 rolling for the entire market constitute a measure with far reaching consequences. In contrast to the rapid pace of change in the equity market, the debt markets both for government debt and corporate debt have seen fewer changes and as a result have suffered from weakness of market design. The fledgling derivatives market in equities is now offering a new opportunity to investors and market participants for hedging, managing risk and as a vehicle for speculation. Growth of this segment will enhance the competitiveness of the entire securities market. Keeping all these aspects and new developments in view, the SEBI has laid down its objectives and initiatives in the short and medium term as follows:

Investor Education:

- Implementation of real time information sharing system
- Enhancing of continuous disclosure standards

Strengthening Primary Market:

- Disclosure in offer documents
- Issue of sweat equity guidelines
- Revisiting IPO Guidelines, including IPO grading (on the lines of credit rating)

Strengthening Secondary Market:

- Enhancing liquidity
- Margin trading
- Call auction markets
- Market making
- Surveillance
- Risk containment
- Insider trading
- Investigation and Enforcement

Strengthening Derivative Segment:

- Surveillance
- Introduction of new products
- Physical settlements
- Enlarging base of companies and intermediaries
- Efficiency of derivative market

Review of Market Infrastructure:

- Demutualisation, Corporatisation, Consolidation, Interlinking etc.
- Setting up of Centralised Listing Authority

Review of Regulations concerning:

- Fraudulent and Unfair Practices relating to Securities Markets
- Portfolio Management

- Merchant Bankers
- Brokers

3.7 Setting up of OTCEI

The term "over the counter (OTC)" was initially understood as a way of trading securities other than on an organised stock exchange, i.e., over the counters of different dealers. The traditional stock exchanges have failed to provide facilities such as adequate liquidity to small scrips and access to small investors. Investors are losing the confidence in market because of lack of transparency of operations. Now OTC markets are envisaged as floorless security trading system equipped with computer network through which nationally and internationally scattered buyers and sellers can conduct business more efficiently. Investors can walk into any of the counters of members and dealers, see the quote-display on the screen, decide to deal and conclude the transaction. All the counters of members and dealers are connected by a telecom network to the OTC Central computer. OTC trading also provides for transfer of shares by registrars, up to a certain percentage per folio. This results in faster transfers. The concept of immediate settlement makes it better for the investor. Investor will trade, not with share certificates but with a different tradable document called CR (Counter Receipt).

OTC Exchange of India is a company incorporated under section 25 of the Companies Act 1956, with the objective of setting up a national, ringless, screen-based, automated stock exchange. OTC Exchange, recognised as a stock exchange under Section 4 of the Securities Contract Regulation Act 1957, is promoted by the all-India financial institutions, insurance companies and merchant banking subsidiaries of banks. It was promoted jointly by many financial institutions like ICICI, UTI, LIC, GIC, IDBI, IFCI, SBI Capital etc. Players in this market include members, dealers, companies and investors, supported by registrars/ custodian, settler and banks. OTC operations are supervised by SEBI and Government of India. Trading began in January 1993 with only two scrips but now OTC Exchange is making its presence clearly felt on the capital market scene.

3.8 Entry of Foreign Investment into India

For all practical purposes, foreign investment was not welcome into India until 1991. The policy framework for the inflow of capital was liberalised in pieces through the 1990s. Foreign Institutional Investors (FII) investment into portfolios was permitted and Indian companies were permitted to raise resources through the international markets in the form of European Convertible Bonds (ECBs) and Global Depository Receipts (GDRs). Foreign direct investments were liberalised and multinational companies were sought by state governments to invest into infrastructure and other projects. The dramatic change in the environment led to a surge in capital flows during mid-1990s.

FIIs were allowed to invest in the capital market securities from September i992. However, investments by them were first made in January 1993.

Foreign investment has entered India mainly in three ways: through direct investment, through FIIs and in the form of ADRs/GDRs. The dramatic changes have come essentially from FII's investments. All this led to an enormous increase in the market capitalization, and also the volatility, at the BSE.

3.9 Establishment of the NSE

National Stock Exchange of India Limited (NSE) was given recognition as a stock exchange in April 1993. NSE was set up with the objectives of (a) establishing a nationwide trading facility for all types of securities, (b) ensuring equal access to all investors all over the country through an appropriate communication network, (c) providing a fair, efficient and transparent securities market using electronic trading system, (d) enabling shorter settlement cycles and book entry settlements, and (e) meeting the international benchmarks and standards. Within a short span of life, above objectives have been largely realized and the Exchange has played a leading role as a change agent in transforming the Indian Capital Markets to its present form. NSE has set up infrastructure that serves as a role model for the securities industry in terms of trading systems, clearing and settlement practices and procedures, fine-tuned risk management system etc. The standards set by NSE in terms of market practices, products, technology and service standards have become industry benchmarks and are being replicated by other market participants. It provides screen-based automated trading system with a high degree of transparency and equal access to investors irrespective of geographical location. The high level of information dissemination through on-line system has helped in integrating retail investors on a nation-wide basis. The Exchange currently operates three market segments, namely Capital Market Segment, Wholesale Debt Market Segment and Futures and Options segment.

NSE has been playing the role of a catalytic agent in reforming the market in terms of microstructure and market practices. Right from its inception, the exchange has adopted the purest form of demutualised set up whereby the ownership, management and trading rights are in the hands of three different sets of people. This has completely eliminated any conflict of interest and helped NSE to aggressively pursue policies and practices within a public interest framework. It has helped in shifting the trading platform and NSE is the first exchange in the world to use satellite communication technology for trading. It uses satellite communication technology to energise participation from about 2800 VSATs from nearly 358 cities spread all over the country. Its trading system, called National Exchange for Automated Trading (NEAT), is a state of-the-art client server based application. At the server end all trading information is stored in an in-memory database to achieve minimum response time and maximum system availability for users. For all trades entered into NEAT system, there is uniform response time of less than 1.5 seconds. NSE has been continuously undertaking capacity enhancement measures so as to effectively meet the requirements of increased users and associated trading loads. With recent upgradation of trading hardware, NSE can handle up to 2.5 million trades per day. NSE has also put in place NIBIS (NSE's Internet Based Information System) for on-line real-time dissemination of trading information over the Internet. Today NSE is the world's fourth largest stock exchange in terms of volume of trades undertaken.

S&P CNX Nifty: S&P CNX Nifty is a well diversified 50 stock index accounting for 22 sectors of the economy. It is used for a variety of purposes such as benchmarking fund portfolios, index based derivatives and index funds. S&P CNX Nifty is owned and managed by India Index Services and Products Ltd. (IISL), which is a joint venture between NSE and CRISIL. IISL is India's first specialised company focused upon the index as a core product. IISL have a consulting and licensing agreement with Standard & Poor's (S&P), who are world leaders in index services. The index is professionally maintained and is ideal for derivatives trading. Nifty stocks represented about 63% of the free float market capitalization as on December 31, 2009.

CNX Nifty Junior: The next rung of liquid securities after S&P CNX Nifty is the CNX Nifty Junior (next 50 stocks). It may be useful to think of the S&P CNX Nifty and the CNX Nifty Junior as making up the 100 most liquid stocks in India. As with the S&P CNX Nifty, stocks in the CNX Nifty Junior are filtered for liquidity, so they are the most liquid of the stocks excluded from the S&P CNX Nifty. The maintenance of the S&P CNX Nifty and the CNX Nifty Junior are synchronised so that the two indices will always be disjoint sets; i.e. a stock will never appear in both indices at the same time. Hence it is always meaningful to pool the S&P CNX Nifty and the CNX Nifty Junior into a composite 100 stock index or portfolio.

Table 3.1: NSE: Achievements/Milestones

November 1992	Incorporation
April 1993	Recognition as a stock exchange
April 1995	Establishment of NSCCL, the first Clearing Corporation
June 1995	Introduction of centralised insurance cover for all trading members
July 1995	Establishment of Investor Protection Fund
October 1995	Became largest stock exchange in the country
April 1996	Commencement of clearing and settlement by NSCCL
April 1996	Launch of S&P CNX Nifty
June 1996	Establishment of Settlement Guarantee Fund
November 1996	Setting up of National Securities Depository Limited, first depository in India, co-promoted by NSE
December 1996	Commencement of trading/settlement in dematerialised securities
December 1996	Launch of CNX Nifty Junior
May 1998	Promotion of joint venture, India Index Services & Products Limited (IISL)
February 1999	Launch of Automated Lending and Borrowing Mechanism
February 2000	Commencement of Internet Trading
June 2000	Commencement of Derivatives Trading (Index Futures)
December 2000	Commencement of WAP trading
June 2001	Commencement of trading in Index Options
November 2001	Commencement of trading in Futures on Individual Securities
December 2001	Launch of NSE VaR for Government Securities
January 2002	Launch of Exchange Traded Funds (ETFs)
October 2002	Launch of NSE Government Securities Index
January 2003	Commencement of trading in Retail Debt Market
June 2003	Launch of Interest Rate Futures
August 2003	Launch of Futures & options in CNXIT Index
June 2004	Launch of STP Interoperability
June 2005	Launch of Futures & options in BANK Nifty Index

June 2007	NSE launches derivatives on Nifty Junior & CNX 100
October 2007	NSE launches derivatives on Nifty Midcap 50
January 2008	Introduction of Mini Nifty derivative contracts on 1st January 2008
March 2008	Introduction of long term option contracts on S&P CNX Nifty Index
April 2008	Launch of India VIX
April 2008	Launch of Securities Lending & Borrowing Scheme
August 2008	Launch of Currency Derivatives
August 2009	Launch of Interest Rate Futures
November 2009	Launch of Mutual Fund Service System
December 2009	Commencement of settlement of corporate bonds
February 2010	Launch of Currency Futures on additional currency pairs

(Source: www.nse-india.com)

3.10 Central Depositories

In order to solve myriad of problems associated with trading in physical securities, NSE joined hands with IDBI and UTI to promote dematerialisation of securities and set up National Securities Depository Limited (NSDL) which commenced operations in November 1996. The system of trading based on physical transfer/custody of securities militated against efficient functioning of markets. The main problems faced by the investors were: (a) delays in transfers of securities, (b) bad deliveries on account of forged signatures/mismatch of signatures or fake certificate/forged transfer deed, (c) delay in the receipt/non-receipt of securities after allotment/refund to non-allottees and (d) inadequate infrastructure in banking and postal segments to handle a large volume of application and store the share certificates.

To overcome the problem of large number of transfer deeds and share certificates, the concept of jumbo transfer deed and jumbo certificate had been introduced. Under this system, all certificates are surrendered to the Issuer Company, which has issued securities. On the receipt of the certificates through the depository participants and on the advice of the depository with whom the company has already entered into an agreement, the certificates are cancelled. The depositories' name is entered in the Register of Members of the company in respect of these securities, and the names of the beneficial owners whose names are recorded as such with a depository are deleted. This has eradicated physical paper from trading and settlement of securities, got rid of risks associated with fake/ forged/stolen/bad paper and has made transfer of securities automatic and instantaneous. The depository system in India operates within the framework of Depositories Act, 1996 and SEBI (Depositories and Participants) Regulation, 1996. This reform has brought the Indian stock markets at par with the international markets. Demat delivery today constitutes 99.99 percent of total delivery-based settlement.

3.11 Clearing Operations and Risk Management on Stock Exchanges

The National Securities Clearing Corporation Ltd. (NSCCL), a wholly owned subsidiary of NSE, was incorporated in August 1995. It was set up to bring and sustain confidence in clearing and settlement of securities; to promote and maintain, short and consistent settlement cycles; to provide counter-party risk guarantee, and to operate a tight risk containment system. NSCCL commenced clearing operations in April 1996. NSCCL carries out the clearing and settlement of the trades executed in the Equities and Derivatives segments and operates Subsidiary General Ledger (SGL) for settlement of trades in government securities. It assumes the counter-party risk of each member and guarantees financial settlement. It also undertakes settlement of transactions on other stock exchanges like, the Over the Counter Exchange of India. NSCCL has successfully brought about an up-gradation of the clearing and settlement procedures and has brought Indian financial markets in line with international markets.

3.11.1 Clearing: NSCCL carries out clearing and

settlement functions as per the settlement cycles of different sub-segments in the Equities segment. The clearing function of the clearing corporation is designed to work out a) what counter parties owe and b) what counter parties are due to receive on the settlement date. Settlement is a two way process which involves legal transfer of title to funds and securities or other assets on the settlement date.

NSCCL has also devised mechanism to handle various exceptional situations like security shortages, bad delivery, company objections, auction settlement etc.

3.11.2 Guarantee: NSCCL assumes the counter-party risk of each member and guarantees settlement through a fine-tuned risk management system and an innovative method of on-line position monitoring. A large Settlement Guarantee Fund provides the cushion for any residual risk. It operates like a self-insurance mechanism where members contribute to the Fund. In the event of failure of a trading member to meet settlement obligations or committing default, the Fund is utilised to the extent required for successful completion of the settlement. This has eliminated counter-party risk of trading on the Exchange. As a consequence, credit risk no longer poses any threat in the market place. The market has full confidence that settlement shall take place in time and shall be completed irrespective of default by isolated trading members. A separate Settlement Guarantee Fund is maintained for the Futures & Options segment.

3.11.3 Risk Management: A sound risk management system is integral to an efficient clearing and settlement system. NSE introduced for the first time in India, risk containment measures that were common internationally but were absent from the Indian securities markets. NSCCL has put in place a comprehensive risk management system, which is constantly upgraded to pre-empt market failures. The Clearing Corporation ensures that trading member obligations are commensurate with their net worth. There is a system of imposition of Margins based on the categorisation of stocks.

Many kinds of Margins are imposed for comprehensive risk management. Daily margins payable by members consists of the following: Value at Risk Margin, Extreme Loss Margin, and Mark to Market Margin. In case of any shortfall in margin, the members shall not be permitted to trade with immediate effect and in addition there are penalties. Members should, in turn, have a prudent system of risk management to protect themselves from client default. However, the quantum of these margins and the form and mode of collection are left to the discretion of the members.

3.12 Risk Management System Adopted by SEBI

The key risk management measures initiated by SEBI include:

- Categorization of securities into groups 1, 2 and 3 for imposition of margins based on their liquidity and volatility.

3.12.1 VaR-based Margining System:

- VaR based margining system has been put in place based on the categorization of stocks based on the liquidity of stocks depending on its impact cost and volatility. It addresses 99 percent of the risks in the market.
- Specification of mark to Market margins.
- Specification of Intra-day trading limits and Gross Exposure Limits.
- Capital adequacy requirements of members.
- Real time monitoring of the Intra-day trading limits and Gross Exposure Limits by the Stock Exchanges.
- Collection of margins on T+1 basis, although settlement done T+2.
- Index based market wide circuit breakers.
- Automatic de-activation of trading terminals in case of breach of exposure limits.

SEBI issued a circular modifying the above mentioned present risk management framework to move to upfront collection of VaR margins (instead of margin collection on

T+1 basis). The new framework was made effective from May 30, 2005. In the revised framework the liquid assets deposited by the broker with the exchange should be sufficient to cover upfront VaR margins, Extreme Loss Margin, MTM (Mark to Market Losses) etc.

3.13 Stock Lending Scheme

To facilitate securities lending for short sellers, who sell shares without owing them, SEBI approved a scheme in 1997. Short sellers provide liquidity to genuine investors. In a falling market, the purchases of short sellers to cover their sales lead to recovery in prices. In a rising market, short sales can arrest further rise. The scheme enables lending of securities through an approved intermediary registered with the SEBI, to a borrower under an agreement for a specified period with the condition that the borrower would return equivalent securities of the same type/class at the end of the period along with the corporate benefits accruing on the securities including dividends, rights, bonus, redemption benefits, interest pr any other right/benefit accruing on the securities lent. The borrower cannot discharge his liabilities through payment in cash or kind. In the event of failure of the borrower, the intermediary would be liable to make good the loss caused to the lender. The intermediary is entitled to receive from the borrower collateral security and fee for lending securities.

The Securities Lending Scheme also provides for mobilisation of idle stock in the hands of lenders such as FIs, MFs, FIIs and large investors. This also gives an additional income to the lender, who can lend securities to the clearing corporation. Securities lending are an essential element for smooth functioning of modern securities market. Securities lending contributes to the liquidity in the market. It smoothens the settlement system and improves efficiency of the settlement system by facilitating timely delivery of securities and correcting temporary imbalances between demand and supply.

For securities borrowing and lending system, clearing corporations of the stock exchange would be the nodal agency and be registered as the "Approved Intermediaries" (AIs). A lender, under an agreement with the AI can lend his securities to the AI with the guarantee that the AI shall return the equivalent securities of the same class and type. A borrower can also borrow from the AI on the specified terms of the AI and shall also return the equivalent securities of the same class and type. The AI is the complete interface between the borrower and the lender. In the event of the defaulted selling broker failing to make the delivery within the specified period, the clearing corporation has to buy the securities from the open market and return the same to the lender within seven trading days. There are at present 4 approved intermediaries under the scheme. At present, SEBI is not granting any fresh registrations to the Approved Intermediaries.

In 2005, SEBI referred the original stock lending scheme of 1997 to its secondary Market Advisory Committee (SMAC), in order to explore alternative models of stock lending, since the scheme had almost failed to take off. Moreover, it was advocated that a mechanism for lending and borrowing wherein the ordinary investor can also participate should be put in place. After discussing five different models and examining the prevailing situation, SMAC felt that it might be worthwhile to re-launch the same scheme and allow it to operate for sometime, since T+2 was now operative and lending/ borrowing will make greater sense in the absence of *badla*. It also suggested reviewing the scheme after six months.

3.14 Introduction of Derivatives

It is the internationally popular and standard method of speculative trading on stock exchange, which gives the benefits of speculation to the market without giving the losses of speculation to the average investors. Derivative securities (popularly known as Futures & Options or F&O) refer to securities which have no tangible worth of their own and which derive their value from the underlying main security.

Options contract/option security is a contract which gives the option holder an option to buy or sell a specified quantity of a security at a predetermined price on or before a specified date. In other words an option holder has a right but not the obligation to buy or sell a specified security at pre-determined price. Futures differ from options in the sense that whereas an option gives the right but not the obligation to buy or sell a specified number of underlying securities at a future date at past prices, a future is a contract to buy/sell a predetermined number of underlying securities at a future date on past prices (i.e. the contract incorporates a right as well as obligation to carry out the transaction). In India, through a gradual progress, now the full range of derivatives is allowed in equity derivatives. Index Futures, Index Options, Stock Options and Stock Futures were introduced in June 2000, June 2001, July 2001 and November 2001 respectively. Stock derivatives are more popular in India. India is one of the few countries to have stock futures. The equity derivatives market has grown dramatically ever since its inception in June 2000 and has become one of the most successful derivatives markets amongst all countries in the third world.

3.14.1 Advantages of Derivatives:

1. Increased volume of trading (from market point of view).
2. Segregation of market into speculative i.e. derivative trading, and investment market i.e. non-derivative/basic security market. Thus the losses on account of excessive speculation, excessive volatility of share prices and market defaults doesn't go against the interest of small innocent investors. For financial institutions like financial intermediaries, investment companies, mutual funds etc. and also for expert individuals derivatives are a good way of engaging in speculation in the stock market.
3. Risk management, especially through option derivatives, which gives benefit of hedging i.e. limiting the loss.

4. Benefit of portfolio diversification, as the market participants can now choose derivative securities in addition to stocks

Despite all the charms of derivative products, there are certain systemic inefficiencies. Currently the settlement is done in cash, favouring traders, increasing the scope for speculation. A trader can sell futures of a particular stock without owning even a single share of the stock. As trades do not need to be backed by an actual delivery, it gives enough leeway to manipulators to rig prices and make profits. Reduction in contract size is another important aspect. The minimum contract size is currently a huge Rs.2 lakh, which acts as a constraint to the entry of retail investors. Once all the systemic inefficiencies are sorted out, a further rise in derivative volumes will hardly come as a surprise. The world over, the turnover in the derivatives segment is double that of cash segment. Keeping the trend, derivative volumes in India, too, were also expected to be twice that of the cash market.

3.15 Rolling Settlement

The account period settlement mechanisms which was being followed in the stock exchanges before the introduction of rolling settlement provided for settlement of transactions on a fixed day only, irrespective of when the transaction took place. The system earlier had a fortnightly account period settlement, which was changed in September 1996 into a weekly settlement with the settlement period being Monday to Friday. The account period based settlement hampered the liquidity of the market as well as the liquidity of individual investors. Moreover there was a system of carry over of the settlement wherein the transaction could remain unsettled and could be carried over to the next settlement period (by paying badla charges). With a view to introduce greater transparency, liquidity and with a view to reduce the excessive speculation and problems of defaults, the mechanism of rolling settlements was introduced and has been gradually extended in coverage and scope. Under this mechanism every transaction is to be settled within a specified number of days, rather than on a fixed weekly or fortnightly day (e.g, T+3 means transaction plus 3 days is the settlement period).

The shift from the traditional account period settlement marks an important change in the market design and age old practices. Rolling settlement is an important measure to enhance the efficiency and integrity of the securities market. In January 1998, SEBI had introduced rolling settlement on a voluntary basis for D-mat securities. However, as there was hardly any response to the voluntary scheme, SEBI introduced compulsory rolling settlement, initially for 10 scrips in January 2000 and then increased the number of scrips in a phased manner. In July 2001, soon after the market crash in March 2001, SEBI shifted 414 stocks to the rolling T+5 settlement mode and made settlement cycles uniform across all exchanges for the remaining stocks. (All stocks were included in rolling settlement in January 2002.) In April 2002, the T+5 settlement cycle was further reduced to T+3. And from April 2003, the settlement cycle has been further compressed to T+2, with the aim being to move to T+1.

Shorter settlement cycles lower the trading costs for market participants and reduce the risk of counter-party failure. It has improved the attractiveness of Indian stock market.

3.16 Operation of Fully Electronic Trading Platforms

NSE was the first exchange in the world to use satellite communication technology for trading. It has helped in shifting the trading platform from the trading hall in the premises of the exchange to the computer terminals at the premises of the trading members located country-wide and subsequently to the personal computers in the homes of investors. Its trading system, called National Exchange for Automated Trading (NEAT), is a state of-the-art client server based application. At the server end all trading information is stored in an in-memory database to achieve minimum response time and maximum system availability for users. For all trades entered into NEAT system, there is uniform response time of less than 1.5 seconds. With recent upgradation of trading hardware, NSE can handle up to 2.5 million trades per day. NSE has also put in place NIBIS (NSE's Internet Based Information System) for on-line real-time dissemination of trading information over the Internet. Similarly, the values of all BSE indices are presently updated every 15 seconds during the market hours and displayed through the BSE Online Trading (BOLT) system, BSE website and news wire agencies.

3.17 Internet Based Trading

The Securities & Exchange Board of India (SEBI) approved the report on Internet Trading brought out by the SEBI Committee on Internet Based Trading and Services In January 2000. Internet trading can take place through order routing systems, which will route client orders to exchange trading systems for execution. Thus a client sitting in any part of the country would be able to trade using the Internet as a medium through brokers' Internet trading systems. SEBI-registered brokers can introduce Internet based trading after obtaining permission from respective Stock Exchanges.

3.18 Wireless Application Protocol (WAP) Trading

Since august 2000, SEBI-registered brokers who have been granted permission to provide Internet based trading services can introduce Wireless Application Protocol (WAP) platform based trading, after obtaining permission from respective stock exchanges. NSE became the first exchange to grant permission to its members for providing WAP trading services. NSE has granted permission to one of its trading members M/s. Gogia Capital Services Ltd. to provide securities trading through WAP. This is the first WAP enabled online stock trading facility in the country, leading to convenience of live stock trading for people on the move.

3.19 Margin Trading Facility

In the context of present market structure and reforms taken, there was an apprehension that the liquidity may be affected. It was, therefore, felt necessary to provide the facility of margin trading as an alternative for infusing liquidity in the market. The RBI had issued guidelines in November 2001 for allowing banks to finance margin trading subject to various parameters and risk containment measures. Margin Trading is trading with borrowed funds/securities. It is essentially a leveraging mechanism which enables investors to take exposure in the market over and above what is possible with their own resources. SEBI has been prescribing eligibility conditions and procedural details for allowing the Margin Trading Facility from time to time.

Corporate brokers with net worth of at least Rs. 3 crore are eligible for providing Margin trading facility to their clients subject to their entering into an agreement to that effect. Before providing margin trading facility to a client, the member and the client have been mandated to sign an agreement for this purpose in the format specified by SEBI. It has also been specified that the client shall not avail the facility from more than one broker at any time. The facility of margin trading is available for Group 1 securities and those securities which are offered in the initial public offers and meet the conditions for inclusion in the derivatives segment of the stock exchanges. For providing the margin trading facility, a broker may use his own funds or borrow from scheduled commercial banks or NBFCs regulated by the RBI. A broker is not allowed to borrow funds from any other source. The "total exposure" of the broker towards the margin trading facility is regulated by SEBI.

In 2005 the SMAC of SEBI noted that despite these enabling provisions, margin trading has not truly taken off as all banks are not lending under the scheme and it advocated for new models like the one where brokers directly finance their clients for margin trading. It was considered suitable in the

Indian context subject to legal feasibility. Another variant of the traditional model was also discussed, where the banks and RBI recognised NBFC's finance the margin trading and the brokers merely act as facilitator. In this model, the broker would only be bringing the borrowers (clients) to the lenders (banks/NBFCs) for financing and will be intermediary and such borrowing would not be reflected in the balance sheet of the broker. The risk containment measures recommended for the traditional model will apply mutatis mutandis to this model. The SMAC felt that this model can be launched immediately since it does not require any legal amendments / clarifications and margin trading may be immediately started with this model.

3.20 Installation of Circuit Breaker on BSE

SEBI introduced the index based market wide circuit breaker system from July 2, 2001. These circuit breakers would apply at three stages of the index movement either way at 10 percent, 15 percent and 20 percent and would bring about a coordinated halt trading in all equity and equity derivative markets nationwide.

- In case of a 10 percent movement of either of these indices, there would be a 1 hour market halt if the movement takes place before 1 pm. In case the movement takes place at or after 1 pm but before 2:30 pm there will be a trading halt for ½ hour. In case the movement takes place at or after 2:30 p.m. there will be no trading halt at the 10 percent level and the market will continue trading.
- In case of a 15 percent movement of either index, there will be a 2-hour halt if the movement takes place before 1 p.m. If the 15 percent trigger is reached on or after 1 p.m. but before 2 p.m., there will be a 1 hour halt. If the 15 percent trigger is reached on or after 2 p.m. the trading will halt for the remainder of the day.
- In case of a 20 percent movement of the index, the trading will be halted for the remainder of the day.

Movement of either BSE Sensex or the NSE S&P CNX Nifty, whichever is breached earlier, would trigger the market wide circuit breakers. These percentages will be translated in to absolute points index variations on quarterly basis and at the end of each quarter would be revised and be applicable for the next quarter. The above mentioned percentages would be translated into absolute points would be calculated on the closing level of the index on the last day of the trading in a quarter and rounded off to nearest 25 points in case of BSE Sensex and nearest 10 points in case of S&P CNX Nifty. In addition to the market wide index based circuit filters, there are individual scrip wise price bands of 20 percent either way, for all scrips in the compulsory rolling settlement except for scrips on which derivatives products are available or scrips including in indices on which derivatives products are available.

3.21 BSE-TEC*k* Index

This is a stock index constituted of companies in the Technology, Media and Telecom sectors (TMT Sectors). It would track the performance of TMT sectors through a basket of 21 quality stocks. The BSE TEC*k* Index would provide a quality benchmark for the investment community in the knowledge-based sectors. The Technology orientation of the current economy has primarily marked a paradigm shift from manufacturing based activities to knowledge based activities. The TMT sectors have seen heightened activity in recent years and the stock valuations of the companies in these sectors have witnessed unprecedented volatility. This led to a strong bull run in the TMT stocks in 1999 and early 2000. The market subsequently witnessed the most unexpected sell-off in the stocks of the TMT sectors which led to a huge market capitalisation erosion on the bourses and scared away genuine investors. Despite this, the TMT stocks have kept investors fascinated. It is without doubt that the world is closely tracking the performance of the TMT sectors to infer future trends in the economy. Globally a lot of investment is being committed to the TMT sectors. Even in India, the last 2 years have seen a lot of international and local money flowing into the TMT sectors. Going by the trading pattern, around 68 percent of the turnover on the stock exchanges is taking place in TMT sector stocks. These stocks collectively account for 23 percent of the total market capitalisation. It was felt that in the absence of a proper benchmark, the performance of the TMT sectors remained inadequately tracked. In order to fill this void, the BSE-TEC*k* index is being positioned as an index for benchmarking the performance of the TMT sectors.

'TEC*k*' stands for the following:

- **'T' - Technology** (BSE Sector: Information Technology)
- **'E' - Entertainment**(BSE Sector: Media & Publishing)
- **'C' - Communication** (BSE Sector:Telecom)
- **'*k*' - Other Knowledge based** companies not falling in any of the above 3 sectors. There are 21 constituents in the BSE-TEC*k* Index.

3.22 Straight through Processing

Straight Through Processing (STP) is a process driven mechanism to control all elements of the work flow in a financial transaction that allows electronic capturing and processing of transactions in one pass from the point of origination to settlement. STP was launched in India in November 2002. STP is currently being used by the market participants on a voluntary basis. Several STP Service Providers have been providing STP service to the market participants; however, there was no inter-operability between the STP Service Providers. NSE has now set up the STP Central Hub (2004) to provide inter-operability between the STP service providers. The STP service providers connect to the STP central hub for the purpose of sending and receiving messages between them. The STP Central Hub facilitates the smooth flow of messages between users of different service providers. With interoperability in place, the market participants can avail of the STP services offered by any of the service providers. SEBI has directed that all the institutional trades executed on the stock exchanges shall be mandatorily processed through the STP System with effect from July 01, 2004. The messages like contract notes, delivery instructions etc can be exchanged by the market participants by utilizing the STP services offered by the four service providers, BSE, FT, NSDL and NSE.IT.

SEBI has been working towards further shortening the two-day delay between the transaction date and settlement date, and aims to more to the T+1 settlement from the present T+2. This effort was constrained by the limited ability of the payments system to move funds across the country, and also required electronic dada exchanges within the securities industry, called "straight through processing" (STP) mechanism. Now with the first phase of the STP implementation in place, focusing on the transaction flow between` institutional investors, custodian banks and brokers, it is hoped that movement towards T+1 settlement would be facilitated.

3.23 Unique Client Code

SEBI made mandatory for all brokers and sub-broker to use unique client codes for all clients which will act as an exclusive identification for the client and will facilitate maintaining database of their clients. For this purpose, brokers would collect and maintain in their back office the Permanent Account Number (PAN) allotted by Income Tax Department for all their clients. Sub-brokers would similarly maintain for their clients. If a client does not have PAN number, such a client would furnish passport number and place and date of issue. If the client does not have a PAN number or a passport, such a client would furnish driving license number, place and date of issue. If none of the above is available, the client would give his voter ID number. These requirements have become applicable for clients having order value of Rs.1 lakh or more and shall be enforced w.e.f. August 1, 2001. This would help in easing audit trail. An extended endeavour in this context has been the MAPIN scheme of SEBI, discussed later in the chapter.

3.24 Exchange Traded Funds

ETFs are just what their name implies: baskets of securities that are traded, like individual stocks, on an exchange. Unlike regular open-end mutual funds, ETFs can be bought and sold throughout the trading day like any stock. Most ETFs charge lower annual expenses than index mutual funds. However, as with stocks, one must pay a brokerage to buy and sell ETF units, which can be a significant drawback for those who trade frequently or invest regular sums of money. About 60 percent of trading volumes on the American Stock Exchange are from ETFs. The most popular ETFs are QQQs (Cubes) based on the Nasdaq-100 Index and SPDRs (Spiders) based on the S&P 500 Index. Their passive nature is a necessity: The funds rely on an arbitrage mechanism to keep the prices at which they trade roughly in line with the net asset values of their underlying portfolios. For the mechanism to work, potential arbitragers need to have full, timely knowledge of a fund's holdings.

ETFs are different from Mutual funds in the sense that ETF units are not sold to the public for cash. Instead, the Asset Management Company that sponsors the ETF (Fund) takes the shares of companies comprising the index from various categories of investors like authorized participants, large investors and institutions. In turn, it issues them as large block of ETF units. They offer a number of advantages over traditional open-ended index funds as follows:

- While redemptions of Index fund units takes place at a fixed NAV price (usually end of day), ETFs offer the convenience of intra-day purchase and sale on the Exchange, to take advantage of the prevailing price, which is close to the actual NAV of the scheme at any point in time.

- They provide investors a fund that closely tracks the performance of an index throughout the day with the ability to buy/sell at any time, whereby trading opportunities that arise during a day may be better utilized.
- Unlike listed closed-ended funds, which trade at substantial premia or more frequently at discounts to NAV, ETFs are structured in a manner which allows Authorized Participants and Large Institutions to create new units and redeem outstanding units directly with the fund, thereby ensuring that ETFs trade close to their actual NAVs.
- Since an ETF is listed on an Exchange, costs of distribution are much lower and the reach is wider. These savings in cost are passed on to the investors in the form of lower costs. Further, the structure helps reduce collection, disbursement and other processing charges.
- Tracking error, which is divergence between the NAV of the ETF and the underlying Index, is generally observed to be low as compared to a normal index fund due to lower expenses and the unique in-kind creation/ redemption process.

The first ETF in India, **"Nifty BeEs"** (Nifty Benchmark Exchange Traded Scheme) based on S&P CNX Nifty, was launched in January 2002 by Benchmark Mutual Fund. It may be bought and sold like any other stock on NSE. Its symbol on NSE is "NIFTYBEES".

3.25 Demutualisation and Corporatisation of Stock Exchanges

Keeping up with global standards, the Government had announced that the stock exchanges will be corporatised and their ownership, management and trading/operating membership would be segregated from each. In accordance with the above policy announcement, the SEBI Board decided that henceforth no stock broker member of any stock exchange shall be an office bearer of the exchange. All recognised stock exchanges were also directed to amend their rules accordingly. Simultaneously, the SEBI also examined the administrative and legal modalities for corporatisation.

SEBI constituted a Group under the chairmanship of Justice M. H. Kania, former Chief Justice of India to recommend the steps that need to be taken to implement the announcement of the Government policy on Demutualisation and Corporatisation. The terms of reference of this Group were as under:

- to review and examine the present structure of stock exchanges including stock exchanges which are set up as company and those set up as un-incorporated bodies, mainly as AOPs
- to examine the legal, financial and fiscal issues involved to corporatisation and demutualisation of stock exchanges, recommend the specific steps that need to be taken for implementation, and
- to advise on the consolidation and merger of the stock exchanges.

The group gave its recommendations that called for converting the stock exchanges set up as the association of the persons and as limited companies by guarantee into companies limited by shares, and that a common model for corporatisation and demutualisation be adopted for all stock exchanges. This will turn the status of the stock exchanges from non-profit entities to pro-profit institutions.

3.26 Sensex with Free-float Methodology

The free float is a methodology that uses calculations to ascertain the amount of shares that are freely available to investors, and excludes that part of the full market capitalization that is held by promoters. In order to further the process of globalisation of the capital markets, India's most tracked stock market index, the BSE Sensex has turned free float from September, 2003. This method of index weightage will be in-line with the major stock exchanges like the Morgan Stanley Capital Indices (MSCI), Nasdaq-100, Dow Jones, FTSE, Standard and Poor's 500 and STOXX. The new Sensex will reflect market movements better as there will be no undue influence of closely held large-cap stock on the index movement, and only the capitalization that is available to the public influences the market. It would exclude promoters' holding, government holding, controlling/strategic holding and other locked-in shares that will not come to the market for trading in the normal course. In doing so there would be minor changes in weightage of Sensex components, but the value of the index would remain unchanged. This will not erode the comparability of the Sensex to the past.

In India, BSE pioneered the concept of Free-float by launching BSE TECk in July 2001 and BANKEX in June 2003. While BSE TECk Index is a TMT benchmark, BANKEX is positioned as a benchmark for the banking sector stocks. SENSEX becomes the third index in India to be based on the globally accepted Free-float Methodology. Major advantages of Free-float Methodology are:

- A Free-float index reflects the market trends more rationally as it takes into consideration only those shares that are available for trading in the market.
- Free-float Methodology makes the index more broad-based by reducing the concentration of top few companies in Index. For example, the concentration of top five companies in SENSEX has fallen under the free-float scenario thereby making the SENSEX more diversified and broad-based.

3.27 Central Listing Authority

Central Listing Authority (CLA) is a regulatory body established by the SEBI. CLA shall be charged with the responsibility of scrutinizing and approving all applications for letter of permission to list securities on stock exchanges, and make recommendations to SEBI on matters relating to listing conditions and listing standards. The CLA has been empowered to make recommendations to the Securities and Exchange Board of India (SEBI) on issues concerning the protection of interests of investors in securities and the development and regulation of the securities market.

CLA will bring uniformity in the due diligence process and in scrutinising listing applications across the stock exchanges. It would centralise the listing function which currently takes place at the exchange level. Once CLA is fully functional, it may take up ongoing monitoring of compliance of listing requirements by firms. The main function of CLA will be to process applications made by any body corporate, mutual fund or collective investment scheme for a letter of listing on a stock exchange, make recommendations for listing. No company, mutual fund or collective investment scheme apply for listing of its securities to a recognised stock exchange unless it has obtained a letter of recommendation for listing from CLA.

Besides the principal function of receiving and processing applications for "letter precedent to listing", the CLA can now specifically make suggestions on investor protection, development and regulation of the securities market, including listing agreements, listing conditions and disclosures to be made in offer documents. SEBI has come up with a new set of regulations on CLA that has broad-based the functions of the authority, besides making alterations in its composition.

3.28 Introduction of Fund of Funds Schemes

A fund of funds (FOF) scheme is a mutual fund scheme that invests in other mutual funds schemes instead of investing in securities. Such schemes are prevalent in international markets. These schemes can have different investment patterns and investment strategies as disclosed in offer documents. The investors may invest their funds in those FOF schemes which meet their investment objectives instead of investing in different schemes of a mutual fund and keeping track of their NAVs. Such FOF schemes may invest in other sector specific schemes or those schemes which have more weightage of certain stocks and can exit from those schemes when growth prospects of those sectors are not good. The investors putting their money in one sector specific scheme may not be able to decide when to exit.

Earlier, mutual funds had a small number of schemes and hence the concept of FOF was not much feasible. Over the years, all mutual funds have launched a number of schemes and it is now possible for them to launch such FOF schemes. It is also likely that a FOF scheme may like to invest in mutual funds schemes of other mutual funds subject to disclosures in the offer documents. Therefore, the aforesaid Regulations would need amendments so that Clause 4 of the Seventh Schedule of SEBI (Mutual Funds) Regulations, which prohibits a mutual fund scheme from investing in another mutual fund, is not made applicable to FOF schemes.

3.29 Electronic Date Information Filing & Retrieval System (EDIFAR)

A number of the SEBI Regulations impose reporting or filing obligations on the intermediaries and other persons. Further, some intermediaries are also required to issue contract notes or enter agreements with clients or other intermediaries. Presently, these requirements have to be met by physically filing the required documents with SEBI or physical issue of contract note or entering into agreement physically. Section 4 of the IT Act says that any information or other matter required by any law to be in writing can be in electronic form. Section 5 says that where any law requires any information or other matter to be authenticated by the signature of any person, when such requirement shall be deemed to be satisfied, if such information or matter is authenticated by means of digital signature digital signature, using what is known as "public key cryptography", affixed in the manner provided by the Rules.

In case of Foreign Institutional Investors, SEBI is already allowing direct uploading of daily reports through a secure network designed by the Information Systems Division of SEBI. A virtual private network (VPN) has been created through the internet having safety features such as encryption. A terminal specific connectivity has been set up with many custodians who upload the data in respect of each FII as required by the Regulations. In the US, the Securities Exchange Commission (SEC) requires electronic filings through the EDGAR system through the internet. It seems that more than a lakh filers use it. SEBI seeks to facilitate electronic filing of documents by intermediaries etc, e.g., Reports or draft offer documents of schemes of Mutual Funds, Collective Investment Schemes or returns in respect of portfolio investments, annual accounts etc., filed by existing intermediaries who are few in number such as Mutual Funds to whom the present arrangement of VPNs can be extended and which can be integrated in the database maintained by the concerned Department; and,

SEBI is also considering and introducing, in a phased manner, various other e-initiatives like, electronic issue of contract notes, electronic maintenance of record, electronic transmission of documents to unit holders, electronic underwriting agreements with clients etc.

3.30 Development of Self-regulatory Organizations (SROs) in Indian Securities Market

Globally, regulators are debating on the development of the Self Regulatory Organizations (SROs) in the Securities Market more than ever before. Major thinking behind this concept is that some of the regulatory responsibilities of the regulators like SEBI may be shared with these SROs so that they can focus on much bigger and macro level issues. Another dimension of the concept is that it amounts to the self discipline approach, which helps the industry itself in winning the confidence of the market participants.

Financial Markets, across the globe, are undergoing profound, unprecedented and fast-paced changes.

Unquestionably, Regulations need to keep pace with the dynamically changing business environment because Regulators cannot deal with the complexities of the new age business environment with archaic rules, regulations and a rudimentary perspective. At the global level, Regulators' focus is shifting dramatically from regulations to the Development of the Markets. Today, Regulations focus on simply defining the broad framework/parameters for the game and within that framework; market participants are allowed to operate without any intervention. This approach is all about having confidence in the market and systems.

SEBI, accordingly, has been trying to co-design the structure of the Indian Securities Market with the help of the market participants. These organizations operate under the overall regulatory supervision of the main regulator and help the main regulators in accomplishing their Regulatory Objectives. SROs would have their own memorandum of articles and association. They would also have the Bye-laws, which will be approved by SEBI. Broadly, SROs are expected to work on the delegation by SEBI in addition to carrying out the general activities for the market development like investors' education and professional up-gradation among the members. They may also provide the certification facility among their members for the purpose of creating professionalism among the market players. Some of the existing organizations like Association of Merchant Bankers (AMBI), Association of Mutual Funds (AMFI), if desired to be recognized as SROs, would be required to make an application to SEBI on the lines of the regulations finally formulated by SEBI on the subject. SROs provide benefits like:

- **Industry Specialized Knowledge:** As market participants are the members of the SROs, SROs posses good knowledge base. Their interaction with the regulator on day to day basis improves the overall quality of the regulations in the market.
- **Industry Motivation:** Industry participants want to reflect

a clean image to their associates and other operators in the market. Being the part of an SRO helps them do the same.

- **Flexibility in Regulations:** Continuous dialogue of a market oriented body with the main regulator helps the regulations being more dynamic and market oriented. The change becomes easy to implement when both the main regulators and the markets interact on day to day basis and co-design the regulations.
- **Lower Cost of Regulation:** Self-regulation is less costly than the statutory regulation.

3.31 Market Participants and Investors Integrated Database (MAPIN)

Creation of the efficiency and effectiveness in the system has been the concern of all Market Developers and Regulators globally. Numerous initiatives are taken by them to develop a clean market place, which attracts investing community based on its own inherent capabilities, efficiency and credibility. One such initiative in the global markets is the development of an inventory of Market Participants and Investors. On lines of global trends and underlying delivery of the concept, Indian Securities Market is planning to take the steps towards creation of the central database of the Securities Market Participants and Investors. The SEBI (Central Database of Market Participants) Regulations, 2003 were notified on November 20, 2003. As per these regulations, all the participants in the Indian Securities Market viz., SEBI registered intermediaries, listed companies and their associates and the investors would need to get registered and obtain a Unique Identification Number (UIN). The system for allotment of UIN involves the use of biometric impressions for natural persons. This data base is to be designed with cutting edge web based technology so that it is dynamic in nature.

The major objective is creation of a comprehensive database of market participants. Once created, the database would not only help the regulator in establishing the identity of person(s) who have taken large exposures in the market and/or who are trading through a large number of different brokers but also enable the regulator to take adequate risk containment measures such as imposition of margins, trading or exposure limits etc., depending upon the exposures of various investors. Hence, in the event of a failure of market integrity, an immediate audit trail would be possible and the regulator would be able to take early preventive and/or remedial measures and track down the defaulters and/or manipulators. The database would contain comprehensive information of market participants which would be available for view by regulators, SROs and the investing public, giving them advance information of various entities before they actually enter into securities transactions. As it has been decided to introduce the system in a phased manner, it was decided to suspend all fresh registrations for obtaining UIN and the requirement to obtain/quote UIN under the MAPIN Regulations/Circulars with effect from July 01, 2005.

3.32 BSE Indo*Next*:

Regional stock exchanges (RSEs) have registered negligible business during the last few years. As a result, small and medium-sized companies (SMEs) listed there find it difficult to raise fresh resources in the absence of price discovery for their securities in the secondary market. Investors in such small and medium companies are therefore unable to find an exit route and to realise a fair market value for their investments. The companies listed only at RSEs find it extremely difficult, if not impossible, to raise fresh resources from the capital markets in the absence of price discovery of their securities in the secondary market. New small and medium enterprises (SMEs) have also been unable to tap the markets to raise equity and debt, to fund their plans.

The BSE Indo*Next* would help the investors to reach the BSE Indo*Next* traded scrips in addition to the network of BSE, also through the network of about 7,000 members of RSEs, who cater to the investors in the far-flung areas of the country and, thus, contribute to the development of the capital market. BSE Indo*Next* thus, envisages harnessing advantages of creating a single national trading platform, with a large number of member participation, which would help achieve a fairly vibrant trading platform for SMEs.

The BSE Indo*Next* Segment has the following objectives:

- To allow companies listed only with RSEs to raise fresh resources from the capital market, given higher liquidity in their shares.
- To create liquidity in all the scrips listed on the Exchanges.
- To provide an avenue for new SMEs from various regions of the country to raise fresh resources from the capital markets, which would help, achieve balanced regional growth.
- To harness the infrastructure at RSEs.
- BSE Indo*Next* is an initiative being formulated by BSE and FISE (representing 20 RSEs). BSE would be a Central Participating Exchange and the RSEs, which have indicated their willingness to participate in the formation of BSE Indo*Next* would be referred to as Participating RSEs.
- The Stock Exchanges at Ahmedabad, Bangalore, Delhi, Madras,, Hyderabad, Jaipur, U.P., Ludhiania, Pune, Saurashtra-Kutch, Vadodara,, Cochiin, Magadh, Coimbatore, Guwahati, Bhubaneshwar Stock, Madhya Pradesh and the Inter-connected Stock Exchange of India Ltd. the participating RSEs.

BSE Indo*Next* was launched on 7h January 2005. To first establish the trading platform expeditiously, the BSE has set up the BSE Indo*Next* market as separate trading market on its BOLT system as 'S' group. All the eligible securities in the B1 groups of the BSE would be transferred to the 'S' group. Eligible scrips from the participating RSEs would also be introduced in the 'S' group under the permitted category at BSE. The members of the BSE and the sub brokers of the subsidiaries which are members of the BSE will be allowed to trade in this market. The clearing and settlement as well as the risk management will be the sole responsibility of the BSE at this stage. Implementation may not require any change in the Bye-laws of the BSE. All members of the BSE, including the subsidiaries of the RSEs would thus have an opportunity to trade on this market without any difficulty. The participating RSEs whose listed securities are permitted to be traded on BSE Indo*Next* shall ensure the compliance of all listing requirements.

3.33 BSE Mid-Cap Index and BSE Small-Cap Index

BSE introduced the new index series called 'BSE Mid-Cap' index and 'BSE Small-Cap' index to track the performance of the companies with relatively small market capitalization that would exclusively represent the mid and small cap companies listed on the Stock Exchange. Companies with large market capitalization bias the movement of BSE-500 index, which covers 93 percent of the listed universe. This necessitated construction of a separate indicator to capture the trend in the specific class of companies (with lower market capitalisation). BSE Mid-Cap and BSE Small-Cap index would prove to be a great utility to the investing community as they would truly capture the movement of the segments they are represent (mid and small). Salient feature of these indices are:

- Base year of these indices would be 2002-2003.
- Base index value would be 1000 for each of these indices.
- These would be based on a free-float methodology.
- Constructed on 80 percent-15 percent-5 percent method whereby BSE Mid-Cap tracks the performance of scrips between 80 & 95 percent of aggregate market capitalisation and BSE Small-Cap index tracks the performance of remaining 5 percent scrips (95-100 percent).
- Number of companies in each of these indices would be variable. Constituents of these indices are reviewed on a

quarterly basis. On the date of launch (April 11, 2005), these indices comprised of 231 and 425 constituents in BSE Mid-Cap and BSE Small-Cap index respectively.

3.34 Proposed Regulation of Investment Advisers

Section 12 of the SEBI Act, 1992 provides for registration and regulation of investment advisers. However, presently SEBI does not register and regulate investment advisers as a separate class of intermediary. Investment advisory services rendered by market intermediaries such as portfolio managers, stock brokers, merchant bankers and credit rating agencies are regulated by SEBI through separate regulations. Portfolio Managers regulations, in particular, cover investment advisers who have discretion over and hold custody of client assets.

The entities involved in investment advice and not covered by SEBI regulations often operate as one stop shops calling themselves financial/investment consultants or advisers, who are engaged in distribution of retail financial products rendering investment advice to specific clients, without any formal contract and who have no discretion over and do not hold custody of client assets. These could also include Banks, Certified Financial planners, Chartered Accountants, Tax Consultants and those rendering investment advice on publicly accessible media like television, newspapers, radio, internet, mobile phone services, etc. There have been concerns in India regarding misuse of investment advice particularly in publicly accessible media like the electronic and print media.

There are likely to be lakh of advisers and distributors in India and it is not feasible for SEBI to regulate such a large number directly. One view is that a private sector self-financing Regulatory Organization (RO) should be created to be the first level regulator for investment advisers. The RO should develop principle based regulations with risk based examinations and implement regulation of discrete market segments in phases. These should include regulations on advertising, performance reporting and presentation, disclosure of conduct, experience and conflicts, disclosure of services and fees, prices and commissions and fair dealing.

Typically, investment advisers deal not only in securities but also other products such as insurance, commodities, pension products and government products including bonds and postal deposits, company deposits, NBFC deposits and mortgages. It has also been suggested, therefore, that for effective regulation of investment advice, the RO should regulate investment advice relating to all the products. However, these products fall under the jurisdiction of different regulators/agencies. While it is legally not possible for any of the regulatory bodies/agencies to regulate a product outside its jurisdiction, same RO reporting to various regulatory bodies/agencies would lead to undesirable multiplicity of authorities over the RO.

3.35 Plan for a Unified Exchange Traded Corporate Bond Market

In his Budget speech on February 28, 2006, the Finance Minister indicated that steps would be taken to create a single unified exchange traded market for corporate bonds and the task of development of the capital market was entrusted to SEBI. SEBI constituted a High Level Committee under the Chairmanship of Dr. T.C. Nair, Whole Time Member to work out a plan for implementation of a single unified exchange traded corporate bond market in India by identification of an appropriate mechanism and institutional framework to implement the proposal

Creation of a single unified exchange traded market for corporate bonds would mean development of infrastructure to support secondary debt market trading system which allows efficient price discovery and reliable clearing and settlement. The Committee observed that in most countries, the majority of bonds are traded on over-the-counter (OTC) markets which make it difficult to have real time data for price comparisons, trading and analysis. In India, secondary market trading in corporate bonds, like in most other markets, is done over the counter (OTC) between the counterparties directly or through brokers. The Committee observed that the corporate bond market in India does not have any common clearing and settlement infrastructure in place, unlike in the case of the government securities market. There is, thus a pronounced need for a compulsory trade reporting to a central authority by all participants along with an organized set up for clearing and settlement.

The internal Committee noted that both NSE and BSE have already in place electronic trading platforms for government securities along with the clearing and settlement arrangements. The exchange traded debt market in India, as elaborated earlier will take off in three phases. Since the two exchanges viz. NSE and BSE already have most of the required infrastructure in place, internal Committee felt that one of them, preferably BSE, could make a beginning towards setting up a reporting platform and thereafter a platform for trading. In the second phase, BSE will provide facility for trading through electronic order matching based on price time priority through online trading system as operational in equities.

In the third phase of development, the corporate bond trading activity could be hived off from BSE to a subsidiary jointly set up by NSE and BSE for corporate bond market trading, clearing and settlement as suggested above. SEBI will confine its role here, to regulation of the corporate debt market.

It will accordingly issue guidelines to bring about coordination initially in respect of trade reporting and later on, implementation of the anonymous order matching system for corporate bonds. SEBI would, also initiate a plethora of other measures which have been recommended by the High Level Committee to widen and deepen the corporate debt market in the country, in consultation with RBI and IRDA.

3.36 Some Proposed New Innovations in the Securities Market

A discussion paper on "Innovations in the Securities Market" has been prepared by SEBI. The new innovations which have been contemplated and have been put into public domain for inviting suggestions from the general public are:

3.36.1 Trading of rights on the Stock Exchanges in Electronic Form: Rights offered in the rights issues confer choice to the existing shareholders of the company, to buy additional shares. These rights essentially are call options on the issuer's stock to the existing shareholders of the company. These rights are traded in over the counter (OTC) market. The proposal here is two fold – First, migrate from OTC to exchange driven environment and second, shift from physical to electronic mode of rights, crediting them directly to D-mat account. In other words, proposal is to trade rights in electronic form in the organized fashion on the stock exchanges to ensure better liquidity, price discovery and other values. In addition, this migration would result in enormous administrative convenience and cost saving through elimination of the renunciation and split forms etc.

3.36.2 Strategic Use of Put Options in the Fixed price Buy Back and Takeovers Cases: The concept of Buy back of shares by the listed companies was pioneered in the Indian Capital Market in 1998. As stipulated in the Regulations, companies may buy back their shares through the fixed price tender offer on proportionate basis, through book building route (called reverse book building) or through open market purchase. It is proposed that the companies coming out with the fixed price buy back/tender offers, issue the put warrants to the investors on proportionate basis. Put warrants are essentially the put options (option to sell), which offer the right to the investors to sell their shares to the company back, at a specific price (strike price of options). Because there is a specific price on the put option, it is a perfect substitute to the fixed price offers in the prevailing form. But, the operational mechanism of the product would be different and would offer host of advantages to the investors, issuers and market. It would offer benefits like Risk arbitrage and consistent pricing of the stock, immediate availability of the funds to the investors, savings of the cost to the company because no need to issue fresh share certificates, and flexibility to the investors as these would operate like put options American type i.e. exercisable any time till the maturity.

3.37 Future Prospects

Today, Indian Securities Market can claim to be one among the best across the world. Indeed, we are at par with international standards on almost all operational and structural parameters. SEBI is consistently evolving improved market mechanisms, processes and regulations. RBI and SEBI are jointly working on mechanisms like 'margin trading', corporate bond market, SROs etc.

The market has made enormous progress in terms of obtaining liquidity and improving the operational efficiency, apart from achieving a growth in size and outreach. However, as the results of our empirical study would indicate in later chapters, there is much to be desired in terms of the pricing efficiency. Recent studies have revealed that the prices of equity derivatives often diverge from those consistent with logic, with the lack of arbitrage opportunities. There is a need for policy efforts at the level of exchanges, SEBI and the RBI in resolving the impediments to arbitrage. Excessive, and often manipulative, speculation with a desire to become rich overnight is the biggest culprit that robs the market of the transparency and efficiency in price discovery.

The most difficult area in terms of obtaining a sound secondary market relates to the problems of market manipulation, and those of establishing sound procedures for surveillance. One key element for making progress in this regard would be a requirement that every trade should be tagged with the PAN number of the customer. This would simultaneously serve to establish the identity of the customer, and limit the extent to which the parallel economy is able to trade on the public securities market.

This effort must be linked with a greater effort on regulation of listed firms. A prime issue here is that of disclosure. Improvement in accounting disclosure, handling of news and continuous disclosure of all material information, are all areas where much new work is still required. There is a need for greater regulatory and market-based mechanisms to give firms incentives for better disclosure.

Another major issue which will influence India's securities markets in future is the challenge of globalisation. RBI has increasingly moved in the direction of giving access to international diversification to institutional investors and individual investors in India. Financial intermediaries and exchanges in India will also experience global competition. There is a need for greater thought and policy initiatives, in fully integrating a global perspective into the plans of firms, exchanges, regulators and policy-makers. Financial Markets, across the globe, are undergoing profound, unprecedented and fast-paced changes. Technology has revolutionized the processes and the information explosion has sparked off remarkable changes in the way the world has been operating. Though organizations, their competencies and product portfolios are expanding and going global, their profit margins are shrinking, competition is intensifying and their lives are becoming more and more complex and tougher day by day. Opportunity zones are encountering a blood bath, globally.

Investors' confidence has become a precious commodity across the Global Securities Markets. Market misconducts have drastically shaken the confidence of the investing community, globally. Reputed Market Intermediaries are also victimized by the erring act of some of the industry players and blood bath is apparent in the markets. After all that, markets are exploring all the possible means to restore that extremely critical piece "confidence" among the investing community and discipline among the market participants as without them in place, markets can never encounter sustainable long term growth. Debates on the subject are on and on in the global markets.

Interestingly, amidst all this, markets are expanding ruthlessly. Trading platforms, clearing and settlement mechanisms, regulatory frameworks, positing of various industry players are being redefined on day to day basis. One of the primary reasons of this rethinking all around in the market places is the prevailing market misconducts. Each misconduct in the market has offered a great opportunity to the market to take initiatives to prevent the recurrence of such events in the future. All must appreciate that no market in the world is both fail proof and fail proof at any point in time. Therefore, misconducts prevail but their degree varies and so does their impact on the overall market. Indian Securities Market has encountered its fair proportion of market misconducts over the period of time. But, every such event has lifted the system to better standards. The attempts of the regulators have always been to improve the overall systems by taking the appropriate cues from every such damaging event.

Analysis of various market misconducts reveals that lack of proper identity of persons operating in the market is a constraint in making an audit trail and regulators have great difficulty in trying the real beneficiaries of irregularities. Illegal activities such as terrorist financing, money laundering are also major concerns of regulators around the globe. Regulators need to identify the violators and take speedy and stringent enforcement action. Therefore the regulators are turning to creation of a comprehensive database of market participants.

The ultimate aim of this and the other ongoing reforms would be to enhance the transparency and to check the volatility in the market. A growing but inefficient market cannot benefit the economy as much as an efficient and growing market.

3.38 Conclusion

The Indian stock market has come a long way, from the earlier days of floor trading system to the present day screen-based and net-based trading. It has seen the phasing out of the century old "badla" system with the introduction of a plethora of new products and mechanisms. As discussed above, post 1990s many important policy initiatives have focused on fostering liquidity and efficiency of the securities markets. The securities market in India has become more modern in terms of infrastructure, adoption of international practices in accounting standards as well as disclosure norms, settlement cycle through rolling settlement, derivatives trading, implementation of corporate governance etc. The dematerialization of shares has enhanced the 'ease' quotient for investors. Indian stock market has experienced some revolutionary changes in its functioning. It would also be relevant to mention here that on the following paradigms Indian Securities Market is ahead of the international standards:

- Fully electronic and state of the art trading platforms
- Shift of the settlement cycle to T+2 rolling settlement.
- Establishment of Central Listing Authority (CLA).
- Corporate governance index as a measure of wealth creation, management and distribution.
- On-line position monitoring and risk management by the exchanges.

The effect of all these ongoing reforms and adoption of international standard practices has already been felt and its reflection is seen in the growth of sensex and BSE market capitalisation.

4

Secondary Securities Market: Recent Reforms

4.1 Short Selling

Hon'ble Finance Minister, in the Union Budget 2007-08, had proposed inter alia "to allow short selling settled by delivery, and securities lending and borrowing to facilitate delivery, by institutions." Subsequently, after a series of discussions with the stock exchanges, depositories and market participants, SEBI specified a broad regulatory framework for short selling and a full-fledged securities lending and borrowing scheme by institutional investors. Relevant amendments were made to SEBI (FII) Regulations, 1995 and SEBI (Mutual Funds) Regulations, 1996, enabling FIIs and Mutual Funds to participate in the framework for short selling and SLB. RBI also made the necessary amendments to Foreign Exchange Management Act, 1999 (FEMA) and vide circular dated January 01, 2008, enabled FIIs to participate in short selling and SLB. Central Board of Direct Taxes (CBDT) vide circular dated February 22, 2008, clarified that SLB transactions would not attract capital gains tax and STT. The aforesaid framework for short selling and SLB would be operationalised with effect from April 21, 2008.

Pursuant to feedback from the market participants, the scheme for Securities Lending and Borrowing was revised. Key modifications made to SLB were: (i) increasing the tenure of SLB, (ii) extending the duration of SLB session (iii) allowing margins in SLB to be taken in the form of cash and cash equivalents and (iv) clarifying how to deal with corporate actions.

Short selling is defined as selling a stock which the seller does not own at the time of trade. The seller would have either borrowed the securities temporarily for delivery to the buyer or would not have made any provision at all i.e. naked short sale.

Short selling is used for many purposes, including to profit from an expected downward price movement, to provide liquidity in response to unanticipated buyer demand, or to hedge the risk of a long position in the same security or a related security. Short selling is considered as a desirable feature as it enhances market efficiency through price discovery and improves liquidity in the permitted securities. Empirical analysis suggests that when short-selling is possible, market returns are less volatile and there is greater liquidity. However, it is also viewed as potential risk than can accentuate a downtrend and thus destabilise the market.

Short selling is central to the theoretical foundations of the Efficient Markets Hypothesis and Asset Pricing theory. Short selling as a trading tool is important from the broad perspective of global equity market development. A recent research study by Cornell University, examines effectiveness of short selling across different types of sellers including individuals, institutions and proprietary accounts. According to the study, heavy short-sellers, mainly institutional, have in fact identified and acted on important value-relevant information that has not yet been impounded into prices. The price effects are permanent, which suggest that short sellers are not manipulating or otherwise temporarily depressing the share price. They found that shorting accounts for more than 12.9 percent of NYSE volume, suggesting that shorting constraints are easily surmounted for even the smallest-cap NYSE stocks.

The securities markets across the world have permitted short sales subject to certain safeguards like disclosures and tick rules. The US SEC has introduced Regulation SHO in 2005 which was an updated version in light of numerous market developments since short sale regulation was first adopted in 1938. Naked short selling is not necessarily a violation of the federal securities laws or the SEC's rules. SEC recognises a tolerance level of unsettled trades for five consecutive settlements, before taking action under SHO.

On the other hand in UK, the Financial Services Authority (FSA) UK, emphasises on transparency and disclosure of short sales rather than putting restrictive rules.

In Hong Kong, short selling is permitted on certain designated securities like those that were part of the benchmark indices or those in which futures and options have been made available. Further, the tick rule has been specified, i.e., it cannot be effected below the best current ask price. At the time of putting the order, investors are required to communicate to broker dealers that it is a short selling transaction.

Many emerging markets like Korea, Japan, Singapore, etc., have also permitted short selling subject to disclosure of such transactions and tick rules. Certain jurisdictions prohibit short selling during specific corporate activities like acquisitions/takeovers, new issuances, strategic policy announcements etc.

In India, short sale was permitted for retail investors in 1996 subject to the disclosure requirements. It was banned twice in 1998 and 2001 in response to market volatility. With the introduction of rolling settlement, with effect from July 2, 2001, SEBI permitted short sales by retail investors. However, institutional investors were not permitted to do the same.

Pursuant to the recommendations of the Secondary Market Advisory Committee (SMAC) of SEBI and the decision of the SEBI Board, it has been decided to permit all classes of investors to short sell. The mechanism for short selling would be supplemented by a full-fledged Securities Lending and Borrowing (SLB) scheme. SEBI has issued guidelines to implement and put in place a broad framework to short-sell and for the introduction of SLB.

4.2 Securities Lending and Borrowing (SLB)

Securities lending is a temporary transfer of securities from the owner of the securities to a third party, for a fee. At the end of loan term, securities must generally be returned to the owner. Securities lending arrangements are governed by commercial agreement entered into between the lender and borrower. Securities lending and borrowing has become an inevitable mechanism in capital markets. SLB complements short selling in securities and also enables the investors to earn returns on their idle securities.

SLB was first introduced in United States in the 1980s. It now supports trading and settlement in all developed and emerging markets. A recent study by World Federation of Exchanges has enumerated how securities lending is affecting the business of stock exchanges through corporate governance norms and market surveillance. SLB confers liquidity and improves efficiency of securities markets. Securities lending provides the lender of securities with a low risk yield enhancement to his portfolio, while enabling the borrower to cover failed trades and to hedge/ arbitrage in the market.

In most markets, the securities lending and borrowing transactions are by and large, over-the-counter (OTC) contractual obligations executed between lenders and borrowers. Regulators do not directly regulate the lending and borrowing transactions. In some emerging market jurisdictions like Hong Kong, Korea, Singapore etc., the depositories and custodians provide an electronic platform for execution of securities lending and borrowing transactions. For example the State Street, Bank of Depository Association run the SLB for their clients who register with them through electronic trading screen which matches the demand and supply for the designated securities.

In India, SLB was introduced in 1997 with a view to handling settlement shortages. There was no scope for investors to capitalise on the demand for their securities in the market and thus earn a return by lending them. Later, there was a need for a full-fledged SLB to include participation of all classes of investors. SLB has been introduced by SEBI within the overall framework of Securities Lending Scheme,

1997. All market participants are eligible to participate in the scheme. The SLB takes place on an automated, screen-based, order-matching platform which will be provided by the approved intermediaries (AIs). The AIs includes Clearing Corporation/Clearing House of stock exchanges having nation-wide terminals. The securities traded in F&O segment are eligible for lending and borrowing under the scheme.

4.3 Introduction of DMA

With a view to increase liquidity, bring about greater transparency, lower impact cost for large orders and reduce risk of error associated with manual execution of client orders, the facility of Direct Market Access (DMA) was introduced. This facility allows brokers to offer its clients direct access to the exchange trading system through the broker's infrastructure without manual intervention by the broker.

The DMA framework places onus on the broker to do proper risk assessment of clients before providing DMA facility and broker is responsible for risk management, setting trading/exposure/positions limits and maintaining adequate audit trails.

The facility was initially provided to institutional investors. It was clarified that Institutional investors may use DMA facility through investment managers after due authorisation and upon furnishing to the broker/exchange suitable agreements/undertakings between the institution and investment manager stating, *inter alia*, that the institutional investor shall be responsible for all actions undertaken by its authorized investment manager. Such investment managers may execute necessary documents on behalf of the institutional investor.

Direct Market Access (DMA) is a facility which allows brokers to offer clients direct access to the exchange trading system through the broker's infrastructure without manual intervention by the broker. Some of the advantages offered by DMA are direct control of clients over orders, faster execution of client orders, reduced risk of errors associated with manual order entry, greater transparency, increased liquidity, lower impact costs for large orders, better audit trails and better use of hedging and arbitrage opportunities through the use of decision support tools/algorithms for trading.

As per IOSCO definition, Direct Electronic Access (DEA) refers to the process by which a person transmits orders on his own (i.e. without handling or re-entry by another person) directly into the market's trade matching system for execution. DEA falls into two key categories: intermediated and non-intermediated.

Intermediated DEA refers to:

- Customers being given direct access to the market through a registered intermediary's system/infrastructure, *i.e.*, automated "order routing;" or
- Customers of an intermediary being given direct access to the market without going through the intermediary's system/infrastructure, *i.e.*, "sponsored" access.

In either case, however, the order is sent to the market as the intermediary's order, *i.e.*, using the intermediary's trading ID. The intermediary therefore retains full responsibility for the order.

Non-intermediated direct access generally refers to markets providing direct access to non-intermediaries (*i.e.*, parties other than registered brokerage firms), as market members and in that capacity connecting directly to the market, without going through an intermediary. This type of DEA is referred as direct access by non-registrant/non-intermediary market-members.

In India, the High Powered Expert Committee on Making Mumbai an International Finance Centre (MIFC) talked about the potential of DMA and algorithmic trading to achieve a role in international finance here. Algorithmic trading or programme trading refers to orders that are automatically placed in the market by software programmes, built on certain mathematical models. Simply put, in algorithmic trading, the software is programmed in a manner to detect arbitrage opportunities between the cash and the futures market and place orders on exchanges in real time through DMA. Thus, DMA helps in reducing "high latency" or loss of time and enhances the profit making potential of programme traders and arbitragers.

SEBI allowed intermediated DMA in India whereby customers can access the market directly through a registered broker's system/infrastructure.

Brokers interested to offer DMA facility shall apply to the respective stock exchanges ensuring that software and systems are in place that support direct access. SEBI asked stock exchanges to facilitate direct market access to institutional investors.

The brokers shall be fully responsible and liable for all orders emanating through their DMA systems. They shall specifically authorize clients for providing DMA facility after fulfilling Know-Your-Client requirements and carrying out due diligence regarding clients' credit worthiness, risk taking ability, track record of compliance and financial soundness.

Brokers shall ensure that only those clients who are deemed fit and proper for this facility are allowed access to the DMA facility. Brokers shall maintain proper records of such due diligence. Brokers using DMA facility for routing client orders shall not be allowed to cross trades of their clients with each other. All orders must be offered to the market for matching.

4.4 Mandatory Requirement of PAN

SEBI stipulated that PAN would be the sole identification number for all participants in the securities market, irrespective of the amount of transaction with effect from July 02, 2007. Market intermediaries were advised to ensure that their clients' transactions are linked to the PAN details of the client with which detailed analysis could be made and to build the necessary infrastructure for enabling accessibility and query based on PAN thereby enabling retrieval of all the details of the clients that was available including the transactions done by them. The objective was to strengthen the 'Know Your Client' (KYC) norms through a single identification number for all participants in the securities market for facilitating sound audit trail. In accordance with the above mentioned policy, SEBI discontinued with the requirement of Unique Identification Number (UIN) under the SEBI (Central Database of Market Participants) Regulations, 2003 (MAPIN Regulations).

The Central government has exempted the persons resident in Sikkim from Direct Income taxes. In view of this, SEBI exempted investors residing in the state of Sikkim from the mandatory requirement of PAN for their investments in mutual funds.

In view of Rule 114 C (1) (c) of Income Tax Rules, requirement of PAN was also relaxed in the case of securities market transactions undertaken on behalf of Central and State Governments and by the officials appointed by the Courts e.g., official liquidator, court receiver etc. (under the category of Government).

4.5 Supervision of Branches of Depository Participants

In terms of Regulation 46 of the SEBI (Depositories and Participants) Regulations, 1996, every Depository Participant (DP) shall have adequate mechanism for the purpose of reviewing, monitoring and evaluating its internal accounting controls and systems. It had been clarified that these provisions apply to DPs in respect of all their branches also. DPs were, therefore, required in terms of these provisions to put in place appropriate mechanisms to ensure that their branches were carrying on the operations in compliance with the applicable regulations, bye-laws, etc. Further, DPs were also required to put in place suitable internal control systems to ensure that all branches were exercising due diligence in opening accounts, complying with KYC requirements, ensuring systems safety in complying with client instructions, manner of uploading client instructions, verifying signatures and maintaining client records, etc.

Depositories shall examine the adequacy of the above mechanisms during their inspections of DPs. Depositories shall also put in place appropriate mechanisms for monitoring opening of branches by DPs.

4.6 Corporatisation and Demutualisation of Stock Exchanges

The Securities Contracts (Regulation) Act, 1956 (SCRA) was amended in October 2004 to facilitate the Corporatisation and Demutualisation of stock exchanges, mandating all recognised stock exchanges, if not already corporatised and demutualised, to be corporatised and demutualised on and from the appointed date as notified by SEBI. It obligated on all non-corporate and mutual stock exchanges to submit their C and D Scheme to SEBI for approval.

SEBI notified C and D schemes of 19 stock exchanges in the year 2005. As per the C and D schemes, the stock exchanges were required to complete their corporatisation process within three months from the date of notification of their respective Schemes.

The process of corporatisation includes incorporation of for-profit company limited by shares, re-registration/conversion from company limited by guarantee to company limited by shares, allotment of shares to eligible members, etc. Accordingly, all the stock exchanges were converted into corporate entities in the year 2006-07.

In order to fully complete their demutualisation process, the stock exchanges were required to ensure that at least 51 percent of their equity share capital is held by public other than shareholders having trading rights as per section 4B (8) of the SCRA. The stock exchanges were required to complete the same within twelve months from the publication of the Order, approving their respective schemes (further extendable by SEBI by another period of twelve months as per the SCRA).

As requested by the stock exchanges, SEBI extended the above time period by another period of twelve months for all 19 stock exchanges.

To facilitate the divestment process, SEBI notified the Securities Contracts (Regulation) (Manner of Increasing and Maintaining Public Shareholding in Recognised Stock exchanges) Regulations, 2006 (MIMPS Regulations) on November 13, 2006. Subsequently, the Government of India policy regarding foreign investments in infrastructure companies in securities markets, viz. stock exchanges, depositories and clearing corporations was issued by SEBI on December 22, 2006. In conformity with the provisions of the MIMPS Regulations and the aforesaid FDI policy, 16 stock exchanges had completed their demutualisation process by diluting at least 51 percent of their equity shareholding to public other than shareholders having trading rights. Appointed dates were also notified for these stock exchanges.

As for the remaining three stock exchanges, SEBI withdrew the recognition of Saurashtra Kutch Stock Exchange Limited and Magadh Stock Exchange Limited for failing to comply with observations in the inspection report and Hyderabad Stock Exchange Limited was de-recognised for its failure to complete the demutualization process within the prescribed time.

As part of the aforesaid divestment process, in all 521 investors (146 corporates and 375 individuals) had subscribed to the equity share capital of 16 stock exchanges. The 146 corporates who had taken stake in various stock exchanges include 43 listed companies. Some of the major banks/ institutions that had taken stake in various stock exchanges include State Bank of India, Central Bank of India, Bank of India, Life Insurance Corporation of India, TIDCO and WBIDFC.

The aforesaid 521 investors include six foreign entities that had taken stake in Bombay Stock Exchange Limited namely Deutsche Boerse A.G., Singapore Exchange Limited,

Caldwell India Holdings Inc, Atticus Mauritius Ltd, Dubai Financial LLC and Acacia Banyan Partners Ltd. In the case of Delhi Stock Exchange Association Limited, three foreign entities had taken stake viz., New Vernon Pvt. Equity Ltd., Passport Global Master Fund SPC Ltd., and Wilmette Holdings Ltd. Though NSE was already incorporated as a demutualised exchange, eight foreign stakeholders namely, NYSE Group, Inc. New York, GA Global Investments Limited, Cyprus, GS Strategic Investments Limited, Mauritius, SAIF II Mauritius Company Limited, Mauritius, Saturn India Limited, Mauritius, Saturn South Asia Limited, Mauritius, Citigroup Strategic Holdings Mauritius Limited, Mauritius and MS Strategic (Mauritius) Limited, Mauritius had equity stake in NSE as on March 31, 2007.

4.7 Policy Initiatives for Derivatives

India is presently reckoned as one of the most established markets in the world for exchange traded derivatives products. In order to further deepen the derivatives market and to cater to the growing needs of investors for more sophisticated derivatives products, SEBI decided to come up with three new products i.e. mini contracts, option contracts with longer life/tenure and volatility Index. The three products would provide investors more flexibility in terms of executing their trading strategies.

4.7.1 New Products for Futures and Options Segment: Derivatives Market Review Committee (DMRC) was set up on April 3, 2007 under the Chairmanship of Professor M. Rammohan Rao to carry out a comprehensive review of the developments in the derivatives market in India and to suggest the future course of action. SEBI on November 14, 2007, approved, in principle, the interim recommendations on 'New products for futures and options segment'. Accordingly, four new derivative products have been introduced. It is expected that these new derivative products will provide investors with a wider range of risk mitigation products and create more activity in the Indian derivatives markets. The four products are as follows:

A. Mini Contracts in Equity Indices: Exchanges (NSE and BSE) were permitted to introduce mini contracts in equity indices with minimum contract size of Rs. One lakh. It was expected that the availability of mini contracts with lower contract size i.e. Rs one lakh will facilitate small retail investors to effectively hedge their portfolios. The existing risk containment and other measures applicable for existing exchange traded equity Index derivative contracts were also extended to the mini derivative contract on Index.

B. Options Contracts with Longer Life/Tenure: Exchanges (NSE and BSE) were permitted to launch options contracts with longer tenure up to five years. To begin with, at any point in time, there would be options contract with at least three year tenure available for investors. The options cycle would be as under:

- The three serial month contracts would continue to exist.
- The following three quarterly months of the cycle March/June/September/December would be available.
- After these, five following semi-annual months of the cycle June/ December would be available, so that at any point in time there would be options contract with at least three year tenure available for investors.

The risk containment and other measures applicable for existing exchange traded equity Index option contracts would be extended suitably to long term option contracts on Index.

It was expected that these contracts will provide liquidity at the longer end of the market and will enable investors to hedge their positions for a longer duration.

C. Volatility Index and F&O Contracts: Exchanges (NSE and BSE) were permitted to construct volatility index and disseminate the same. The Exchanges were free to decide whether they want to adopt any of the Volatility Index computation models available globally or may like to develop their own model for computation of Volatility Index. Based on experience gained and awareness generated, derivatives on Volatility Index would be considered for introduction in due course of time.

D. Bond Index and F&O Contracts: Exchanges were permitted to construct the bond index (both corporate and GOI) and disseminate the same. Bond index reflects expectations about the term structure of interest rate in the economy. It was expected that futures and options on bond index will enable market participants to hedge their interest rate risk. The exchanges were free to decide whether they want to adopt any of the Bond Index computation models available globally or may like to develop their own model for computation of Bond Index.

4.7.2 Acceptance of Foreign Sovereign Securities: SEBI permitted clearing members to accept Foreign Sovereign Securities as collateral from Foreign Institutional Investors (FIIs) for Exchange Traded Derivative Transactions. Presently, in Exchange traded derivative transactions, FIIs are depositing the collateral with the clearing members, in the form of cash. Under the existing guidelines for clearing members, for collateral purposes, at least 50 percent of the liquid assets would be in the form of cash or cash equivalents, and the rest can be in the form of non-cash components. Clearing members were now permitted to accept foreign sovereign securities with 'AAA' rating, ("sovereign securities") as collateral from FII client with the following necessary safeguards:

- Before accepting sovereign securities as collateral from FII, the clearing member would enter into a written agreement with the FII and also with the clearing corporation.
- The clearing member would take due care to ensure that the sovereign securities tendered as collateral would be available for liquidation in the event of insolvency of the FII or any intermediary or any other person located overseas through whom the securities were held.
- The clearing corporation would also take due care to

ensure that sovereign securities tendered as collateral are available for liquidation in the event of insolvency of the clearing member or any intermediary or other person located overseas through whom the securities were held.

- The clearing corporation would take adequate care to ensure that the sovereign securities accepted by it as margin were tendered under a mechanism which does not unduly hinder timely liquidation in the event of default by the clearing member.

The clearing corporation would value the collateral tendered by applying due haircuts. The haircut may either be a fixed percentage or VaR based. A higher haircut may be considered to cover the expected time frame for liquidation. A market determined price as obtained from an internationally recognized data vendor shall be considered for valuation. The prices shall be converted into rupee terms on a daily basis. The rupee value so used for conversion shall be the "RBI Reference rate". The RBI reference rate shall be disclosed by the clearing corporation to the clearing members, so as to enable them to report the value of the margins collected from FIIs.

The sovereign securities tendered as collateral shall be treated as part of the cash component of the liquid assets of the clearing member, and shall be subject to the condition that the value of the sovereign securities shall not be more than 10 percent of the total value of the cash component of the liquid assets of the clearing member.

The existing procedure for acceptance and release of collateral tendered by domestic investors in the case of domestic securities shall be adopted mutatis mutandis for the sovereign securities tendered by FII, except to the extent specifically provided otherwise.

4.7.3 Exchange Traded Currency Derivatives: Based on the recommendation of RBI-SEBI Standing Technical Committee on Exchange-Traded Currency Futures, SEBI laid down the framework for the launch of Exchange-traded

Currency Futures in respect of eligibility norms for existing and new Exchanges and their Clearing Corporations/Houses, eligibility criteria for members of such Exchanges/Clearing Corporations/Houses, product design, risk management measures, surveillance mechanism and other related issues.

4.7.4 Extending Calendar Spread Treatment till Expiry of the Near Month Contract: SEBI extended the benefit of calendar spread treatment till the expiry of the near month contract to avoid sudden rise in margins without any corresponding increase in the risk of the spread position. The margin on calendar spread remains unchanged at a flat rate of 0.5 percent per month of spread on the far month contract subject to a minimum margin of 1 percent and a maximum margin of 3 percent on the far side of the spread with legs up to one year apart.

4.7.5 Eligibility Criteria for Permitting Derivatives on Shares: With a view to rationalise the eligibility criteria for permitting derivatives on shares, SEBI specified that the exchanges may introduce derivatives on shares fulfilling the following criteria irrespective of their date of listing and/or size of issue.

- The stock shall be chosen from amongst the top 500 stocks in terms of average daily market capitalisation and average daily traded value in the previous six months on a rolling basis.
- The stock's median quarter-sigma order size over the last six months shall be not less than Rs. 1 lakh.
- The market wide position limit in the stock shall not be less than Rs. 50 crore.

4.7.6 Revised Exposure Margin for Exchange-Traded Equity Derivatives: SEBI modified the exposure margin to be the higher of 10 percent or 1.5 times the standard deviation (of daily logarithmic returns of the stock price) of the notional value of the gross open position in single stock futures and gross short open position in stock options from the earlier prescribed limit of the higher of 5 percent or 1.5 times the standard deviation.

4.7.7 Issuance of Electronic Contract Notes (ECNs) in Equity Derivatives Segment: SEBI extended the facility of issuance of ECNs as a legal document using Straight Through Processing (STP) to the equity derivatives segment.

4.7.8 Cross Margining across Exchange-traded Equity and Exchange-traded Equity Derivatives Segments: In order to improve the use of capital by market participants, SEBI extended the facility of cross margining across cash and derivatives segments to all categories of market participants. To begin with, a spread margin of 25 percent of the total applicable margin on the eligible off-setting positions is levied in the respective cash and derivatives segment. In the first phase introduced in May 2008, cross margin benefit to the extent of VaR margin was provided for institutional investors on cash market positions having off setting futures positions. In the second phase, introduced in December 2008, this facility was extended to all market participants for offsetting positions in cash and derivatives market.

4.7.9 Exchange-traded Interest Rate Derivatives: A RBI-SEBI Standing Technical Committee was constituted to lay down the operational and risk management norms for three products i.e., 91-day Treasury Bill Futures, Short Term Interest Rate Future based on an Index of actual call rates and Notional Coupon Bearing 10 Year Long Bond Futures.

4.7.10 Revised Position Limits in the Exchange-traded Currency Derivatives Segment: Based on the feedback received from the market participants, the client level and non-bank trading member level position limits for Exchange Traded Currency Derivatives were modified. Accordingly, SEBI specified that the gross open position of a client across all contracts shall not exceed 6 percent of the total open interest or USD 10 million, whichever is higher, instead of 6 percent of the total open interest or USD 5 million, prescribed earlier. Further, the gross open position of a Trading Member, who is not a bank, across all contracts shall not exceed 15 percent of the total open interest or USD 50 million whichever is higher, instead of 15 percent of the total open interest or USD 25 million, prescribed earlier. The position limits were made specific to an exchange and not to the Exchange-Traded Currency Derivatives market as a whole, as prescribed earlier.

4.8 Amendment to Securities Contracts (Regulations), 2006

SEBI vide notification dated December 23, 2008 amended the Securities Contracts (Regulation) (Manner of Increasing and Maintaining Public Shareholding in Recognised Stock Exchanges) Regulations, 2006 relaxing the shareholding restrictions in recognised stock exchanges. The amendment *inter-alia* provide for:

- Six categories of entities, viz., stock exchanges, depositories, clearing corporations, banks, insurance companies; and public financial institutions may hold, directly or indirectly, a maximum of 15 percent of the paid-up equity share capital of a stock exchange.
- Any shareholder, other than the aforesaid six categories of investors, may hold either directly or indirectly, not more than 5 percent of the paid-up equity share capital of a recognized stock exchange.
- No person shall, directly or indirectly, either individually or together with persons acting in concert with him, acquire and/or hold more than five percent of the paid up equity capital of a recognised stock exchange, unless he is a fit and proper person and has taken prior approval of the Board for doing so.
- In respect of exchanges that are not listed, FIIs may purchase shares of such exchanges through transactions outside of the exchange provided it is not an initial allotment. However, if the exchange is listed, transactions by FIIs should be done through the exchange platform.

4.9 Internal Audit for Stock Brokers, Trading Members and Clearing Members

SEBI advised stock exchanges to direct their stock

brokers/trading members/clearing members to carry out complete internal audit on a half-yearly basis, starting with October 2008–March 2009, by chartered accountants, company secretaries or cost and management accountants who are in practice and who do not have any conflict of interest. The scope of such audit shall cover, *inter alia*, the existence, scope and efficiency of the internal control system, compliance with the provisions of the SEBI Act, 1992, Securities Contracts (Regulation) Act 1956, SEBI (Stock Brokers and Sub-Brokers) Regulations, 1992, circulars issued by SEBI, agreements, KYC requirements, byelaws of the exchanges, data security and insurance in respect of the operations of stock brokers/clearing members.

5

Secondary Securities Market: Recent Trends

5.1 Equity Markets in India: 2009-10

Equity markets which witnessed a downward and volatile trend during 2008-09 and remained range bound, exhibited signs of recovery from April 2009. With the revival of foreign institutional investors' (FIIs) interest in emerging market economies including India, the equity markets gained strength during May-July 2009. There was a fresh spell of bullish sentiment in September 2009, with the Bombay Stock Exchange (BSE) Sensex recording a high of 17,126 during the month. The Indian equity markets closed lower at 15,896 in end-October 2009, before showing an improvement during November-December 2009. As on March 31, 2010, the BSE Sensex stood at 17,527 and the S&P CNX Nifty closed at 5,249.

The secondary market staged a handsome recovery in 2009 following stimulus measures implemented by the Government and resurgence of foreign portfolio flows displaying renewed interest by foreign investors. The subdued global commodity prices in the beginning of 2009 also lifted the sentiments in the Indian capital market. Furthermore, election results announced in May 2009 removed uncertainty on economic policies and as such boosted Indian equity markets and both benchmark and sectoral indices rallied.

Though resource mobilization from the primary market through equity investments was sluggish in 2009 both in terms of number of issues and amount raised through public rights issues and follow-on public offerings, there was an increase in debt market activity and private placements. The total amount mobilized through equity issues in 2009 was lower at

Rs. 23,098 crore as compared to Rs. 49,485 crore raised in 2008. An important aspect regards the regulatory measures initiated during the year were clearly in the direction of introducing greater transparency, protecting investors' interests and improving efficiency in the working of Indian equity markets, while also ensuring the soundness and stability of the Indian capital market.

5.1.1 Stock Markets in 2008-09

Notwithstanding the deteriorating international financial crisis, the Indian equity markets performed in orderly manner in the second quarter of 2008-09. Domestic stock markets recovered with intermittent corrections in the second quarter till mid-September 2008. Since then, bankruptcy of world's largest financial institutions had its sway on Indian financial markets. Added to these were the heavy net sales by FIIs, domestic inflation, depreciation of rupee and slowdown in the industrial growth as shown by IIP.

In third quarter of the financial year, weak trend continued in the markets as there was a sharp fall in the share prices. Concerns over the world economy plunging into recession added to the downswing. Substantial net outflows by FII, poor second quarter corporate results, depreciation of rupee and concerns of Indian economy falling into recession on account of weak industrial growth and decline in exports accentuated the downtrend.

The subdued and volatile trend continued in the fourth quarter of 2008-09 mainly reflecting the international equity markets. The BSE Sensex touched a low of 8160 on March 9, 2009. Thereafter, a slight recovery was seen in consonance with the improvements in world equity markets towards the end of 2008-09. In tandem with the decline in stock prices in 2008-09, there was a fall in turnover and market capitalisation across the board.

In the cash segment, the turnover at BSE and NSE declined by 30.3 percent and 22.5 percent, respectively during 2008-09 over the previous year. Derivatives turnover at NSE and BSE declined by 17.3 percent in 2008-09 over the previous year.

5.2 Global Equity Markets

The global equity market was dominated by the financial turmoil and the signs of severe recession inflicted by the deteriorating financial markets. Equity markets across the world—developed and emerging—declined over concerns of economic slowdown in US, Europe and Asia, which was predicted to be the most severe compared the recession of 1930s. Plummeting share prices and heightened volatility across markets and sectors characterised the world stock markets during 2008-09. Collapse of world's leading financial institutions including Lehmann Brother's fuelled the downturn in the second-half. Emerging markets which were till then, shielded from the direct effect of the financial turmoil, came under severe pressure during the period. Downward spiral of share prices, outflows of foreign investment, depreciation of currencies of emerging markets followed. Weak earnings results reported by corporates, tightening of lending norms by banks and overall reduction in consumer confidence precipitated declining trend of indices, especially in mid-October and November. During 2008-09, all the equity markets witnessed downturn. The downtrend was the highest for Russian CRTX index (63.5 percent) followed by Hermes index of Egypt (59.6 percent), BUX index of Hungary (49.0 percent) and SET index of Thailand (47.2 percent). BSE Sensex and S&P CNX Nifty saw a fall of 37.9 percent and 36.2 percent, respectively during 2008-09.

During 2009, the Asian stock markets were on a recovery path. The cumulative change in global indices in end-December 2009 over the end- December 2003 level revealed a significant rise in these indices across countries. The Jakarta Composite index (Indonesia) registered a rise of 264.1 per cent to 2,510 at end-December 2009, while the BSE Sensex was up by 199.1 per cent to 17,465 in end-December 2009. Nikkei

225, Japan, however remained lower than its end- December 2003 level. Notwithstanding an improvement in global stock indices during the year, they were still lower than the levels reached in 2007.

5.3 Performance of Sectoral Indices, 2008-10

Following a subdued performance, the sectoral indices witnessed a remarkable improvement in 2009-2010. During the year the BSE Sensex rose from 9901 as on April 1, 2009 to 17,527 on March 31, 2010 a rise of 77 per cent. The S&P CNX Nifty rose from 3060 on April 1, 2009 to close at 5,249 on March 31, 2010, a jump of 71 per cent.

However, there was an across the board decline in broad-based and sectoral indices in 2008-09. Among the broad-based indices of shares listed on BSE, BSE 100, BSE 200 and BSE 500 recorded a fall of 40.0 percent, 41.0 percent and 42.8 percent respectively over the previous year. Among the indices of shares listed on NSE, the S&P CNX 500, CNX Nifty Junior and CNX Midcap declined by 40.0 percent, 45.6 percent and 45.4 percent, respectively in 2008-09.

The BSE Small-cap index recorded a fall of 58.6 percent in 2008-09. Among the sectoral indices, the highest fall was recorded by BSE Metal index (58.7 percent), BSE Consumer Durables (58.1 percent) and BSE Capital Goods index (53.8 percent). While the metal index reflected the downtrend in metal prices, the general down trend in the economy and industrial production reflected in decline in the capital goods and consumer durables indices.

Among the sectoral indices of NSE, S& P CNX Finance declined by 61.3 percent followed by CNX Bank (37.9 percent) and CNX IT (37.4 percent). Of the other indices at NSE , the highest fall was witnessed in Nifty Midcap 50 (50.9 percent), followed by S&P CNX Defty (49.9 percent), CNX Nifty Junior (45.6 percent) and CNX Midcap (45.4 percent).

5.4 Turnover in Indian Stock Market

In tandem with the downward spiral of equity prices, there was a decline in the trading volumes in stock exchanges in 2008-09. During 2008-09, turnover of all stock exchanges in the cash segment declined by 24.9 percent to Rs. 38,52,579 crore compared to Rs. 51,30,816 crore in 2007-08. BSE and NSE together contributed more than 99.9 percent of the turnover, of which NSE accounted for 71.4 percent in the total turnover in cash market. Apart from NSE and BSE, the only two stock exchanges which recorded turnover during 2008-09 were Kolkata Stock Exchange and UPSE. There was hardly any transaction on other stock exchanges. Month-wise, BSE and NSE recorded the highest turnover in July 2008 followed by May 2008 and April 2008. Despite the declining volumes, Indian exchanges maintained their positions vis-à-vis major exchanges of the world. As per the data released by World Federation of Exchanges (WFE), NSE was ranked fourth and BSE was ranked seventh among the top-most exchanges in terms of the number of trades in equity shares for the calendar year 2008. In terms of the value of shares traded, NSE was ranked 18th among the top-most exchanges for the calendar year 2008.

The total equity turnover at BSE as in March 2010 stood at Rs. 99,492.54 crore.

5.5 Market Capitalisation

Market capitalization of shares traded on the BSE and NSE increased sharply in 2009. Market capitalization, which had reached record levels in 2007, recovered in the case of Nifty, Nifty junior, the BSE Sensex and BSE 500 by end-December 2009. It surpassed the 2007 level in the case of Nifty junior, while for other indices it remained lower than 2007 levels.

The market capitalisation of BSE doubled to Rs. 61,64,157 crore in March 2010, compared to the previous year. The market capitalisation of BSE decreased by 39.9 percent to

Rs. 30,86,075 crore in 2008-09 from Rs. 51,38,014 crore at the end of 2007-08. At NSE also, market capitalisation declined by 40.4 percent to Rs. 28,96,194 crore at the end of March 2009 from Rs. 48,58,122 crore at the end of March 2008. As per the data release of WFE, BSE and NSE were ranked 14th and 15th in the world in terms of market capitalisation at the end of March 2009. The downturn in the stock markets resulted in fall in market capitalisation of many indices in 2008-09. Among the indices of BSE, decline in market capitalisation was the highest for BSE Teck index which fell by 39.7 percent. The market capitalisation of Bankex index also declined by 38.0 percent in 2008-09 over the previous year. The benchmark index of BSE, BSE Sensex witnessed a market capitalization of Rs. 15,07,742 crore reflecting a decline of 32.2 percent in 2008-09.

At NSE, fall in market capitalisation was the highest for CNX Midcap (40.9 percent). This was followed by CNX IT (37.5 percent) and CNX Bank (36.1 percent).

5.6 Stock Market Indicators

The market capitalisation to GDP ratio is one of the parameters for evaluation of stock markets. Also, liquidity of the market can be measured by the traded value to GDP ratio, i.e., value of the shares traded to GDP at current market prices. Since 2002-03, there was a sustained increase in the market capitalization to GDP ratio. The BSE market capitalisation to GDP ratio had increased from 23.3 percent in 2002-03 to 108.8 percent last financial year in 2007-08. Similarly, at NSE also the ratio had increased from 21.9 percent to 102.9 percent during the same period. However, downswing in the stock market in 2008-09 led to a substantial decline of the market capitalisation to GDP ratios of BSE and NSE to a round half of its values in the previous year. The market capitalisation to GDP ratio of BSE was 58.0 percent and that of NSE was 54.4 percent during 2008-09.

Similarly, the turnover-GDP ratio was the highest in 2007-

08 for both the cash and derivative segment. It slid considerably in the 2008-09 in tune with fall in the share prices and the resultant decline in the trading volume. The all-India equity market turnover to GDP ratio declined to 72.4 percent in 2008-09 as compared to 108.6 percent in 2007-08. In the derivative segment also, the turnover ratio declined from 282.3 percent in 2007-08 to 207.1 percent in 2008-09.

The valuation of the shares could be gauged from the price-earning ratio. The AS 30 index of Australia and NASDAQ Composite of the U.S. had the highest P/E ratios in 2008-09. Among the indices of emerging markets analyzed, SHCOMP index of China, TWSE index of Taiwan and KOSPI index of South Korea had higher P/E ratios in 2008-09 than that of Indian benchmark indices.

At the end of March 2009, the P/E ratios of BSE Sensex and S&P CNX Nifty were 13.7 and 14.3, respectively. The valuation of stocks in terms of P/E ratios of the Sensex and Nifty increased to 22.36 and 23.17 respectively as on December 31, 2009. The P/E ratios witnessed steady fall in 2008-09 from the initial highs in the first quarter of the financial year. Towards the last quarter, there was a considerable decline in the valuations of all indices except CNX PSE.

Price to book value ratio (P/B ratio) is a valuation measure which measures the returns left for the shareholders after providing for liabilities of a company. Thus, the P/B ratio of an index shows the asset quality of companies pertaining to that sector. During 2008-09, there was a fall in the P/B ratios of all indices as compared to 2007-08. The P/B ratio was the highest for the CNX IT index at 3.54, followed by the benchmark indices, BSE Sensex and S&P CNX Nifty at 2.66 and 2.50, respectively.

5.7 Volatility in Stock Markets

Volatility is measured by the standard deviation of logarithmic returns during a certain period. During 2008-09, stock markets all over the world witnessed extreme volatility. The domestic stock market also could not remain unaffected from the global volatile trend. The annualised volatility of BSE Sensex soared to 43.6 percent in 2008-09 from 30.6 percent in 2007-08. Similar trend was also observed for S&P CNX Nifty, which recorded annualized volatility of 41.5 percent in 2008-09 compared to 32.1 percent in the previous year. Month-wise, volatility in the benchmark indices was the highest in October 2008 and November 2008.

This was true for the mid-cap and small cap indices as the market witnessed negative cues from other countries, mainly US and Europe. The lowest volatility in the benchmark indices was noticed during April 2008 and May 2008. An international comparison of volatility in stock returns indicates that volatility was quite high in 2008-09 in both emerging and developed markets.

Volatility was extremely high in majority of the markets in the month of October 2008. Indian markets were the seventh most volatile market in the world. Among the developed markets, the annualised volatility was high in Hong Kong (48.4 percent) followed by Japan (46.0 percent) and USA NASDAQ (44.6 percent). Among the emerging markets, annualised volatility was higher for Russia (81.8 percent), Brazil (53.0 percent) and Hungary (45.8 percent).

Market volatility of the Indian indices, declined significantly in 2009. However, the volatility of weekly returns of Indian indices, namely Sensex and BSE 500, in 2009 was even higher than that in 2008, while Nifty indices, namely Nifty and Nifty junior, recorded lower volatility in 2009.

5.8 Trading Frequency

Liquidity in stock markets can be measured by comparing the trading frequency of listed stocks at BSE and NSE. The number of shares listed at the end of March 2009 was 7,729 at BSE. At NSE, the number of companies listed was 1,432 as on March 31, 2009. Trading frequency improved at both the stock exchanges in 2008-09 over the previous financial year.

During 2008-09, the number of shares traded in BSE was 3,246 as compared to 3,166 in 2007-08. On the other hand, the number of shares traded in NSE was higher at 1,301 in 2008-09 compared to 1,266 in 2007-08. The percentage share of shares traded at BSE above 100 days declined from 90.6 percent in 2007-08 to 87.2 percent in 2008-09. At NSE, the percentage of shares traded increased from 93.0 percent in 2007-08 to 97.9 percent in 2008-09. The percentage share of stocks traded for less than 10 days was 4.5 percent at BSE and 0.2 percent at NSE in 2008-09.

5.9 Activities of Stock Exchanges

Over the years, NSE and BSE have emerged as the nation-wide stock exchanges of the country contributing more than 99 percent of the total turnover. Apart from NSE and BSE, only Calcutta and UPSE recorded some transactions. Four stock exchanges viz., Hyderabad, Magadh, SKSE and Mangalore, have recently been de-recognised by SEBI.

The number of shares traded and delivered declined at BSE, NSE, Calcutta and UPSE. The value of shares delivered also declined at these stock exchanges. Of the total shares traded, NSE's share was 65.7 percent, followed by BSE which constituted 34.3 percent of the total shares traded. NSE had a share 72.6 percent in the total value of shares delivered followed by BSE (27.4 percent).

Majority of the other stock exchanges were inactive and their operations were confined to their subsidiaries, which, in turn, have taken membership of BSE and NSE. The turnover of many of the subsidiaries declined in 2008-09 over the previous financial year. Turnover of subsidiaries during 2008-09 was Rs. 1,71,721 crore compared to Rs. 2,53,218 crore in 2007-08, indicating a fall of 32.2 percent. The subsidiaries turnover constituted a miniscule of 1.2 percent of the total turnover of cash and F&O segment of all stock exchanges in India.

5.10 Dematerialisation

There are two depositories in India viz., National Securities Depository Limited (NSDL) and Central Depository Services Limited (CDSL). The depositories have set up nation-wide network with proper infrastructure to handle the securities deposited or settled in dematerialized mode in the Indian stock markets. The number of companies signed up for dematerialisation in NSDL rose to 7,801 in 2008-09 from 7,354 in 2007-08. In CDSL, the number of companies signed up increased from 5,943 in 2007-08 to 6,213 in 2008-09. Similarly, the number of dematerialised shares in NSDL went up by 19.4 percent from 23,68,970 lakh in 2007-08 to 28,28,700 lakh in 2008-09. In CDSL too, the number of shares dematerialised rose significantly by 42.2 percent to 7,08,200 lakh in 2008-09 from 4,98,200 lakh in 2007-08. In both the depositories, there was a decline in the value of shares settled in dematerialized mode. While in NSDL, the total value of demat settled shares declined by 23.4 percent to Rs. 10,88,895 crore in 2008-09 from Rs. 14,20,717 crore in 2007-08, the same in CDSL declined by 41.5 percent from Rs. 3,83,179 crore in 2007-08 to Rs. 2,23,989 crore in 2008-09.

Apart from the shares, dematerialization facility is also offered for other instruments viz., commercial papers and bonds. The total dematerialised value of the commercial papers increased at both NSDL and CDSL. At NSDL, dematerialised value of commercial papers rose from Rs. 37,507 crore in 2007-08 to Rs. 48,922 crore in 2008-09. The dematerialised value of commercial papers also increased at CDSL from Rs.980 crore in 2007-08 to Rs. 1,139 crore in 2008-09. While dematerialised value of debentures /bonds increased at NSDL in 2008-09 over the previous financial year, that in CDSL declined during the same period.

The geographical coverage of depository participants (DPs) of NSDL and CDSL also widened in 2008-09. The DPs of NSDL were available at 946 cities in 2008-09 as compared to 803 cities in 2007-08. In case of CDSL, DPs were available at 815 cities in 2008-09 as compared to 740 cities in 2007-08.

5.11 Derivatives Market in India

5.11.1 Trends in Equity Derivative Market: Exchange traded derivatives is an important segment of Indian stock markets. The derivatives markets have grown substantially over the years in India. Trading in derivatives is dominated by NSE, which has a share of more than 99 percent of the total turnover. Over the years, derivatives market has generated turnover substantially higher than that of the equity segment. During 2008-09, turnover of derivatives market was 2.86 times of the turnover in all-India equity exchanges.

The total number of contracts traded in the derivative segment of NSE rose by 54.7 percent to 65,73,90,497 in 2008-09 from 42,50,13,200 in 2007-08 whereas at BSE, the number of contracts traded declined by 93.3 percent to 4,96,502 in 2008-09 from 74,53,371 in 2007-08. The value of the contracts traded in the derivative segment of NSE declined by 15.9 percent to Rs.1,10,10,482 crore in 2008-09 from Rs. 1,30,90,478 crore in 2007-08, and the turnover at the derivatives segment of BSE declined by 95.1 percent to Rs. 11,775 crore in 2008-09 from Rs. 2,42,309 crore in 2007-08. A clear-cut change was seen in the product composition of turnover in the derivatives market in India. Futures in general and single stock futures, in particular, had so far been actively traded derivatives product in India. But in 2008-09, the largest share in the total derivatives turnover was contributed by index options (33.9 percent). The share of index options in the total turnover was 10.4 percent in 2007-08. This was followed by index futures which increased from 29.2 percent in 2007-08 to 32.4 percent in 2008-09. The share of single stock futures slid from 57.7 percent in 2007-08 to 31.6 percent in 2008-09. The open interest in the derivative segment increased by 17.8 percent to Rs. 57,705 crore at the end of 2008-09 from Rs. 48,974 crore at the end of March 2008. Product-wise share in the open interest shows that the notional value of outstanding contracts was the highest for index options (Rs. 27,402 crore) followed by single stock futures (Rs. 15,722 crore), index futures (Rs. 12,060 crore), and stock options (Rs. 2,521 crore).

5.11.2 Membership of Derivatives Segment: There was a rise in various types of membership for derivative segment at NSE. The number of registered members at NSE increased to 1,076 as on March 31, 2009 from 964 in the previous year. Out of the total, there were 549 trading members at the end of 2008-09 compared to 510 a year ago. There were 207 trading-cum-clearing members and 300 trading-cum-self clearing members at NSE as on March 31, 2009. At BSE, there were 309 trading members and 97 trading-cum-clearing members at the end of March 2009. The transactions undertaken by trading-cum- clearing members constituted 56.5 percent of the total turnover of the F&O segment in 2008-09. The percentage share in the traded value by trading-cum-self clearing members and trading members was 28.1 percent and 15.4 percent, respectively.

5.11.3 Trend in Currency Derivatives Market: Currency futures trading commenced in India in August 2008 at NSE. Later, BSE and MCX were also granted permission in October 2008 to start trading in currency derivatives. During 2008-09, total turnover was the highest at NSE (Rs. 1,62,563 crore) followed by MCX (Rs. 1,48,826 crore) and BSE (Rs. 869 crore). At NSE, the share of top ten members in volumes of currency derivatives segment was 56.8 percent at the end of March 2009. Their share was 34.3 percent in open interest of currency derivatives segment. The share of top ten members in volumes and open interest of MCX was 61.7 percent and 57.2 percent, respectively. In BSE, the share of top ten members in volume and open interest was 100 percent.

5.12 Investor Assistance and Investor Education

5.12.1 Redressal of Investors' Grievances: SEBI has a comprehensive mechanism to facilitate redressal of grievances against intermediaries registered by it and against companies whose securities are/are being listed in Stock Exchanges. The Office of Investor Assistance and Education (OIAE) acts as the single window interface, interacting with investors seeking assistance.

Dedicated investor helpline telephone numbers are available for investors seeking general guidance pertaining to securities markets and to provide assistance in filing grievances. Dedicated personnel manning the helpline also guide the investors in filing up the grievance submission forms as well as in determining the appropriate authority for their first recourse.

SEBI website offers investors the facility of tracking the status of their grievances lodged with SEBI, pertaining to listed companies.

Enforcement actions as provided under the securities laws (including launch of adjudication, prosecution proceedings, direction u/s 11B) are initiated against companies and/or its Directors whose progress in redressal of investor grievances is not satisfactory.

During 2008-09, SEBI received 57,580 grievances from investors and resolved 75,989 grievances as compared to 54,933 grievances received and 31,676 grievances resolved in 2007-08. As on March 31, 2009, there were 1,71,000 grievances pending resolution as compared to 1,89,409 unresolved grievances as on March 31, 2008.

5.13 Retrospect and Prospects

5.13.1 Retrospect: Indian economy, following a sustained high growth rate during Tenth Plan period, witnessed a slowdown during 2008-09 as GDP grew at a moderated pace of 7.1 percent. The slowdown in momentum in manufacturing and industrial activity pulled down the overall growth rate amidst uncertain global business environment.

The securities market remained subdued with the BSE Sensex closing below the 10,000 mark on October 17, 2008. Thereafter, it witnessed its lowest close at 8,160 on March 09,

2009 before embarking on an upward path.

During 2008-09, BSE Sensex lost 37.9 percent and Nifty lost 36.1 percent over March 2008. Reflecting the price depreciation, market capitalisation (of BSE) to GDP ratio and the traded value (of BSE and NSE together) to GDP ratio declined to 58.0 percent and 72.4 percent, respectively in 2008-09 from 108.8 percent and 108.6 percent a year ago. The downslide in securities market was broad-based with a majority of the sectors registering price fall. Besides FIIs, mutual funds and retail investors also pared their positions in the secondary market. Due to weak global and domestic macro-economic fundamentals, overall market sentiment was subdued throughout the major part of the year, except in last quarter of 2009.

The primary market witnessed moderate activity during 2008-09. The number of companies which accessed the primary market was 47 in 2008-09 compared to 124 in 2007-08. Amount mobilised was Rs. 16,220 crore during 2008-09, lower than Rs. 87,029 crore mobilised during 2007-08. The number of Initial Public Offerings (IPOs) declined to 21 in 2008-09 from 85 in 2007-08 and the number of rights issue declined to 25 from 32 during the same period.

There was a net withdrawal of resources from mutual funds in 2008-09. With private sector mutual funds contributing a major part of the redemption, there was a net outflow of resources from all mutual funds at Rs. 28,296 crore during 2008-09 compared to a net accretion of resources of Rs. 1,53,802 crore in 2007-08. The exposure of mutual funds to debt securities increased due to the correction witnessed in the domestic equity market.

The FIIs continued to invest in Indian market. The number of SEBI registered FIIs went up to 1,635 by end March 2009 from 1,319 a year ago. Their net sales in equities was USD 10,324 million in 2008-09 as against a net investment of USD 13,243 million in the previous year.

5.13.2 Prospects: Protection of investor interests, ensuring that the markets are fair, efficient and transparent and reduction of systemic risk should be some of the major objectives of SEBI. In the past few years, SEBI has taken several steps to further these objectives and proposes to continue to take further steps in this direction. With maturing of markets, further specialization and innovations are likely to occur. These generate unknown risks. SEBI should encourage all market players to have better risk management systems to mitigate risks arising out of these activities.

Developing wide and deep markets should continue to be an area of prime importance. Wider investor participation imparts stability to markets and SEBI should continue to reinforce investor protection measures and take further investor education initiatives towards this end.

Wider retail participation in the markets through investor friendly channels is predicated upon low transaction costs. SEBI measures which will reduce transaction costs and encourage retail participation should be taken. SEBI should take such further steps for empowering the small investors through necessary disclosures as necessary. Making available high quality data to public will continue to be of prime importance. In the recent past several new products have been introduced in the Indian securities markets and we hope that SEBI will continue to encourage introduction of relevant innovative products in the markets to fill in the existing needs while taking care of the systemic stability concerns.

Several important steps have been taken by SEBI for developing corporate debt market and further efforts should be made in close coordination with the industry and other regulators. Maintaining market integrity is of prime importance to every securities market regulator. SEBI should further strengthen its integrated market surveillance system to deter market manipulations.

Taking timely and deterrent action against the offenders should be an important part of SEBI's work.

6

Evidence of Weak Level Efficiency

6.1 Introduction

The only way one can reliably ascertain or comment on stock market efficiency is through rigorous empirical testing. The purpose of this chapter is to present the findings of different tests applied to test the weak form efficiency. The weak-form tests are concerned with the utility of using the past history of prices to predict future prices. Direct evidences concerning the market's reaction to the information set relating to past price movement will be collected through various tests.

Tests of weak form of efficiency have their origin in what has come to be known as the random walk model or random walk hypothesis. Strictly speaking this model implies that the abnormal return follows an independent and identical distribution. Although this model is elegant and simple, the restrictions of iid are not plausible in the changing scenario of stock markets. For example, technical equipments, institutional investors, regulatory bodies and social environment have changed over the years. Therefore, there is a need to relax the restrictions of identical distribution and independence. We will see that relaxing these restrictions would broaden the scope of testing of market efficiency. In this study we are using three tests viz. the serial correlation test, the runs test and the variance ratio test. The serial correlation test and the variance ratio test are based on the relaxed version of random walk model whereas the runs test is based on its strictest version.

Even when one kind of test fails to reject the random walk hypothesis, the others may actually reject it. When the monthly prices tend to follow a random walk, the weekly prices or daily prices may not. When the returns on stock prices are independent, the returns on indices may be dependent.

Therefore applying a variety of tests, to different types of data will improve the accuracy of the study. This study tries to reach the above goal with a more comprehensive testing of the random walk hypothesis. In doing so, we will apply all the three tests, as stated above, on index data (BSE-Sensex and NSE-Nifty) as well as on the data pertaining to the individual shares. Extensive tests will be conducted on different data series, of daily data, weekly data and monthly data respectively. Also, at some places, a comparison with other markets is done.

6.2 Serial Correlation Coefficient Test

The serial correlation coefficient or auto-correlation can be used to measure whether or not the returns and the lagged returns in the same time series are correlated. A serial correlation coefficient that is not significantly different from zero implies that the returns and the lagged returns are uncorrelated. Thus, the stochastic process of stock prices exhibits a random walk. Alternatively, a significant non-zero serial correlation coefficient indicates that the returns and the lagged returns are correlated. The stochastic process of stock prices does not follow a random walk. A significant positive serial correlation coefficient means that a trend exists in the stock prices, whereas a significant negative serial correlation coefficient shows the existence of a reversal in the stock prices. Both the significant trend and reversal of returns can be used to predict price movement to obtain abnormal return. Therefore, the significant serial correlation coefficient between the returns in lead and lag is inconsistent with Market efficiency.

The null hypothesis states that the serial correlation coefficient is not significantly different from zero. The alternative hypothesis implies that the series correlation coefficient is not equal to zero. When the absolute value of series correlation coefficient is less than twice the standard error, we accept the null hypothesis, and the market can be concluded to be efficient in the weak form.

Before the results are analysed there is a need to emphasise that the serial correlation of daily returns, weekly returns and monthly returns cannot be compared to each other directly according to the magnitude of their serial correlation coefficients. Since the interval of observations, as well as the numbers of observations of daily, weekly and monthly returns are quite different within the same period; their standard deviations differ greatly. Therefore, the comparison of serial correlation between daily returns, weekly returns and monthly returns in this context are conducted in terms of the serial correlation coefficients and the standard deviation.

The two main indices of the Indian stock Market are BSE-Sensex and NSE-Nifty. The results of BSE- Sensex were divided into three categories namely Sub-period I (1980 to 1990), Sub-Period II (1991-2005) and overall period (1980-2005).

The daily returns in market indices of both the Bombay stock Exchange and National Stock Exchange exhibited correlated return patterns. The serial correlation coefficient of returns in lags one, eight and ten in the BSE were significantly different from zero. Lag one was significant at 1 percent significant level and lags eight and ten were significant at 5 percent significance level. In the NSE, lags one, two and nine were significant at 1 percent significance level and lag three; four and ten were significant at 5 percent significance level. Moreover, the null hypothesis that overall serial correlation coefficient from lag one through ten in the BSE and in the NSE were simultaneously equal to zero was also rejected by BL-statistics at the 1 percent level of significance. A comparison of Sub-Period I and Sub-Period II of BSE-daily returns showed that during Sub-Period I the returns were more correlated with their lag returns (as lags one, three, five, eight and nine were significant) as compared to Sub-Period II. During Sub-Period II only lags one and three were significant. However, the joint test of lag one through lag ten correlation coefficients in Sub-Period I and in Sub-Period II rejected the null hypothesis at the 1 percent significance level with a BL-statistics of 48.462 and 49.097 respectively. Results of daily price returns showed that before liberalization prices were more predicable and dependent than after liberalization. Therefore, it can be said that the process of economic reforms has reduced the dependence of stock prices on their lagged prices.

However, the serial correlation of daily returns in the two main indices on each of the two markets showed mixed results. In BSE, lags one, eight and ten were important whereas in NSE, lags one, two, three, four, nine and ten were significant. This means that the historical information embedded in longer period of lags is as influential in determining the future price as the information embedded in shorter lag lengths. Further, out of ten correlation coefficients four were negative and six were positive in BSE as well as in NSE. Therefore we cannot draw any clear-cut conclusion regarding price reversal or trend. However, lags two and seven were negative in both the indices, which indicated the price reversal on second and seventh trading day. This was true even if we compared daily returns of before and after liberalization period of BSE-Sensex.

The serial correlation figures of weekly returns in the two main indices of Indian stock market were obviously smaller than those of daily returns. Only the serial correlation coefficient in lag two in BSE-Sensex was significantly different from zero at the 5 percent level. The remaining serial correlation coefficient and BL-statistics for BSE were insignificant. Similarly, with the exceptions of the serial correlation coefficient in the lag one in the NSE, all the remaining serial correlation coefficients and BL-statistics were not statistically significant. Thus, the correlated return pattern in weekly return was not as significant as that in daily returns for the two main indices.

Results of the Sub-Period I and Sub-Period II also showed almost the same kind of pattern as shown by the overall period.

Results of Sub-Period I showed that lag two was significant and results of Sub-Period II showed that lag one was statistically significant. No other significant correlation coefficient was found and even BL-statistics of both the periods were also insignificant.

The number of positive serial correlation coefficient of weekly returns was greater than the number of negative coefficient for both the indices. Thus it is seen that the trend is dominating in weekly return, while the reversal appears in seven-week lags of BSE-Sensex and Nifty.

The larger rate of rejection of the null hypothesis of zero correlation coefficients on daily returns versus weekly and monthly returns is common phenomena of the world's stock markets. Apparently this phenomenon reveals that the larger the interval of the observations of prices, the less important is the lag price in determining the future price. But it should be stressed that the explanation about price interval is not applicable to monthly indices as we see that in the Indian case the serial correlation coefficient of monthly returns displays significant correlation at lag six and more negative coefficients as length of lags increases beyond six.

6.3 Runs Test

The runs test is a non-parametric statistic designed to determine whether the changes between observations are correlated or random. A run is a sub-sequence of 'like observations' with the first and the last observation of the run being preceded and followed, respectively, by an unlike observation. The sign "+" stands for a positive return, "–" stands for a negative return; '0' means zero return. The runs test assumes that if the price changes are random, the actual number of runs (r) should be close to the expected number of the runs (μ_r). Too many or too few actual runs are inconsistent with randomness. Thus, when trend in stock prices dominates the series, the actual runs will be less than the expected runs. Conversely, where there is a preponderance of stock price reversal, the actual runs will be greater than the expected runs.

We found that actual runs were less than their relevant expected runs. The Z-statistics significantly rejected the null hypothesis at 1 percent or 5 percent significance level. A comparison of Sub-Period I and Sub-Period II showed that the absolute value of Z-statistic during Period II was larger than that of Period I. The runs tests on daily returns in the two main market indices corroborated the results of the tests of serial correlation coefficient of daily returns. The positive serial correlation of daily returns in the first order results in too few actual runs compared with the expected runs. Thus, both the serial correlation coefficient tests and runs tests on the daily returns in the two main market indices indicated a departure from randomness.

The runs test on weekly returns of both the indices almost replicated the results of daily section. All of the actual runs on weekly returns in different period and for both the indices were lesser than their corresponding expected runs, so that the statistically significant negative Z-statistics rejected the null hypothesis at the 5 percent significance level for overall period. However, the absolute values of the Z-statistics of daily returns of the two indices were larger than those of the weekly returns. Thus, the daily returns behaviour showed more dependence than weekly returns. But as far as the observation periods were concerned, the behaviour of weekly returns remained similar in Sub-Period I (i.e. Pre-liberalisation) and Sub-Period II (Post- liberalisation) as accepting the null hypothesis of efficiency.

The difference between actual runs and expected runs of monthly returns for both the indices and for different time period narrowed visibly. None of the Z-statistics of monthly returns, for all the different periods and for either of the two indices, could reject the null hypothesis. The runs test showed that the daily and weekly performances refuted the random walk hypothesis for the Indian Stock Market, whereas the monthly performance conformed to randomness.

6.4 Variance Ratio Test

The variance ratio test exploits the fact that if the logarithms of the stock prices follow a random walk, the return variance should be proportional to the return horizon. The Variance Ratio (VR) methodology is based on the assumption that the variance of the random walk increments is linear in the sampling interval. Specifically, the variance estimated from the q-period returns should be q times as large as the variance estimated from one-period returns. Therefore, the ratio of the two variances divided by q should be equal to one.

Variance ratio test is much more powerful and reliable than the usual tests of random walk models. A variance ratio of less than one implies that the returns of short intervals tend to have 'mean reversion' feature over a long interval. On the other hand, a variance ratio exceeding one implies that the returns of short intervals have 'trend' feature over a longer interval.

The results of the variance ratio test of the daily returns section indicated that the daily price behaviour of both the indices departed tremendously from randomness. Except the results of the sub period I of BSE-Sensex, all the test statistics of Z(q) rejected the null hypothesis at 5 percent as well as at 1 percent significance level. Furthermore the rejections of the null hypothesis were robust in all intervals.

The variance ratio exceeded one for all other cases in the daily returns section, and most of them were relatively large.

The variance ratio of daily returns in both the indices increased successively as the length of the interval q increased.

The compatibility of the results of variance ratio test and autocorrelation test indicated that the non-random behaviour of the market was not because of the heteroscedasticity, but because of genuine autocorrelations. The serious violation of randomness found in the test of serial correlation and runs test is evidenced again in the variance ratios test.

6.5 Summary of Results

The serial correlation coefficient test, the runs test and the variance ratio test were applied to the data pertaining to the daily returns, weekly returns and monthly returns. Further, each test was conducted on the returns on the two main market indices and also on the individual share prices. The abundant results are briefly summarised in Tables 6.1 and 6.2. The symbol 'R' in a particular cell in these tables denotes rejection of the random walk hypothesis, and conversely, the symbol 'A' denotes acceptance of the random walk hypothesis.

The rejection is given under the following conditions:

- When the test is applied on an index, the test-statistics reject the null hypothesis at the 5 percent level of significance.
- When the test is applied on individual share prices, the test-statistics reject the null hypothesis at the 5 percent level of significance for more than 25 percent individual shares (lower than 36.36 percent, suggested by Fama in 1965). The criterion of 36.36 percent set by Fama (1965) 40 years ago may not be reasonable today. In modern market where information is communicated rapidly, the market predictability has improved with the availability of updated methodologies. This criterion, therefore, needs to be made more stringent. However, having said that, it must also be stated that any benchmark in this respect has to be a subjective estimate at best.

Table 6.1: Brief Conclusions of the Serial Correlation Test, Runs Test and Variance Ratio Test applied on Market Indices

	Serial Correlation Test			Runs Test			Variance Ratio Test		
	D	W	M	D	W	M	D	W	M
Sub Period I	R	A	A	R	A	A	A	A	A
Sub Period II	R	A	A	R	A	A	R	R	A
Overall Period	R	A	A	R	R	A	R	R	A

D = Daily; W = Weekly; M = Monthly; R = Rejection of the random walk hypothesis and A = Acceptance of the random walk hypothesis.

Table 6.2: Brief Conclusions of the Serial Correlation Test, Runs Test and Variance Ratio Test applied on BSE-Individual Shares

	Serial Correlation Test			Runs Test			Variance Ratio Test		
	D	W	M	D	W	M	D	W	M
Sub Period I	R	A	A	A	A	A	A	A	A
Sub Period II	R	R	A	R	A	A	R	R	A
Overall Period	R	R	A	R	A	A	R	R	A

D = Daily; W = Weekly; M = Monthly; R = Rejection of the random walk hypothesis and A = Acceptance of the random walk hypothesis.

Rejection of the null hypothesis at the 5 percent level of significance by more than 25 percent of the individual shares studied is construed as 'R' in the tests for individual shares.

Several features of the test results can be deduced. Firstly, the daily returns in the two main market indices were highly correlated. All the three tests applied on the market indices showed that the daily returns for sub-period I were less correlated than for sub-period II. Nevertheless, it was definitely demonstrated that the daily returns were correlated in the overall period. Secondly, all the three tests showed the existence of trend in weekly returns as the number of positive serial correlation coefficients was more than negative ones, Z-statistics of runs test were negative and the relevant variance ratios were larger than one. All the results of index weekly return for sub-period I supported the efficiency but we found mixed results for sub-period II and overall period. Thirdly, all the results of monthly returns supported the random walk hypothesis across all periods.

Empirical results reported here substantiate that the three tests (the serial correlation coefficient test, the runs test and the variance ratio test) are not completely consistent in rejecting or accepting of the null hypothesis. In other words, individual data sets do not consistently permit rejection of the RWH at high significance level, yet the various data sets together strengthen the case against validity. The daily, weekly and monthly behaviour of stock prices vary remarkably. The properties of the returns in market indices and in individual stocks are different. At first glance it may appear that the conclusions lead us nowhere, yet the comprehensive analysis still gives rise to a discussion towards classifying the market as being efficient or not due to many assorted statistics.

Therefore, this analysis avoids a distorted view that may occur when only one model is used on just one particular type of data. In such a case, the results are more likely to be clearer and homogenous, but whether they would also be more reliable or conclusive cannot be said with any amount of certainty. A research with heterogeneous conclusions for different data sets cannot be undermined for it still captures the confusing, and often realistic, behaviour of the markets. This would not only caution the market participants but would also motivate the policy makers and regulators to work towards greater measures aimed at creating more transparency and efficiency.

7

Volatility and its Implications for Efficiency

7.1 Volatility: A Feature of Stock Markets

If it is stagnant, it cannot be stock market at all! Volatility is an inevitable and significant characteristic of stock markets. It was also one of the first ways to study 'anomalies to simple efficient-market models'. Although there are several other anomalies to efficient-market models like the day of the week effect, small-firm effect, trading mechanisms and seasonality effects but volatility findings are often seen as the most clinching evidence against efficient-market models as a class. Volatility tests are a useful way to show that expected returns vary through time. 'Time varying expected returns', over and above the expected returns that vary according to the information availability, is seen as an exception of Efficient Market Hypothesis.

The Efficient Market Hypothesis contends that financial asset prices provide rational assessments of fundamental values and future payoffs. By implication, price changes should reflect the arrival and processing of all relevant new information. However, the proportion of return variability that can be ascribed to public news is low in the studies of Poterba and Summers (1986). They found that even the largest daily price changes in the stock market generally cannot be associated with any significant economic news. To the extent the volatility, even if huge, is explained by significant information/events affecting the stock price movements, the informational efficiency of the stock markets is not diluted by volatility. In other words, volatile movements in stock prices or in values of market indices do not necessarily make stock markets inefficient. It is only when volatile swings take place without any correlation with the significant information, that such volatility puts a question mark on the pricing efficiency of the stock markets. Thus 'true pricing' versus 'distorted pricing' of financial assets by the stock markets can be understood within the context of stock market volatility. The crucial question is: 'whether the variation in expected returns is rational?'

Therefore, in this study we are trying to associate large price movements with some public announcement or news. More specifically, the study addresses an important question, namely, 'how have the returns in the Indian stock market behaved, following financial liberalisation'? Considering "volatility" an important indicator of stock market efficiency and development, average level of volatility is measured for the period 1980 to 2003, taking BSE-Sensex daily index as the proxy for the market. The data sample period, from January 1, 1980 to December 31, 2003, covers a wide range of political and economic events that may have influenced the economy and, hence, the stocks market. Estimates of the standard deviation of monthly return in a year, daily return in year and daily return in a month are made to have a complete idea of level (size) and nature of volatility. Further, we have tried to study acceptable limits of volatility that may be embedded in the decision making of investors, depending on the type of investors.

Traders trade because the stock is volatile, and because traders trade, the volatility of the stock increases! The first part of the statement is true because if that were not the case, then there would be not much interest in that stock; and the second part is true because as more traders enter the arena, the interest in that stock increase and so does the volatility. At any point of time there are buyers and there are sellers in a particular stock, but with an opposite view and perception. This contrast in view feeds volatility. We know that every investor entering a stock market understands that market would move either way and accepts an 'acceptable' level of volatility either in favour or against, but hopes for a favourable movement and therefore embeds that into his investment decision-making process. In this chapter we have tried to analyse various acceptable levels of volatility so that the same can be embedded into the investment decisions by various types of investors.

Increase in efficiency also causes fluctuations because the speed of discounting the information increases. It has been observed that when markets become open to massive capital flows, the fluctuations become higher and regulators try to control these fluctuations. In the study we have also tried to compare the fluctuations of pre and post liberalization period. In general, it is understood that less volatile market reflects greater market efficiency. However, greater volatility is not necessarily a sign of less developed stock market. In fact, if volatility could be justified in terms of information, it signals the maturity and efficiency of stock market. Therefore, high volatility could be an indicator of development, in so far as revelation of information leads to volatility in a well functioning market [Barker and Harvey 1995]. Hence, from the development point of view, accurate estimation, forecasting, and management of the exposure of the market to high volatility assume greater importance. This portion of our study tries to examine this aspect, with more specific objectives of: measuring the volatility of the Indian stock market, understanding the justification of the large movements of stock market return in terms of arrival of public information and defining the control limits for stock market return and their implications for different types of investors.

7.2 Measurement of Volatility of the Indian Stock Market

The standard deviation of return (r) from a sample of n observations is the square root of the average squared deviation of returns from the average in the sample.

The daily returns were calculated by taking into account the difference between the natural logarithms of the daily closing prices of two consecutive trading days, while the monthly returns were calculated by taking into account the difference between the natural logarithms of the closing prices on the first and the last trading days of the month. From these, three volatility series were generated which are as follows.

- Volatility of monthly returns in a year.
- Volatility of daily returns in a year.
- Volatility of daily returns in a month.

7.2.1 Volatility of Monthly Returns in a Year: For each year, 12 monthly returns were used to calculate standard deviation of a year. Therefore, there was one figure per year for the entire period of study.

For the complete period, the arithmetic mean of the yearly standard deviations (N = 24) was 7.38 percent and standard deviation of yearly standard deviations was 2.65. To see the years with highly volatile fluctuations and less than average level of fluctuations respectively, we used a quality control limit of $\mu \pm 0.5\sigma$ (it covered nearly 66.6 percent observations of the study). Years having standard deviations more than $\mu + 0.5\sigma$ were highly volatile years viz. 1990 (12.45) and 1992 (15.89). Years having standard deviations less than $\mu - 0.5\sigma$, viz. 1980 (4.32), 1981 (5.7), 1982 (5.8), 1983 (3.86), 1984 (3) and 1987 (4.31) were the years representing least volatility. Remaining 16 years were years of moderate fluctuations having moderate standard deviation.

Year 1985 emerges out as the watershed year in the stock market as it set the limits of volatility to a higher level for all time to come. This year took the volatility beyond all previous records. Average monthly return touched a new peak in 1985 with 5.61 percent. This was because of share mania of the 1980s that continued up to 1992 causing a second highest average monthly return of 5.14 percent in 1991. But with a nosedive in share price in 1992, the market experienced its highest volatility level of 15.89 percent till date. Between 1990 and 1994, the market had been through three major crashes. Hence, the market is continuously experiencing the moods of euphoria and despondency, whether we look at the period before liberalization or at the subsequent period.

7.2.2 Volatility of Daily Returns in a Year: Year 1985 experienced the highest average daily return of 0.34 percent, which coincided with our earlier results. Again 1992 topped in volatility level of daily returns, followed by 1990. Therefore, these results do not make an additional contribution at this stage of the study. However, these results are used in setting the quality control limits of volatility in the subsequent section of the study.

7.2.3 Volatility of Daily Returns in a Month: An attempt was made to measure share price fluctuations using standard deviation of daily returns within each month. Each month's standard deviation was measured around a different mean in the same way as in the previous analysis where the standard deviation for each year was measured around each yearly mean.

The period of 1980s could be defined as the period of "lull before the storm". During this period, strong economic fundamentals; a number of liberalized policies and entrance of general public in market pampered the market thoroughly. Interestingly, the forces operating during this period were of great variety and were incorporated in the index. Along with other factors, speculation and over optimism as well affected the market, because of which the market got over-heated and created a speculative "bubble" of 1992. This bubble finally burst in April 1992, causing the highest volatility of 6.02 percent of month.

The average level of monthly volatility was 1.55 percent. Further, a standard deviation of standard deviations (N=288) was measured. If we set the quality control limit at $\mu \pm 1\sigma$ (it covered nearly 78 percent observations of the study) to judge the most volatile months, we get two limits viz. $\mu + 1\sigma$ (i.e. 2.36 percent) and $\mu - 1\sigma$ (i.e. 0.74 percent). These are upper control limits (UCL) and lower control limits (LCL) respectively. Months having volatility above 2.36 percent were most volatile months and below 0.74 percent were quite stable months. The months having the volatility between 0.74 percent and 2.36 percent were moderately volatile months. This analysis reveals that out of 33 most volatile months, which crossed the limit of 2.36 percent, 6 months were from 1992, 6 months from 1990 and 3 months from 1991. Collectively, almost 50 percent of the total sample period's fluctuations related to the period 1990-92. Thus, the year 1992 stands out as the most volatile year of the Indian stock market.

7.3 Events Explaining Volatility

Even with assistance provided by hindsight, the ability of expert to explain stock price changes remains modest. The efficient market hypothesis contends that financial asset price provide rational assessment of fundamental values and future payoffs. By implication price changes should reflect the arrival and processing of all relevant new information. Recently several studies have attempted to study the link between stock return volatility and the economic events. For example, Cutler, Poterba, and Summers (1989) find that even the largest daily price changes in the stock market generally cannot be associated with any significant economic news. Schwert (1989), in an exhaustive study, finds that the volatility of stock return is not closely related to the volatility of other economic variables. Roll (1988) concludes that much of the variance in the equity return series may be related either to private information or occasional "frenzy" unrelated to concrete information. The risk associated with noise in stock return is nevertheless of concern to investors.

In an attempt to identify the causes for the identified volatility shifts, we search for the release of extraordinary information in the vicinity of these unusual dates. It is clear that a number of factors are responsible for these wild fluctuations at different dates. Contrary to the conclusion of Poterba and Summers (1986), we find that majority of volatile changes (60 percent) are associated with the release of significant economic information which implies that Indian stock market is largely responding to economic information.

Moreover, before liberlisation (i.e. till 1990) only 45 percent changes were associated with economic information but after liberlisation (i.e. since 1991) 65 percent changes are associated with economic information. Hence Indian stock market is responding more to economic information after liberlisation. Some of these factors affecting market volatility are discussed here in detail.

First, the release of budget news is of paramount importance in explaining volatility. It is a major macro economic policy document of the government that triggers significant revision in share prices. The budget 1992-93 caused a volatile increase of 6.37 percent and 9.95 percent of return in two successive days as the budget was market friendly. On the other hand, return declined by 5.25 percent after presentation of union budget 2000-01 declaring double dividend tax and progressive withdrawal of tax deduction on export earnings.

Second, we observe that institutional investors sell/buy during large market swings, contributing to market volatility to a great extent. Since institutional investors are more sophisticated and have short horizons, therefore, they herd together with their peers and sell/buy during a market decline/rise. For example sustained selling by FIIs particularly US-based portfolio investors magnified the impact of attack on World Trade Tower causing a decline of 5.41 percent and 5.42 percent of return in two consecutive days. Similarly large-scale disinvestments by financial institutions created nervousness in the market in August and September 1985. We also find that a recovery of 184 points in sensex took place by aggressive purchases by FIIs in March 2001. In nutshell, we can say that institutional investors trade with the momentum of the market on days when there are large movements in the stock market and provide further fuel to volatility.

Third, the most significant announcements by RBI, SEBI or by Central Government too affect the market movements. Apart from these changes in fundamentals, chain reactions to some major news, holidays, and news of socio-political instability are some of the reasons causing volatility.

Therefore, we feel that volatility of share returns may be partly explained by psychological factors, fads, and incorporation of private information. The unexplained volatility on non-news dates indicates not only that private information is being incorporated into prices but also that mania is periodically gripping investors. Perhaps either panic or euphoria drives the market, every now and then, as evident in these spikes.

Thus, we stipulate that the volatility process is driven by the simultaneous interaction of numerous components, some associated with economic news release, some with social political happenings and some unobserved (latent) factors.

7.4 Summary of Results

The main findings of the volatility tests are as follows. First, it is seen that the stock returns do not move in smooth sine waves of constant amplitude and wavelength. Rather, the actual return pattern follows bumpier patterns. Second, we do not find a noticeable pattern of volatility. Although, the period (1990-1992) underwent considerable ups and downs, this period is not throwing up any pattern that could be taken as a distinct, representative pattern for the whole period. Yearly volatility of monthly return as well as of daily return was highest in 1992, followed by 1990. Third, the quality control bands show the area of operation for hedgers. Fourth, some information drives prices away from equilibrium. As a result of this information, the market oscillates or bounces around its mean level. The study also reflects that Indian stock market after liberalisation has become somewhat more responsive to economic information.

8

Conclusions, Explanations and Implications

This study has comprehensively tested the random walk hypothesis to determine the validity of weak form efficiency of Indian stock market. The serial correlation coefficient test, the runs test and the variance ratio test have been applied to the data of the daily returns, weekly returns and monthly returns. Further, each test has been conducted on the returns in the two main market benchmark indices (the BSE Sensex and the NSE Nifty) as well as on the returns on the individual share prices of 57 companies forming part of the BSE Sensex. A comparative evaluation of the efficiency in the pre liberalisation and the post liberalisation period was also attempted. Moreover, tests of volatility were conducted as an alternative but related method of studying the market efficiency.

8.1 Summary of Evidences

Firstly, the daily returns in the two main indices representing two markets are highly correlated. It is also demonstrated by and large that daily returns are correlated in each of the periods under study viz., the pre liberalisation, the post liberalisation and the overall period. All the three tests applied on indices show that the daily returns in sub-period II are more correlated than in sub-period I. Secondly, all the three tests show the existence of trend in weekly returns as the number of positive serial correlation coefficient are more than negative ones, Z-statistics of runs test are negative and the relevant variance ratios are larger than one. All the results of index weekly return of sub-period I support the efficiency but we find mixed results for sub-period II and overall period.

Thirdly, all the results of monthly returns support the random walk hypothesis across all periods.

The main features of the results of individual shares depict similarity with the features of the results for market indices, though with minor differences. In addition to the above stated results, the serial correlation coefficient rejects the RWH for weekly returns on individual shares in sub-period II and overall period. Moreover, runs test accepts the RWH even for daily returns in sub-period I. Thus, individual datasets do not consistently permit rejection of the RWH at high significance level, but at the same time the various data sets together strengthen the case against validity.

Further, the tests of volatility show that the number of all the three types of spikes, in a way representing the departures of minor, moderate and major amplitude from the mean returns, have remarkably increased in the post liberalisation period. However, the percentage of these departures that could be explained in the context of information and events has also moderately gone up in the post liberalisation period.

Empirical results, thus, indicate that the four tests (serial correlation coefficient test, runs test, variance ratio test and the test of volatility) are not completely consistent in rejection or acceptance of the null hypothesis of stock market efficiency. The daily, weekly and monthly behaviour of stock prices varies remarkably.

The properties of the returns in indices and in individual stock prices data are also different. Therefore, though we don't get a clear line of conclusions for all the datasets and by all the testing tools, yet this comprehensive analysis avoids a distorted view that may occur when only one model is used on a particular type of dataset only. The comprehensive analysis still allows and facilitates a thorough discussion in classifying the market as being efficient or not, and studying its evolution in the post liberalisation period, using the variety of statistics generated.

8.2 Conclusions from the Evidences

The various findings as summarized above can be used to draw some interesting and thought provoking conclusions about the behaviour of share prices and, hence, about the relative efficiency or inefficiency of the stock markets. The following key conclusions emerge from the empirical findings:

- The stock market efficiency is directly related to the time interval of study of returns or the investment horizon. As the time interval or the return horizon is increased, the efficiency also increases. The daily returns are highly correlated, the weekly returns are a little less correlated and the monthly returns are random under each of the three tests used. In other words, the Indian stock market is inefficient over the 'daily' interval but efficient over the 'monthly' interval, with the 'weekly' interval lying somewhere in between.
- The inefficiency of the market has increased in the post liberalisation period. This is vouched by the findings that the returns in sub period-II are much more correlated as compared to sub period I, even though the null hypothesis is rejected for both the periods. Moreover, there are more rejections of the null hypothesis in sub period II under the other tests also, as compared to sub period I.
- The volatility of the Indian Stock Market has significantly gone up in the post reforms period. The number of high amplitude departures from the mean returns has gone up significantly in sub period II. It is seen that the stock returns do not move in smooth sine waves of constant amplitude and wave-length in this period. The volatility tests also show that prices are 'too volatile' to be explained by 'efficient market' as the market oscillates or bounces sharply around its mean level.
- The efficiency is a little better depicted for the individual shares as compared to the benchmark market indices, although the difference is not enough to seriously alter the broad conclusions about the rejection of the null

hypothesis at daily interval. This is reflected in more acceptance of the null hypothesis for the daily returns data for individual share as compared to the market indices (both under the runs test and the variance ratio test).

8.3 Explanation of the Findings

Some of the above conclusions are more or less along the expected lines whereas some others may look a little surprising. However, an attempt has been made below to explain the possible causes/factors that could have led to these findings.

As far as the finding on the efficiency varying with the time interval or the return horizon is concerned, we can say that share price have short memory. It is quite possible that economic agents take buy or sell decisions on immediate expectations; based on most recent historical performance, say the price movement of the day(s) just gone by. However, as the current speculative effects get diluted, the prices in a longer period move towards natural prices of stocks through fundamental undercurrents.

Therefore, this kind of behaviour is observed among daily, weekly and monthly closing returns. In this context, we can also mention here that the hypothesis of 'slowly decaying irrational bubble' has been gaining grounds over the period of evolution of the efficiency findings. It is argued that the irrational bubbles or the unexplained, psychological or speculative movements often affect the returns in the short run, but in the longer run they tend to get corrected/reversed. This possibility is re-validated and reinforced by our findings that the daily returns are highly correlated; the weekly returns show a trend and the monthly returns are random. These patterns indicate at an over/under reaction in the short run (day/week), followed by mean reverting behaviour in the longer run (month).

Further, our findings of the volatility test also point at something similar. It is seen that the market oscillates or bounces around its mean level and creates 'spikes'. As with a stretched spring, the greater the distance that a return is from its mean level, the greater will be the force pulling the return back towards its mean level.

The finding that the inefficiency of the market has increased in the post liberalisation period is interesting and may surprise some people at first glance. However, many reasonable explanations may collectively justify this finding. The daily returns in sub period-II are much more correlated as compared to sub period I, even though the monthly returns for both sub periods show randomness. If we relate to this, the other finding, that the volatility has gone up in the sub period II, then these findings can be explained with reference to the speed and cost of information dissemination. As the information dissemination is getting faster, the inefficiency is getting restricted to shorter and shorter period. The time lag between an informed and an uninformed investor has shrunk, to confine only to a day or so and hence better informational efficiency in the longer run. In fact, as the costless information gets disseminated fast in the reformed stock markets, it is argued that the intra day volatility is likely to increase as the informed investor has very little time, even less than a day, to use his information before the uninformed investor catches up and becomes at par with him!

It can also be argued that the more money supply and increased trading may have caused the greater inefficiency in the post liberalisation period. In the post liberalisation period, India has emerged as 'the land of opportunities' and mega bucks are chasing Indian stocks. In such a scenario, in simple macroeconomic terms, it can be argued that as money supply increases, price rise results (in any market, be it product market or share market) and this price rise may have no relation with the fundamentals or information attached to that particular share/index. In other words market participants, including institutional buyers, buy stocks not because 'they should' but because 'they can', and this fuels unexplained volatility. To put it in still different terms, the buy or sell moves of big buyers/sellers themselves have become 'information' for smaller players to react to. As they find it difficult to keep pace with these moves in the short run we find that the weak level inefficiency over short return horizons has gone up in the post liberalisation period.

The world over, efficiency has not yet been conclusively proved even in the most developed and the most liberalized economies. Therefore it would probably be a little naïve to expect the Indian stock markets to quickly respond to the still young reform initiatives. The impact of some of the most significant reforms like stock lending scheme, straight through processing, electronic data filing and dissemination, participation identification and audit trail etc would not have taken place yet, and hence the post reforms period keeps showing the stock markets as still inefficient. Further, in an emerging economy like India, we probably have not yet reached a time threshold where fair pricing of stocks would be a 'given thing'.

Thus we see that the market moves in 'patterns', often created by smart speculative manoeuvrings of a few big players who try to 'affect the market prices' instead of 'being affected by' or reacting to the market prices. A case in the point is that the derivatives markets, a feature of the post reforms period, have crossed the cash markets in terms of monthly turnover. It is seen often that even when the markets have a downward trend, the futures segments of the markets continue growing at a steady pace. Experts consider this to be an unhealthy trend and believe that equity market investors have become too speculative.

Coming to the finding on the increased volatility in the post liberalisation period, part of the explanation has already been given above in the form of the more money supply, increased trading and speculative manoeuvrings in the Indian stock market. Besides, increasing influence of institutional buyers (including FIIs) and the use of excessive 'charting' by them is often seen as a factor adding fuel to fire. Most computerized trading systems in the world follow simple 'trend following trading systems'. These are statistical systems based on some statistical formulae that generate a buy or sell signal based on some predetermined parameters fed into a computerized black box. These are 100 percent non-discretionary systems and the users of these systems follow them blindly. If a 'sell' is generated the fund managers sell, it is as simple as that. Now when a trend changes then it changes for all and if one system generates a 'sell', then the market comes down. That would result in a generation of a sell signal in some other computerized trading system.

In simple terms, the 'sell' is generated in most of the trading systems more or less at the same time and this has a cascading and a domino effect. Thus it can be said that the computerized trading system increases volatility in modern stock markets, and modern India is no exception. Moreover the attempt by big players to profit from the difference between the cash price and the futures prices, or from the arbitrage difference between two markets, causes major shifts in volume, which in turn cause additional volatility.

The finding that the efficiency is a little better illustrated for the individual shares as compared to the benchmark market indices can be explained as the result of more informed decisions regarding individual stocks. This finding about positive autocorrelations for returns on diversified portfolios has been repeatedly observed in many other studies and has been explained as transitory price variation induced by noise trading. It is easier tracking the fundamentals of an individual stock than understanding the volatile sensex movements, which may be much more dominated by psychological fads, internationally sensitive information, perceptions of the world players about India as an economy etc.

8.4 Limitations of the Study

The multi-fold empirical testing has resulted in a more comprehensive analysis and more multi-directional scrutiny of stock market efficiency, showing a true and complete picture of the behaviour of the market. However, the study had its own limitations, and some of them are indicated here. As a result of limited size of the sample for the sub period I, in view of non-availability of data, the results for the sub period I may be contaminated. This study did not carry out a full examination of the question of efficiency in all its form, and many aspects of efficiency, though reviewed in detail, were not put to empirical testing. Examination of anomalies, event studies to examine the semi-strong level of efficiency and the strong form tests for utility of private information fall in this category.

This study covered 57 individual scrips forming part of the BSE Sensex, though in modern stock markets there is now a greater acceptance of the role played by the relatively smaller stocks forming part of more broad based indices like BSE 100 or NSE Nifty Junior. For a better understanding of the structure of price movements in the Indian Stock Market, the study could be extended to a large sample of individual share price series, so that more generalised conclusions can be drawn.

It is now agreed that all models for expected returns are incomplete descriptions of the systematic patterns in average returns during any sample period. Appearance of significant abnormal returns is sensitive to time period, method of estimation, and sampling. As a result, tests of efficiency are always contaminated by a bad-model problem, and this study cannot be an exception.

To try and explain the trends, irrational bubbles & anomalies within the broader framework of efficiency, fine-tunings in the models and the data are required. A more sophisticated model of investor behaviour may be needed to explain the observed pattern of returns.

Notwithstanding the above limitations, it is sincerely hoped that this study takes forward the ongoing research on an issue that is far from settled yet.

8.5 Synthesis with other Studies

Analysis of our findings in comparison with others' can not only help in the synthesis of results and implications, but would also suggest several issues that should be addressed in future research.

Firstly, on the issue of correlation in daily returns but randomness in monthly returns, our findings can be integrated with the results of De Bondt and Thaler (1985), who suggested that most people tend to "overreact" to unexpected and dramatic news events. They held that extreme movements in stock prices will be followed by subsequent price movements in the opposite direction, and this would imply a violation of weak-form of market efficiency.

Similarly, the results of Poterba and Summers (1988) also suggested that stock returns show positive serial correlation over short periods and negative correlation over longer intervals. In their study also, although individual data sets did not consistently permit rejection of the random-walk hypothesis at high significance levels, the various data sets together strengthened the case against its validity. However, studies like those by Barberis, Shleifer and Vishny (1996) and Daniel, Hirshleifer and Subrahmanyam (1997) found results more consistent with the market efficiency prediction, that long-term return continuation and long-term return reversal are equally likely chance results. Anomalies are chance results; apparent over-reaction to information is about as common as under-reaction, and post-event continuation of pre-event abnormal returns is about as frequent as post event reversal. They argued that those apparent anomalies could be due to methodology.

On the findings of reduced efficiency in the post liberalisation period, it is seen that J. C. Sharma (2002) also concluded that despite the liberalisation process, the Indian Stock Market continued to be largely inefficient as the stationary component explained more than half of the expected variations in stock return even after financial liberalisation process was already in full swing. Laeven (2003) also warned that more liberalised does not necessarily mean a better-organised economy, or more well managed financial systems therein, and hence inefficiency and volatility are likely unless real strength comes at the operative levels.

Further, related to our finding of rising volatility in sub period II, Edwards, Biscarri and Gracia (2003) found that liberalisation in some of the Latin American countries like Brazil, Argentina, Chile and Mexico (these economies are often seen as quite similar to India) led to significant increase in volatility in the stock markets. Further, in so far as we do not outrightly reject market efficiency, through the findings on volatility, our results are broadly along similar lines as those of Poterba and Summers (1986). Like our study, they had also found that volatile movements are only partly explained by information. On the finding of weaker demonstration of efficiency for the market indices as compared to individual shares, studies like the ones by Fisher (1966) and Lo and MacKinlay (1988) also found that positive autocorrelations for returns on diversified portfolios, as benchmark indices always are, were more pronounced, than those for individual shares.

Further, to explain the non-uniform results across different datasets and different testing tools, we would like to point out that at first glance it may appear that the conclusions lead us nowhere; yet the comprehensive analysis still gives rise to a discussion towards classifying the market as being efficient or not due to many assorted statistics. Therefore, this comprehensive analysis avoids a distorted view that may occur when only one model is used on just one particular type of data. In such a case, the results are more likely to be clearer and homogenous, but whether they would also be more reliable or conclusive cannot be said with any amount of certainty. More often than not, whenever a single or just a few tests are used, the results for Indian stock market efficiency have been clearer, but whenever more thorough testing methodology has been used the conclusions have been diverse.

For example N. Krishan Rao and K. Mukherjee (1971) examined one company in detail, using only spectral method, J.L. Sharma and Robert E. Kennedy (1977) examined only one market benchmark index (BVDSI) using the runs test and the spectral test, O.P. Gupta (1985) studied only weekly datasets of 39 shares for a 5 year period and S.K. Chaudhuri (1991) used only the serial correlation test. All these studies found reasonable evidence in favour of efficiency. The results of R.P. Mahapatra (1995), who examined 26 individual shares only, disclosed that the Indian Stock Market seemed to be less efficient in the short run but more efficient in the longer run, thereby rejecting RST and accepting EMH in the long run. On the other hand, D. Ray (1976) used comprehensive testing (runs test, serial correlation test and spectral analysis) and got varying results for different tests. A research with heterogeneous conclusions for different data sets, using multiple tools cannot be undermined as it still captures the confusing, and often realistic, behaviour of the markets. This would not only caution the market participants but would also motivate the policy makers and regulators to work towards greater measures aimed at creating more transparency and efficiency.

8.6 Implications and Suggestions

Does the efficiency of the stock markets in an economy need to be proved conclusively before it has practical relevance for investors and others? We would like to answer this question with a strong "No". Stock markets, whether proved to be efficient or not, hold a very significant status in today's economies, particularly in a fast growing economy like India. The findings of our study can hold many possible implications for the market participants, the market regulators and also for future researches.

The trading strategies for an investor in an inefficient market are likely to be different from the trading strategies in an efficient market. Whether the market can be beaten has always been a key question. The results indicate that there is a correlated pattern in daily returns and therefore it may be possible to earn super normal returns using the predictive power of these correlations. However, it should be appreciated that it is one thing to observe a pattern in past data under a statistical research and conclude that the returns were correlated, and hence predictable, and quite another to be actually able to do it in 'real time'. Thus the message may be that 'you may beat the market, but you should not expect to'!

How good are real world predictions? Surprisingly, (given the amount of money spent on investment research), the answer is, "not real good!" Results indicate that institutional research doesn't seem to produce consistently better stock selections. Stand alone investment advisers, like the brokers, sub-brokers, agents, market experts in the media etc who are omnipresent in our country) fare even worse. Many large corporate pension funds and mutual funds are now putting part of their assets in Index funds (a portfolio constructed to replicate the performance of a stock average such as the BSE Sensex or the NSE Nifty). The reason seems to be if you can't hope to beat the market in real time, then why pay brokers fees! Unless the analyst can make meaningful prior predictions concerning the purchase and the sale of individual securities, and unless his choices consistently outperform randomly selected securities of the same general riskiness, his position is weak and his reliability should be no more than that of an astrologer. Thus, rather than being duped by 'tips' of dubious reliability from smart advisers, investors must train themselves in fundamental analysis, which is always useful. Further learning must become an enjoyable compulsion if they want to compete with others in an attempt to make superior profits.

Moreover, if one is trying to beat the market, he must also be prepared for the associated risks. Very often it is seen that the investors want to earn a fast buck in the stock market but when they incur losses they brand the market as inefficient. In fact major crashes and investors losing heavily are often seen as inefficiency or flaws of the market, whereas actually they are the flaws of the investors' psyche and wrong investment objectives. People expect phenomenal overnight gains rather than market fundamentals based 'average gains'. Subconsciously these investors actually desire the market to be inefficient, so that they can use their so-called superior tips or insight. It is only when they burn their fingers that they blame market inefficiency. If investor biases are at work, they are eventually likely to be followed by losses and, more importantly, learning.

Volatility is an evil to some but is an important analytic tool in the arsenal of a skilled technician. What goes up also comes down and what goes down also goes up in the stock markets. Besides exhibiting fluctuations, the market sends signals to those who understand how to make the best use of that. If volatility is the source of problem, the same is a complete solution in itself. As the quality control bands show in the volatility graphs in Appendix V, an investor can operate as a hedger. If he wants to operate within mean $\pm$ 3SD area then his risk is minimised but hedging cost will be high. Now, an investor needs to assess return against cost of hedging. In essence, a hedger should try to identify shocks that have made large price moves relative to their peers, their industry or the market as a whole. The strategy, based on control limits, calls for a trade according to his acceptable level of risk for a recent excess return, unless an explanation for the recent excess return could be found in fundamentals. Thus, an investor has to decide an acceptable level of risk for himself and make the decision accordingly in the logical hope of mean reversion effect as per the 'stretched spring logic'.

It is very important to note that the volatility increases/decreases at the point of turning because the struggle between the buyers and the sellers is at its best at the turning point where buyers become sellers and sellers become buyers. It is this shift in perception and the demand and supply that causes volatility and it is extremely important in forecasting.

Hedge fund managers usually resort to hedging at turning points to protect the portfolio and to take a contrary position in the event the eventful happens.

Thus our suggestion is that market inefficiency is not a terror, it is only a word of caution. An investor must decide about his own trade off between the risk and return. Adventurous investors can indulge in trying to take advantage of the inefficiency and the volatility. Risk-averse investors should resist from overreacting, or taking irrational decisions, and should take decisions based on the fundamentals. This will be conducive for injecting efficiency in the market, so essential for maintaining good investment climate.

For regulatory authorities, the implication of our findings is that they should diagnose the patient's ills, once they know his blood pressure and temperature. That is to say that since at least the suggestive, even if not clinching, evidence towards inefficiency has been generated by the present study, the scope of economic reform agenda in general and financial reforms in particular must be enlarged. At the same time it needs to be realised that increased liberalisation is not necessarily a boon for market efficiency. Better core-strength of the financial system is a more desirable objective for stability and reliable growth. The fickle optimism and euphoria over liberalisation wont make much sense in the absence of streamlining and trustworthiness of procedures and functioning. It has been observed that in a country like India where a major chunk of unaccounted money is channelled to stock market, no empirical studies would reveal the true structural relationships between money supply and stock return; or between fundamentals & stock returns. Thus there is a need to focus on financial stability, through measures like better audit trail through database of participants, electronic information dissemination and more effective market regulation. Liberalise, but with 'Eyes Wide Open', must be the mantra.'

Financial stability can be defined as a condition in which the financial system, comprising of financial intermediaries, market and market infrastructures, is capable of withstanding shocks and the unravelling of financial imbalances, thereby mitigating the likelihood of disruptions in the financial intermediation process which are severe enough to significantly impair the allocation of savings to profitable investment opportunities. Stabilized system is one in which different units perform their parts of the contract without causing undue change in the underlying prices. It is needed in the wake of domestic and external shocks. It would be possible if we have proper trading and risk management systems. Otherwise it will lead to puncturing of the bubbles causing widespread loss of economic value of the held assets, ultimately causing chaos.

Efficiency of stock markets is the best insurance against price manipulations. Since even large security markets, which are by and large efficient, are prone to sporadic bouts of inefficiency and irrational behaviour, it is necessary to establish trading and regularity systems that create and sustain efficiency. In the Indian context, the key operating parameters for achieving and sustaining greater degree of stock market efficiency would include:

- Improving the quality and frequency of disclosure and achieving wider and speedier dissemination of information.
- A much broader range of exchange traded derivative instruments need to be allowed in order to improve the market for bonds.
- Active participation of well trained, independent and regulated analysts in shaping investor opinion and investor perception.
- Flexibility of trading in the market to drive the prices to the correct level speedily.

The Indian stock market suffers from infirmities on all these aspects. It is time for India to adopt international accounting standards and corporate governance practices apart from making it mandatory for firms to disseminate information from the net, in addition to the traditional channels. Opening the bond derivatives market to all participants would help. A more principle-based approach to capital market regulation might help speed up the introduction of new instruments and, as in product markets, supervisory bodies should be subjected to periodic regulatory impact reviews. The analysts operating in the Indian market are typically attached to various market intermediaries.

There are no effective regulations to ensure that the opinions expressed by them are not coloured by the profit motive of the intermediaries they are attached to. No investor or investment advisor can afford to be ignorant of either (1) the major empirical research on stock prices and returns, or (2) the standard statistical tests available for assessing whether high returns are the result of skill and luck. If there are many analysts who are pretty good, they help narrow discrepancies between actual price and intrinsic values. Finally, there is a need to facilitate borrowing and lending of securities and provide funding for taking trading positions so that the prices reflect the aggregate assessment of the market, unencumbered by trading restrictions. For future research, lots of avenues are already known and this study reinforces the need for diverse testing to take the subject of efficiency to its logical conclusion. Both theoretical and empirical considerations suggest the likelihood that market valuations differ frequently and substantially from fundamental values. Indirect empirical evidence suggested the importance of valuation errors, and the market participants must remain cautious about it.

It must be said that the market efficiency issue is yet to be definitely settled and there exists a controversy in the finance literature as to whether or not the major stock markets of the world are 'efficient' in pricing the securities that are traded there. This controversy manifests itself not only in the classical confrontation between the stock market practitioners and the stock market theorists, but also in the research findings that have unearthed evidence both for and against efficiency.

Before we abandon market efficiency in favour of long-run market under reaction (or overreaction) to various events, prudence demands several commonsense steps. These include evaluating evidence gathered over many, many years and over many kinds of markets and making efforts to evaluate the fallibilities of our methods of modelling, sampling, and measuring long-run abnormal returns. If we do conclude that long-run abnormal performance exists after a given event, prudence still demands that we do not rashly conclude that markets are so inefficient that prices are routinely biased by large amounts, such as 50 to 100 percent.

What causes variations in expected returns, are these variations rational, and can these be predicted are the vital questions which will still be asked and to which concrete answers still need to be found out. There are ever-growing dimensions of further research in this field and more coherent explanations need to be developed about the link between the expected returns and business conditions on one hand, and between variations in expected returns and macro-economic variables like consumption, investment and saving on the other.

For a better understanding of the structure of price movements in the Indian Stock Market, the use of further research, through tighter models, on a large sample of individual share price series is called for. A fascinating area for future research will be to find acceptable level of volatility at industry and firm level. Moreover, intra-day fluctuations can also be studied, hence leaving a vast area for future research.

Further, chartist theories implicitly assume that there is dependence in series of successive price changes. That is, the history of the series can be used to make meaningful predictions concerning the future. There is precious little published discussion of rigorous empirical tests of various technical theories. Thus there is a need of subjecting the chartist theories to equally rigorous tests.

In an uncertain world, however, no amount of empirical

testing may be sufficient to establish the validity of a hypothesis beyond any shadow of doubt.

Appendices

Appendix I

Frequently Asked Questions on Dematerialisation

Disclaimer: These FAQs are not the interpretation of law but provide only a simplistic explanation of terms / concepts related to the depository system. All information has been updated till September 30, 2008. For full particulars of laws governing the depository system, please refer to the Acts/Regulations/Guidelines/Circulars appearing under the Legal Framework Section.

Understanding Depository System

1. What is a Depository?

A depository is an organisation which holds securities (like shares, debentures, bonds, government securities, mutual fund units etc.) of investors in electronic form at the request of the investors through a registered Depository Participant. It also provides services related to transactions in securities.

2. How many Depositories are registered with SEBI?

At present two Depositories viz. National Securities Depository Limited (NSDL) and Central Depository Services (India) Limited (CDSL) are registered with SEBI.

3. What is the minimum net worth required for a depository?

The minimum net worth stipulated by SEBI for a depository is Rs. 100 crore.

4. How is a depository similar to a bank?

It can be compared with a bank, which holds the funds for depositors. A Bank--Depository analogy is given in the following table:

Bank	Depository
Holds funds in an account	Holds securities in an account
Transfers funds between accounts on the instruction of the account holder	Transfers securities between accounts on the instruction of the BO account holder
Facilitates transfer without having to handle money	Facilitates transfer of ownership without having to handle securities
Facilitates safekeeping of money	Facilitates safekeeping of securities

5. Who is a Depository Participant?

A Depository Participant (DP) is an agent of the depository through which it interfaces with the investor and provides depository services. Public financial institutions, scheduled commercial banks, foreign banks operating in India with the approval of the Reserve Bank of India, state financial corporations, custodians, stock-brokers, clearing corporations /clearing houses, NBFCs and Registrar to an Issue or Share Transfer Agent complying with the requirements prescribed by SEBI can be registered as DP. Banking services can be availed through a branch whereas depository services can be availed through a DP.

6. How many Depository Participants are registered with SEBI?

As on September 30, 2008, a total of 711 DPs (266 NSDL, 445 CDSL) are registered with SEBI.

7. Is it compulsory for every investor to open a beneficial owner (BO) account to trade in the capital market?

As per the available statistics at BSE and NSE, 99.9 percent transactions take place in dematerialised mode only. Therefore, in view of the convenience of trading in dematerialised mode, it is advisable to have a beneficial owner (BO) account for trading at the exchanges.

However to facilitate trading by small investors (Maximum 500 shares, irrespective of their value) in physical mode the stock exchanges provide an additional trading window, which gives one time facility for small investors to sell physical shares which are in compulsory demat list. The buyer of these shares has to demat such shares before further selling.

8. What are the benefits of availing depository services?

The benefits are enumerated below:

- A safe and convenient way to hold securities;
- Immediate transfer of securities;
- No stamp duty on transfer of securities;
- Elimination of risks associated with physical certificates such as bad delivery, fake securities, delays, thefts etc.
- Reduction in paperwork involved in transfer of securities;
- Reduction in transaction cost;
- No odd lot problem, even one share can be traded;
- Nomination facility;
- Change in address recorded with DP gets registered with all companies in which investor holds securities electronically eliminating the need to correspond with each of them separately;
- Transmission of securities is done by DP eliminating correspondence with companies;
- Automatic credit into demat account of shares, arising out of bonus/split/consolidation/merger etc.;
- Holding investments in equity and debt instruments in a single account.

Account Opening

9. How can services of a depository be availed?

To avail the services of a depository an investor is required to open a Beneficial Owner (BO) account with a Depository Participant (DP) of any depository.

10. How can one open an account?

First an investor has to approach a DP and fill up an account opening form. The account opening form must be supported by copies of any one of the approved documents which serve as proof of identity (POI) and proof of address (POA) as specified by SEBI. Apart from these PAN card has to be shown in original at the time of account opening from April 01, 2006.

All applicants should carry original documents for verification by an authorized official of the DP, under his signature.

Investor has to sign an agreement with DP in a depository prescribed standard format, which gives details of rights and duties of investor and DP. DP should provide the investor with a copy of the agreement and schedule of charges for their future reference. The DP will open the account in the system and give a unique account number, which is also called BO ID (Beneficial Owner Identification number) and used for all future transactions.

11. What are all charges an investor has to pay for opening and maintenance of a BO account?

SEBI has rationalised the cost structure for dematerialisation by removing account opening charges, transaction charges (for credit or *buy transactions* of securities), custody charges and account closing charges. Custody charges are now paid by the issuer companies. Broadly, investors are required to pay the charges towards:

- Dematerialisation and Rematerialisation of their securities
- Annual account maintenance charges

- Transactions fees (only for sell transactions)

The DP may revise the charges by giving 30 days notice in advance.

Further, SEBI has also advised the DPs to submit to their Depository their tariff/charge structure every year latest by 30th April and changes made therein, along with the date of effect to enable the investors to have a comparative analysis of the tariff/charge structure of various DP's. The information received by the depositories is put up on their websites.

12. Why should an investor give his bank account details at the time of BO account opening?

Bank account details are necessary for the protection of interest of investors. When any cash or non cash corporate benefits such as rights or bonus or dividend is announced for a particular scrip, depositories provide to the concerned issuer /it's RTA, the details of the investors, their electronic holdings as on record/book closure date for reckoning the entitlement of corporate benefit.

The disbursement of cash benefits such as dividend is credited directly by the Issuer/it's RTA to the beneficiary owner through the ECS (Electronic Clearing Service wherever available) facility or by issuing warrants on which bank account details are printed for places where ECS facility is not available. The bank account number is mentioned on the dividend and warrant to avoid any fraudulent misuse. The bank account details will be those which are mentioned in account opening form or modified details that had been intimated subsequently by the investor to the DP.

13. Can an investor change the details of his bank account?

Yes. However, the investor must inform the DP regarding change in the bank account and corresponding change in MICR/IFSC code while updating their bank account details with DP. In the depository system monetary benefits on the security balances are paid as per the bank account details provided by the investor at the time of account opening. The investor must ensure that any subsequent changes in bank account details are informed to the DP.

14. What should be done if the address of the investor changes?

Investor should immediately inform his DP along with necessary documents, who in turn will update the records. This will obviate the need of informing different companies.

15. What would be the charges for account closure and securities transfer due to account closing?

SEBI has advised that from January 09, 2006, no charges shall be levied by a depository on DP and consequently, by a DP on a BO, when a BO transfers all the securities lying in his account to another branch of the same DP or to another DP of the same depository or another depository, provided the BO Account/s at transferee DP and at transferor DP are identical in all respects. In case the BO Account at transferor DP is a joint account, the BO account at transferee DP should also be a joint account in the same sequence of ownership.

All other transfer of securities consequent to closure of account, not fulfilling the above-stated criteria, would be treated like any other transaction and charged as per the schedule of charges agreed upon between the BO and the DP.

16. Can multiple accounts be opened?

Yes. An investor can open more than one account in the same name with the same DP and also with different DPs. For all the accounts, investor has to strictly comply with KYC norms including Proof of Identity, Proof of Address requirements as stipulated by SEBI and also provide PAN number. The investor has to show the original PAN card at the time of opening of demat account.

17. Does the investor have to keep any minimum balance of securities in his account?

No.

18. Is it necessary to have account with the same DP as broker has?

No. Depository/DP can be chosen by investor as per convenience irrespective of the DP of the broker.

19. Can an investor open a single account for securities owned in different ownership patterns such as securities owned individually and securities owned jointly with others?

No. The Demat account must be opened in the same ownership pattern in which the securities are held in the physical form. e. g. if one share certificate is in the individual name and another certificate is jointly with somebody, two different accounts would have to be opened.

20. What is required to be done if one has physical certificates with the same combination of names, but the sequence of names is different i.e. some certificates with 'A' as first holder and 'B' as second holder and other set of certificates with 'B' as first holder and 'A' as the second holder?

In this case the investor may open only one account with 'A' & 'B' as the account holders and lodge the security certificates with different order of names for dematerialisation in the same account. An additional form called "Transposition cum Demat" form will have to be filled in. This would help you to effect change in the order of names as well as dematerialise the securities.

21. Can an investor operate a joint account on "either or survivor" basis just like a bank account?

No. The demat account cannot be operated on "either or

survivor" basis like the bank account.

22. Can someone else operate the account on behalf of the BO on the basis of a power of attorney?

Yes. If the BO authorises any person to operate the account by executing a power of attorney and submit it to the DP, that person can operate the account on behalf of the BO.

23. Can addition or deletion of names of accountholders is permitted after opening the account?

No. The names of the account holders of a BO account cannot be changed. If any change has to be effected by addition or deletion, a new account has to be opened in the desired holding pattern (names) and then transfer the securities to the newly opened account. The old account may be closed.

24. Can an investor close his demat account with one DP and transfer all securities to another account with another DP?

Yes. The investor can submit account closure request to his DP in the prescribed form. The DP will transfer all the securities lying in the account, as per the instruction, and close the demat account.

25. What if there are any discrepancies in the statement of holdings?

In case of any discrepancy in the statement of holdings, investor can contact his DP and in case of discrepancies in corporate benefits, one can approach the company/its Registrar and Transfer Agent. If the discrepancy is not resolved, the investor may approach concerned Depository (NSDL or CDSL).

26. Whether investor can freeze his account(s)?

Investor can freeze his account and/or ISIN and/or specific number of securities under an ISIN for any given period of time as per applicable Regulations of SEBI and Bye Laws of the respective depository.

Dematerialisation

27. What is dematerialisation?

Dematerialisation is the process by which physical certificates of an investor are converted to an equivalent number of securities in electronic form and credited into the BO's account with his DP.

28. How can one convert physical holding into electronic holding i.e. how can one dematerialise securities?

In order to dematerialise physical securities one has to fill in a DRF (Demat Request Form) which is available with the DP and submit the same along with physical certificates that are to be dematerialised. Separate DRF has to be filled for each ISIN. The complete process of dematerialisation is outlined below:

- Surrender certificates for dematerialisation to your DP.
- DP intimates to the Depository regarding the request through the system.
- DP submits the certificates to the registrar of the Issuer Company.
- Registrar confirms the dematerialisation request from depository.
- After dematerialising the certificates, Registrar updates accounts and informs depository regarding completion of dematerialisation.
- Depository updates its accounts and informs the DP.
- DP updates the demat account of the investor.

29. What is an ISIN?

ISIN (International Securities Identification Number) is a unique 12 digit alpha-numeric identification number allotted for a security (e.g. INE383C01018). Equity-fully paid up, equity-partly paid up, equity with differential voting /dividend rights issued by the same issuer will have different ISINs.

30. Can odd lot shares be dematerialised?

Yes, odd lot share certificates can also be dematerialised.

31. Do dematerialised shares have distinctive numbers?

Dematerialised shares do not have any distinctive numbers. These shares are fungible, which means that all the holdings of a particular security will be identical and interchangeable.

32. Can electronic holdings be converted back into physical certificates?

Yes. The process is called rematerialisation. If one wishes to get back his securities in the physical form he has to fill in the RRF (Remat Request Form) and request his DP for rematerialisation of the balances in his securities account. The process of rematerialisation is outlined below:

- Make a request for rematerialisation.
- Depository participant intimates depository regarding the request through the system.
- Depository confirms rematerialisation request to the registrar.
- Registrar updates accounts and prints certificates.
- Depository updates accounts and downloads details to depository participant.
- Registrar dispatches certificates to investor.

Trading/Settlement

33. What is the procedure for selling dematerialised securities?

The procedure for buying and selling dematerialised securities is similar to the procedure for buying and selling physical securities. The difference lies in the process of delivery (in case of sale) and receipt (in case of purchase) of securities.

In case of purchase:

- The broker will receive the securities in his account on the payout day.
- The broker will give instruction to its DP to debit his account and credit BO's account.
- BO will give 'Receipt Instruction' to DP for receiving credit by filling appropriate form. However BO can give standing instruction for credit to his account that will obviate the need of giving Receipt Instruction every time.

In case of sale:

BO will give delivery instruction through Delivery Instruction Slip (DIS) to DP to debit his account and credit the broker's account. Such instruction should reach the DP's office at least 24 hours before the pay-in, failing which, DP will accept the instruction only at the BO's risk.

34. What 'Standing Instruction' is given in the account opening form?

In a bank account, credit to the account is given only when a 'pay in' slip is submitted together with cash/cheque. Similarly, in a depository account 'Receipt in' form has to be submitted to receive securities in the account. However, for the convenience of BOs, facility of 'standing instruction' is given. If you say 'Yes' for standing instruction, you need not submit 'Receipt in' slip every time you buy securities. If you are particular that securities can be credited to your account only with your consent, then do not say 'yes' [or tick] to standing instruction in the application form.

35. What is delivery instruction slip (DIS)? What precautions do one need to observe with respect to Delivery Instruction Slips?

To give the delivery one has to fill a form called Delivery Instruction Slip (DIS). DIS may be compared to cheque book of a bank account. The following precautions are to be taken in respect of DIS:

- Ensure and insist with DP to issue DIS book.

- Ensure that DIS numbers are pre-printed and DP takes acknowledgment for the DIS booklet issued to investor.
- Ensure that your account number [client id] is pre-stamped.
- If the account is a joint account, all the joint holders have to sign the instruction slips. Instruction cannot be executed if all joint holders have not signed.
- Avoid using loose slips.
- Do not leave signed blank DIS with anyone viz., broker/sub-broker, DPs or any other person/entity.
- Keep the DIS book under lock and key when not in use.
- If only one entry is made in the DIS book, strike out remaining space to prevent misuse by any one.
- BO should personally fill in target account-id and all details in the DIS.
- If the DIS booklet is lost/stolen/not traceable, the same must be intimated to the DP immediately in writing. On receipt of such intimation, the DP will cancel the unused DIS of the said booklet.

36. Is it possible to give delivery instructions to the DP over Internet and if yes, how?

Yes. Both NSDL and CDSL have launched this facility for delivering instructions to your DP over Internet, called SPEED-e and EASI respectively. The facility can be used by all registered BOs after paying the applicable charges.

37. Is it possible to get securities allotted in public offering directly in the electronic form?

Yes, it is possible to get securities allotted to in Public Offerings directly in the electronic form. In the public issue application form, there is a provision to indicate the manner in which an investor wants the securities to be allotted. He has to mention the BO ID, name and DP ID on the application form. Any allotment made will be credited into the BO account.

Pledging

38. Can one pledge the dematerialised securities?

Yes. Pledging dematerialised securities is easier and more advantageous as compared to pledging physical securities.

39. What should one do to pledge electronic securities?

The procedure to pledge electronic securities is as follows:

- Both BOs, investor (pledgor) and the lender (pledgee) must have BO account with the same depository;
- Pledgor will have to instruct DP to create pledge in prescribed standard form (Pledge Request Form) with the details of the securities;
- The lender (pledgee) has to confirm the request through his/her DP;
- Once this is done, securities are pledged.
- All financial transactions between the pledgor and the pledgee are handled as per usual practice outside the depository system.

40. What is the procedure for closure of pledge after repayment of loan?

After the repayment of loan, pledgor can request for a closure of pledge by instructing the DP in a prescribed format. The pledgee on receiving the repayment will instruct his DP accordingly for the closure of the pledge.

41. Can pledgor (investor) change the securities offered in a pledge?

Yes, if the pledge (lender) agrees, pledgor (investor) may change the securities offered in a pledge.

42. Who will receive the corporate benefits on the pledged securities?

The securities pledged are only blocked in the account of pledgor (investor) in favour of the pledge (lender). The pledgor would continue to receive all the corporate benefits.

Transaction Statement

43. How does one know that the DP has updated the account after each transaction?

The DP provides a Transaction Statement periodically, which gives details of current balances and various transactions made through the depository account. If desired, DP may provide the Transaction Statement at intervals shorter than the stipulated ones, probably at a cost.

Depositories also provide SMS Alert facility for demat account holders whereby investors can receive alerts for debits (transfers) to their demat accounts and for credits in respect of corporate actions for IPO and offer for sale. Under this facility, investors can receive alerts, a day after such debits (transfers)/credits take place. These alerts are sent to those account holders who have provided their mobile numbers to their Depository Participants (DPs).

44. At what frequency will the investor receive his Transaction Statement from his DP?

DPs have to provide transaction statements to their clients once in a month, if there is any transaction and if there is no transaction, then once in a quarter.

DPs also provide transaction statement in electronic form under digital signature subject to their entering into a legally enforceable arrangement with the BOs to this effect.

45. What is to be done if there are any discrepancies in transaction statement?

In case of any discrepancy in the transaction statement, BO can contact his DP. If the discrepancy cannot be resolved at the DP level, BO should approach the Depository.

46. Whom should BO contact in case of any investor complaint/problem/query?

In case of any investor complaint/problem/query one may first contact his DP. If DP is unable to solve the complaint/problem/query one should approach concerned depository. If one is not satisfied one may approach SEBI. One may also approach SEBI directly.

Nomination

47. Who can nominate?

Nomination can be made only by individuals holding beneficial accounts either singly or jointly. Non-individuals including society, trust, body corporate, karta of Hindu Undivided Family, holder of power of attorney cannot nominate.

48. Who can be a nominee?

Only an individual can be a nominee. A nominee shall not be a society, trust, body corporate, partnership firm, Karta of Hindu Undivided Family or a power of attorney holder.

49. Why is it important to nominate?

Nomination is helpful in smooth transmission of shares upon the death of the BO/s. The nomination once made can be changed at a later date as desired by the BO/s.

Transmission of dematerialised securities

50. What is transmission of dematerialised securities?

Transmission is the process by which securities of a deceased account holder are transferred to the account of his legal heirs/nominee.

Process of transmission in case of dematerialised holdings is more convenient as the transmission formalities for all securities held in a demat account can be completed by submitting documents to the DP, whereas in case of physical securities the legal heirs/nominee/surviving joint holder has to independently correspond with each company in which securities are held.

51. In the event of death of the sole holder, how the successors should claim the securities lying in the demat account?

The claimant should submit to the concerned DP an application Transmission Request Form (TRF) along with the following supporting documents

1. In case of death of sole holder; where the sole holder has appointed a nominee

- Notarised copy of the death certificate

2. In case of death of the sole holder; where the sole holder has not appointed a nominee

- Notarised copy of the death certificate and anyone of the below mentioned documents
- Succession certificate
- Copy of probated will
- Letter of Administration

The DP, after ensuring that the application is genuine, will transfer securities to the account of the claimant.

The major advantage in case of dematerialised holdings is that the transmission formalities for all securities held with a DP can be completed by interaction with the DP alone, unlike in the case of physical share certificates, where the claimant will have to interact with each Issuing company or its Registrar separately.

Inter Depository Transfers

52. If a BO holds an account with NSDL/CDSL, can he receive securities from an account in CDSL/NSDL?

Yes. Inter depository transfers are possible without any additional costs.

Appendix 2

Frequently Asked Questions on Equity and Currency Derivatives

---

1. What are Derivatives?

The term "Derivative" indicates that it has no independent value, i.e. its value is entirely "derived" from the value of the underlying asset. The underlying asset can be securities, commodities, bullion, currency, live stock or anything else. In other words, Derivative means a forward, future, option or any other hybrid contract of pre determined fixed duration, linked for the purpose of contract fulfilment to the value of a specified real or financial asset or to an index of securities.

With Securities Laws (Second Amendment) Act, 1999, Derivatives has been included in the definition of Securities. The term Derivative has been defined in Securities Contracts (Regulations) Act, as:

"A Derivative includes: (a) a security derived from a debt instrument, share, loan, whether secured or unsecured, risk instrument or contract for differences or any other form of security; (b) a contract which derives its value from the prices, or index of prices, of underlying securities".

2. What is a Futures Contract?

Futures Contract means a legally binding agreement to buy or sell the underlying security on a future date. Future contracts are the organized/standardized contracts in terms of quantity, quality (in case of commodities), delivery time and place for settlement on any date in future. The contract expires on a pre-specified date which is called the expiry date of the contract. On expiry, futures can be settled by delivery of the underlying asset or cash. Cash settlement enables the settlement of obligations arising out of the future/option contract in cash.

3. What is an Option contract?

Options Contract is a type of Derivatives Contract which gives the buyer/holder of the contract the right (but not the obligation) to buy/sell the underlying asset at a predetermined price within or at end of a specified period. The buyer/holder of the option purchases the right from the seller/writer for a consideration which is called the premium. The seller/writer of an option is obligated to settle the option as per the terms of the contract when the buyer/holder exercises his right. The underlying asset could include securities, an index of prices of securities etc.

Under Securities Contracts (Regulations) Act, 1956 options on securities has been defined as "option in securities" meaning a contract for the purchase or sale of a right to buy or sell, or a right to buy and sell, securities in future, and includes a teji, a mandi, a teji mandi, a galli, a put, a call or a put and call in securities.

An Option to buy is called Call option and option to sell is called Put option. Further, if an option that is exercisable on or before the expiry date is called American option and one that is exercisable only on expiry date, is called European option. The price at which the option is to be exercised is called Strike price or Exercise price.

Therefore, in the case of American options the buyer has the right to exercise the option at anytime on or before the expiry date. This request for exercise is submitted to the Exchange, which randomly assigns the exercise request to the sellers of the options, who are obligated to settle the terms of the contract within a specified time frame.

As in the case of futures contracts, option contracts can be also be settled by delivery of the underlying asset or cash. However, unlike futures cash settlement in option contract entails paying/receiving the difference between the strike price/exercise price and the price of the underlying asset either at the time of expiry of the contract or at the time of exercise/assignment of the option contract.

4. What are Index Futures and Index Option Contracts?

Futures contract based on an index i.e. the underlying asset is the index, are known as Index Futures Contracts. For example, futures contract on NIFTY Index and BSE-30 Index. These contracts derive their value from the value of the underlying index.

Similarly, the options contracts, which are based on some index, are known as Index options contract. However, unlike Index Futures, the buyer of Index Option Contracts has only the right but not the obligation to buy/sell the underlying index on expiry. Index Option Contracts are generally European Style options i.e. they can be exercised/assigned only on the expiry date.

An index in turn derives its value from the prices of securities that constitute the index and is created to represent the sentiments of the market as a whole or of a particular sector of the economy. Indices that represent the whole market are broad based indices and those that represent a particular sector are sectoral indices.

In the beginning futures and options were permitted only on S&P Nifty and BSE Sensex. Subsequently, sectoral indices were also permitted for derivatives trading subject to fulfilling the eligibility criteria. Derivative contracts may be permitted on an index if 80 percent of the index constituents are individually eligible for derivatives trading. However, no single ineligible stock in the index shall have a weightage of more than 5 percent in the index. The index is required to fulfil the eligibility criteria even after derivatives trading on the index has begun. If the index does not fulfil the criteria for 3 consecutive months, then derivative contracts on such index would be discontinued.

By its very nature, index cannot be delivered on maturity of the Index futures or Index option contracts therefore, these contracts are essentially cash settled on Expiry.

5. Why mini derivative contract?

The minimum contract size for the mini derivative contract on Index (Sensex and Nifty) is Rs. 1 lakh at the time of its introduction in the market. The lower minimum contract size means that smaller investors are able to hedge their portfolio using these contracts with a lower capital outlay. This means a better hedge for portfolio, and also results in more liquidity in the market.

6. Why longer dated index options?

Longer dated derivatives products are useful for those investors who want to have a long term hedge or long term exposure in derivative market. The premiums for longer term derivatives products are higher than for standard options in the same stock because the increased expiration date gives the underlying asset more time to make a substantial move and for the investor to make a healthy profit. Presently, longer dated options on Sensex and Nifty with tenure of up to 3 years are available for the investors.

7. What is Bond Index?

A bond index is used to measure the performance of bond markets. The index is used as a benchmark against which investment managers measure their performance. It is also used as a measure to compare the performance of different asset classes. The government bond market is the most liquid segment of the bond market.

8. What is Volatility Index?

Volatility Index is a measure of expected stock market volatility, over a specified time period, conveyed by the prices of stock/index options. It depicts the collective sentiment of the market on the implied future volatility.

9. What is the structure of Derivative Markets in India?

Derivative trading in India takes can place either on a separate and independent Derivative Exchange or on a separate segment of an existing Stock Exchange. Derivative Exchange/Segment function as a Self-Regulatory Organisation (SRO) and SEBI acts as the oversight regulator. The clearing & settlement of all trades on the Derivative Exchange/Segment would have to be through a Clearing Corporation/House, which is independent in governance and membership from the Derivative Exchange/Segment.

10. What are the various membership categories in the equity derivatives market?

The various types of membership in the derivatives market are as follows:

- Trading Member (TM): A TM is a member of the derivatives exchange and can trade on his own behalf and on behalf of his clients.
- Clearing Member (CM): These members are permitted to settle their own trades as well as the trades of the other non-clearing members known as Trading Members who have agreed to settle the trades through them.
- Self-clearing Member (SCM): A SCM are those clearing members who can clear and settle their own trades only.

11. What are the requirements to be a member of the equity derivatives exchange/clearing corporation?

- Balance Sheet Net worth Requirements: SEBI has prescribed a net worth requirement of Rs. 3 crore for clearing members. The clearing members are required to furnish an auditor's certificate for the net worth every 6 months to the exchange. The net worth requirement is Rs. 1 crore for a self-clearing member. SEBI has not specified any net worth requirement for a trading member.
- Liquid Net worth Requirements: Every clearing member (both clearing members and self-clearing members) has to

maintain at least Rs. 50 lakh as Liquid Net worth with the exchange/clearing corporation.

- Certification requirements: The Members are required to pass the certification programme approved by SEBI. Further, every trading member is required to appoint at least two approved users who have passed the certification programme. Only the approved users are permitted to operate the derivatives trading terminal.

12. What are requirements for a Member with regard to the conduct of his business?

The derivatives member is required to adhere to the code of conduct specified under the SEBI Broker Sub-Broker regulations. The following conditions stipulations have been laid by SEBI on the regulation of sales practices:

- **Sales Personnel:** The derivatives exchange recognizes the persons recommended by the Trading Member and only such persons are authorized to act as sales personnel of the TM. These persons who represent the TM are known as Authorised Persons.
- **Know-your-client:** The member is required to get the Know-your-client form filled by every one of client.
- **Risk disclosure document:** The derivatives member must educate his client on the risks of derivatives by providing a copy of the Risk disclosure document to the client.
- **Member-client agreement:** The Member is also required to enter into the Member-client agreement with all his clients.

13. Which derivative contracts are permitted by SEBI?

Derivative products have been introduced in a phased manner starting with Index Futures Contracts in June 2000. Index Options and Stock Options were introduced in June 2001 and July 2001 followed by Stock Futures in November 2001. Sectoral indices were permitted for derivatives trading in December 2002. During December 2007 SEBI permitted mini derivative (F&O) contract on Index (Sensex and Nifty). Further, in January 2008, longer tenure Index options contracts and Volatility Index and in April 2008, Bond Index was introduced. In addition to the above, during August 2008, SEBI permitted Exchange traded Currency Derivatives.

14. What is the eligibility criterion for stocks on which derivatives trading may be permitted?

A stock on which stock option and single stock future contracts are proposed to be introduced is required to fulfil the following broad eligibility criteria:-

- The stock shall be chosen from amongst the top 500 stock in terms of average daily market capitalisation and average daily traded value in the previous six month on a rolling basis.
- The stock's median quarter-sigma order size over the last six months shall be not less than Rs.1 Lakh. A stock's quarter-sigma order size is the mean order size (in value terms) required to cause a change in the stock price equal to one-quarter of a standard deviation.
- The market wide position limit in the stock shall not be less than Rs.50 crore.

A stock can be included for derivatives trading as soon as it becomes eligible. However, if the stock does not fulfil the eligibility criteria for 3 consecutive months after being admitted to derivatives trading, then derivative contracts on such a stock would be discontinued.

15. What is the lot size of contract in the equity derivatives market?

Lot size refers to number of underlying securities in one contract. The lot size is determined keeping in mind the minimum contract size requirement at the time of introduction of derivative contracts on a particular underlying.

For example, if shares of XYZ Ltd are quoted at Rs. 1000 each and the minimum contract size is Rs. 2 lakh, then the lot size for that particular scrips stands to be 200000/1000 = 200 shares i.e. one contract in XYZ Ltd. covers 200 shares.

16. What is corporate adjustment?

The basis for any adjustment for corporate action is such that the value of the position of the market participant on cum and ex-date for corporate action continues to remain the same as far as possible. This will facilitate in retaining the relative status of positions viz. in-the-money, at-the-money and out-of-the-money. Any adjustment for corporate actions is carried out on the last day on which a security is traded on a cum basis in the underlying cash market. Adjustments mean modifications to positions and/or contract specifications as listed below:

- Strike price
- Position
- Market/Lot/ Multiplier

The adjustments are carried out on any or all of the above based on the nature of the corporate action. The adjustments for corporate action are carried out on all open, exercised as well as assigned positions.

The corporate actions are broadly classified under stock benefits and cash benefits. The various stock benefits declared by the issuer of capital are:

- Bonus
- Rights
- Merger/demerger
- Amalgamation
- Splits
- Consolidations
- Hive-off
- Warrants, and
- Secured Premium Notes (SPNs) among others

17. What is the margining system in the equity derivatives market?

Two type of margins have been specified -

- **Initial Margin:** Based on 99 percent VaR and worst case loss over a specified horizon, which depends on the time in which Mark to Market margin is collected.
- **Mark to Market Margin (MTM):** Collected in cash for all Futures contracts and adjusted against the available Liquid Net worth for option positions. In the case of Futures Contracts MTM may be considered as Mark to Market Settlement.

18. What are the exposure limits in equity derivatives market?

It has been prescribed that the notional value of gross open positions at any point in time in the case of Index Futures and all Short Index Option Contracts shall not exceed 33 1/3 (thirty three one by three) times the available liquid net worth of a member, and in the case of Stock Option and Stock Futures Contracts, the exposure limit shall be higher of 5 percent or 1.5 sigma of the notional value of gross open position.

19. What are the position limits in equity derivatives market?

The position limits specified are as under-

Client/Customer level position limits:

For index based products there is a disclosure requirement for clients whose position exceeds 15 percent of the open interest of the market in index products.

For stock specific products the gross open position across all derivative contracts on a particular underlying of a customer/client should not exceed the higher of –

- 1 percent of the free float market capitalisation (in terms of number of shares) or,
- 5 percent of the open interest in the derivative contracts on a particular underlying stock (in terms of number of contracts).

This position limits are applicable on the combine position in all derivative contracts on an underlying stock at an exchange. The exchanges are required to achieve client level position monitoring in stages.

Trading Member Level Position Limits:

For Index options the Trading Member position limits are Rs. 250 crore or 15 percent of the total open interest in Index Options whichever is higher and for Index futures the Trading Member position limits are Rs. 250 crore or 15 percent of the total open interest in Index Futures whichever is higher.

For stocks specific products, the trading member position limit is 20 percent of the market wide limit subject to a ceiling of Rs. 50 crore.

20. What are the requirements for a FII and its sub-account to invest in equity derivatives market?

A SEBI registered FIIs and its sub-account are required to pay initial margins, exposure margins and mark to market settlements in the derivatives market as required by any other investor. Further, the FII and its sub-account are also subject to position limits for trading in derivative contracts.

21. What are the requirements for a NRI to invest in equity derivatives market?

NRIs are permitted in invest in exchange traded derivative contracts subject to the margin and other requirements which are in place for other investors.

22. What are Currency Futures?

Currency futures are contracts to buy or sell a specific underlying currency at a specific time in the future, for a specific price. Currency futures are exchange-traded contracts and they are standardized in terms of delivery date, amount and contract terms.

Currency future contracts allow investors to hedge against foreign exchange risk. Since these contracts are marked-to-market daily, investors can--by closing out their position--exit from their obligation to buy or sell the currency prior to the contract's delivery date.

23. What are the eligibility criteria for members of the currency futures segment?

The trading member is subject to a balance sheet net worth requirement of Rs. 1 crore while the clearing member is subject to a balance sheet net worth requirement of Rs. 10 crores. The clearing member is subject to a liquid net worth requirement of Rs. 50 lakh.

24. What are the eligibility criteria for setting up of currency futures segment in a recognized stock exchange?

A recognized stock exchange having nationwide terminals or a new exchange recognized by SEBI may set up currency futures segment after obtaining SEBI's approval. The currency futures segment should fulfil the following eligibility conditions for approval:

- The trading should take place through an online screen-based trading system, which also has a disaster recovery site.
- The clearing of the currency derivatives market should be done by an independent Clearing Corporation, which satisfies the eligibility for a clearing corporation.
- The exchange must have an online surveillance capability which monitors positions, prices and volumes in real time so as to deter market manipulation.
- The exchange shall have a balance sheet net worth of at least Rs. 100 crore.
- Information about trades, quantities, and quotes should be disseminated by the exchange in real time to at least two information vending networks which are accessible to investors in the country.
- The per-half-hour capacity of the computers and the network should be at least 4 to 5 times of the anticipated peak load in any half hour, or of the actual peak load seen in any half-hour during the preceding six months,

whichever is higher. This shall be reviewed from time to time on the basis of experience.

- The segment should have at least 50 members to start currency derivatives trading.
- The exchange should have arbitration and investor grievances redressal mechanism operative from all the four areas/regions of the country.
- The exchange should have adequate inspection capability.
- If already existing, the exchange should have a satisfactory record of monitoring its members, handling investor complaints and preventing irregularities in trading.

25. What measures have been specified by SEBI to protect the rights of investor in Derivatives Market?

The measures specified by SEBI include:

- Investor's money has to be kept separate at all levels and is permitted to be used only against the liability of the Investor and is not available to the trading member or clearing member or even any other investor.
- The Trading Member is required to provide every investor with a risk disclosure document which will disclose the risks associated with the derivatives trading so that investors can take a conscious decision to trade in derivatives.
- Investor would get the contract note duly time stamped for receipt of the order and execution of the order. The order will be executed with the identity of the client and without client ID order will not be accepted by the system. The investor could also demand the trade confirmation slip with his ID in support of the contract note. This will protect him from the risk of price favour, if any, extended by the Member.
- In the derivative markets all money paid by the Investor towards margins on all open positions is kept in trust with the Clearing House/Clearing corporation and in the event of default of the Trading or Clearing Member the amounts

paid by the client towards margins are segregated and not utilized towards the default of the member. However, in the event of a default of a member, losses suffered by the Investor, if any, on settled/closed out position are compensated from the Investor Protection Fund, as per the rules, bye-laws and regulations of the derivative segment of the exchanges.

- The Exchanges are required to set up arbitration and investor grievances redressal mechanism operative from all the four areas/regions of the country.

Appendix 3

Frequently Asked Questions on Straight-through Processing (STP)

1. What is STP?

Straight-through Processing (STP) is a mechanism that automates the end-to-end processing of transactions of the financial instruments. It involves use of a single system to process or control all elements of the work-flow of a financial transaction, including what is commonly known as the Front, Middle, and Back office, and General Ledger. In other words, STP can be defined as electronically capturing and processing transactions in one pass, from the point of first 'deal' to final settlement.

2. What is the advantage of using STP over the traditional method?

In the traditional method, each and every transaction involves costly multiple data re-entry from paper documents and other sources which are susceptible to errors, discrepancies, delays and possible fraud. Further, the traditional means and methods of capturing and processing of information such as phone, fax, email etc. requires human intervention which slows the entire cycle, introduces errors and delays settlement. Usage of STP enables orders to be processed, confirmed, cleared and settled in a shorter time period, more cost effectively and with fewer errors. Apart from compressing the clearing and settlement time, STP also provides a flexible, cost-effective infrastructure, which enables e-business expansion through real-time processing and access to enterprise data. STP also streamlines back-office activities, leading to fewer failures, lower risks and drastically reduces costs per transaction. It embraces a set of applications, business processes and standards, which are set to revolutionize the settlement and processing standards within the capital markets industry.

3. What is the status of STP usage in the international scenario?

Internationally, STP can be found in use at the organization level or at the most at the closed group level. However, none of the markets in the world have adopted STP at broader level i.e. STP across the market including participation across the majority of the market participants. As such, no standards for messaging or for interoperability although attempted have been implemented that could be used for adopting STP across the market. The organizations using STP in their own organizational functions are using different messaging standards. Moreover there is STP but only within clients who are networked with one Service Provider. The issue of inter-operability between STP Service Providers has not been resolved. However Internationally it has been accepted that whether it is viewed as an obligation or an opportunity, markets will have no choice but to adopt the system; they will have to spend money to stay in business.

4. What is the current settlement cycle in India?

There has been a move from account settlement period to rolling settlement system. The settlement cycle has been gradually brought down from 15 days to just 2 days thus putting the Indian capital market in the elite group of advanced markets of the world.

5. What are the benefits of adopting STP in India?

- Facilitates shortening of the settlement cycle.
- Increases transparency.
- Avoids costly duplication of work and manual intervention.
- Reduction in Risks and errors.

- Faster data capturing, processing and report generation.
- Increases the overall efficiencies.
- Makes the market cost effective.
- Better regulation by systematic audit trial.

6. What is the genesis of STP in India?

The need for STP or any other mean to achieve a quicker, safer, economical and automated system in the Indian capital market was actually felt with the shortening of the settlement cycle, increase in the number of products traded and number of players who participated it the market. Coupled with the technical advancements taking place, the various limitations arising out of the traditional system of trading and settlement, compelled the industry to revisit the viability and feasibility of the systems they had been adopting. Sensing the need of the market, SEBI set up the Committee on 19-February-2002, to assess the feasibility and suitability of introducing STP in Indian markets. The committee was formed to propose a scheme of STP and undertaking a cost-benefit analysis of implementing STP in India. The SEBI Committee for implementation of STP in Indian markets approached the matter under reference through the following steps:

- Identification of components of the current life-cycle of a trade that involves manual intervention.
- Identifying and establishing messaging standards for information communication.
- Identifying options for establishment of a communications backbone that will enable data transfer across participants in a secure and efficient manner.

The committee made a comparison of the various processes involved in the trade cycle (both domestic and international) and identified the following areas which were needed to be automated on a priority basis:

- Post Trade activities like contract note transfer from broker-dealer to sub-custodian and the mutual fund/FII.
- Pre-match advice to the broker-dealer.

- Domestic Mutual Funds' trade data flow to/from the sub-custodian.

In order to implement STP in Indian market, the committee set up by SEBI recommended the following:

- On-line Connectivity between the depositories to permit easier settlement.
- Recognition of electronic contract notes as a legal document as an alternative to paper based contract notes.
- Adoption of ISO 15022 standards for financial messaging with Digital Signature using PKI (Public Key Infrastructure).
- Encourage multiple STP Service Providers to set-up infrastructure to provide STP to bring in competition for higher efficiency and economy.
- Amendment to the legal framework (laws/regulations/bye-laws etc.) to provide for recognition of paperless form of data and records. The Committee identified and made a list of bye-laws/regulations etc. that needed to be changed in order to move to a paperless environment.
- There were certain issues relating to the payment system that needed to be addressed on a priority basis. However, these did not fall under the purview of SEBI and the matter had to be referred to RBI for action at their end. The Committee recommended a strong need to implement Real Time Gross Settlement system. The RBI has already indicated that the RTGS system would be in place by June 2003 (which has later been revised to mid 2004). This would help in creating better synergy between settlement of funds and securities at the same time and true Delivery v/s Payment system can be achieved. Meanwhile, in the interim period, Electronic Funds Transfer (EFT) facility of the RBI was also proposed to be increased in terms of its coverage and the value so that payments may be made faster.

The STP committee also set out the viability and the road map for STP including the following key dependencies/comments:

- The carrier must be able to deliver a consistent communications platform that meets the security criteria recommended, and offers connectivity to all participants.
- The carrier must be cost-efficient.
- While there is no constraint on the number of carriers, each carrier must, before launch, establish continuous connectivity with other carriers, so that a participant needs only to sign up to one carrier.

7. What are the circulars regarding STP issued by SEBI?

- 17-Mar-98: L C Gupta Committee on Derivatives.
- 30-Jul-98: Varma Committee Report on risk containment in the derivatives market.
- September-02: SEBI Advisory Committee on Derivatives Report on Development and Regulation of Derivative Markets in India.
- 5-Feb-03: Report of the K.R. Ramamoorthy Committee on Participation by Securities Brokers in Commodity Futures Markets.
- 5-Oct-04: Market Integrity Related Disclosures.

8. On what lines was STP mandated?

SEBI vide letter dated October 03, 2002[1] (Ref: FITTC/FII/19320/2002) mandated introduction of STP for electronic trade processing with a common messaging standard with effect from December 02, 2002 on the following lines:

- Adoption of ISO 15022 messaging standards by the market participants.
- Electronic delivery of Contract Notes.
- Connectivity among the market participants and implementation of STP.

9. When was STP first introduced in India?

STP was launched in India on a voluntary basis on November 30, 2002.

10. What were the issues due to which the system could not initially nourish?

- Lack of Inter-operability between all the STP Service Providers. (a) message Handshake Protocols, (b) lack of Common Authentication of Digital Signatures across the STP Service Providers, (c) lack of end to end compliance to ISO messaging formats from sender to the recipient and absence of standardisation of file formats for client's back office development, and (d) technological Issues.
- Absence of a common agreement among the STP Service Providers.
- Lack of Service Legal Agreement between the STP Service Providers to guarantee delivery of the entire message in a secure and confidential manner.
- High inter-connectivity charges to interconnect different STP Service Providers.
- Commercial considerations–bearing of the additional cost of developing and maintaining such interfaces.

11. How was the issue of inter-operability addressed?

To address the issue of inter-operability, a committee consisting of the 4 existing STP Service Providers was formed with NSDL as the convener. The Committee had various deliberations and raised issues of regulatory non-clarity of the issue of electronic contract notes, issues relating to payment of consolidated stamp duty, technological issues, absence of inter-operability between the STP Service Providers due to non-verification of the digital signature of one STP Service Provider (obtained from one Certifying Authority) by another STP Service Provider (who has obtained digital signature from another Certifying Authority), legal and operational issues subsequent to finalization of the operational issues.

NSDL on behalf of the Committee on July 4, 2003, forwarded a consolidated document highlighting the communication protocol & message structure standards/discussions which in their opinion would suit the inter-connectivity between the STP Service Providers through a centralized hub. However one of the STP Service Provider, Financial Technologies had their reservations in adapting the specified customized protocol to suit the inter-operability needs. They preferred adopting the readymade standard messaging platforms.

12. Why was ISP chosen over CUG by the STP Centralised Hub?

There were two options available for the STP centralised hub, one to set it up as a CUG or as an Internet Service Provider (ISP). It was informed that in the current scenario, registering the STP centralised hub as a CUG would necessitate a special permission to waive the inter-connection charges between the STP Service Providers and the STP centralised hub. According to them, the waiver of interconnection charges would take more time. Further, under the existing scenario, CUG networks do not have the flexibility to interconnect to other networks. Compared to this, ISP license has the required flexibility & the following advantages:

- The STP centralised hub set up as an ISP can be connected by an existing CUG network as a client.
- The centralized hub could also be connected through a leased line connection or through dial-up connections. However it had been opined that a leased line connection would be a more secure form of connection and the dial-up connectivity should be used as a back-up form of communication.
- Interconnection to other ISP or any other network including CUG network does not attract any interconnect charges based on the directive issued by TRAI. Only leased line charges based on bandwidth and distance shall be applicable. As such, connectivity of STP centralised hub with any other CUG networks can be achieved without any licensing issues. It has also been confirmed that the STP centralised hub as an ISP would have the

flexibility of connecting with any other CUG network like RBI's INFINET CUG network (to facilitate STP for funds).

- International connectivity is permitted.
- IP/VPN connection is permitted.
- Present ISP's license charges applicable are Rs. 1 per annum.
- No major roll-out obligations. Even one customer with an ISP is regarded as the same having gone live considering the requirement of roll-out within 18 months as per the license requirements.
- The STP centralised hub as an ISP could also be used for other allied services like a standard communication platform for various exchanges, depositories, and market participants and the STP centralised hub could be made scaleable to include STP among retail clients also.

13. What is the constitution of the STP Centralised Hub?

The STP centralised hub was registered as an Internet Service Provider (ISP) with TRAI. The next issue was the mechanism in which the STP centralised hub would be constituted and owned. After various deliberations, it was agreed that since the exchanges are the originators of trade and the trade gets finally settled with the Clearing Corporation/house associated with the exchange, the exchange and its Clearing Corporation is the focal point for all post trade, pre-settlement and post settlement activities. Hence it would be desirable for the exchanges to constitute the STP centralised hub to bring in the inherent synergies and efficiencies to make the whole framework economically viable. NSE and BSE had shown interest in setting up the STP centralised hub. However setting up two centralized hubs would not solve the issue of inter-operability and would complicate the issue further. BSE endorsed the proposal but desired that the centralized hub be set up as a joint venture between BSE and NSE. NSE also agreed with the proposition of setting up the centralized hub as a joint venture. However NSE recommended implementing the proposed plan in two phases. In Phase I NSE would setup the centralized hub by earmarking some of its existing infrastructure to implement STP for institutional trades where the number of trades is not very large. In Phase II BSE and NSE could jointly develop a project to set up an independent STP centralised hub with an independent system architecture and infrastructure. This plan was accepted by both the exchanges.

It was also confirmed that an ISP license taken up by NSE in Phase I could be later reconstituted to enable joint ownership by BSE and NSE in Phase II. Accordingly, NSE made an application for the ISP (for the STP centralised hub) with Department of Telecommunication (DoT) and has procured the necessary registration of the STP centralised hub as an ISP.

14. How was the issue of Electronic Contract Note operationalised by SEBI?

In order to operationalise the issue of an electronic contract note, SEBI had issued a circular no. SMDRP/POLICY/Cir-15/00 dated December 15, 2000 and a clarification vide letter dated SEBI/SMD/SE/15/2003/29/04 dated April 29, 2003 whereby SEBI had permitted the issue of electronic contract notes with digital signature obtained from a valid Certifying Authority provided under the Information Technology Act, 2000 (IT Act). The exchanges were directed to make the necessary amendments to the bye-laws, rules and regulations for the implementation of the same.

15. What was the format prescribed by SEBI in order to streamline the issuance of electronic contract notes as a legal document like the physical contract note?

In order to streamline the issuance of electronic contract notes as a legal document like the physical contract note, SEBI prescribed a format for the electronic contract note and advised the exchanges to implement the following vide SEBI circular no. DNPD/Cir-9/04 dated February 3, 2004:

- The exchanges would prescribe a standard format for the electronic contract note (based on the prescribed model format prescribed in Annexure A) in its bye-laws, rules and regulations.
- The exchange bye-laws, rules and regulations for issuance of electronic contract note were amended to include all the standard pre-printed terms and conditions in the physical contract note. The electronic contract note would mention the relevant bye-laws / rules / regulations of the exchange subject to which the said contract note is being issued.
- The exchanges were also advised to modify / amend other relevant bye-laws, rules and regulations with respect to signing of the electronic contract note with a digital signature so as to make the modified format of the electronic contract note a valid legal document like the physical contract note.
- The exchanges were asked to prescribe the mechanism of record keeping of electronic contract notes in a soft non-tamperable form in compliance with the provisions of the IT Act, 2000.

16. When did the mandatory use of STP come into existence?

SEBI decided vide circular no. DNPD/Cir- 22 /04 dated April 1, 2004 that all the institutional trades executed on the stock exchanges would be mandatorily processed through the STP System w. e. f. July 01, 2004.

17. What was the system flow of transactions in the STP framework as prescribed by SEBI?

In order bring in standardisation and objectivity, SEBI vide circular no. DNPD/Cir- 23/04 dated April 27, 2004 prescribed the following system flow of transactions in the STP framework:

- A STP user intending to send an instruction would send the message to his STP service provider after digitally signing the same.
- The STP service provider would verify the signature of the STP user and forward it to the: (i) recipient STP user, if the recipient STP user is availing services of the same STP service provider; or the (ii) STP centralised hub if the recipient STP user is not with the same STP service provider. In such a case the STP service provider would be required to prepare a message as per the STP centralised hub prescribed message format, enclose the user's message, digitally sign the message and then send it to the STP Centralised Hub.
- On receipt of the message by the STP centralised hub, the STP Centralised Hub would: (i) verify the signature of the sending STP service provider only, (ii) send an acknowledgment to the sending STP service provider.
- The STP centralised hub would forward the message to the recipient STP service provider after digitally signing on the message.
- The recipient STP service provider on receipt of the message from the STP centralised hub, shall verify the signature of the STP centralised hub, verify if the recipient STP user is associated with itself and send an appropriate acknowledgment with digital signature to the STP centralised hub. The STP centralised hub would in turn forward the acknowledgment (received from the recipient STP service provider) duly signed to the sending STP service provider.
- The recipient STP service provider shall forward the message to the recipient STP user. The recipient STP user would receive the message and verify the signature of the recipient STP service provider and sending STP user.
- To enable inter-operation, the STP centralised hub would provide a utility / client software to the STP service provider. The STP service provider's point of interface

with the STP centralised hub would be through this utility/ client software. The PKI (Public key infrastructure) system for the interface shall be implemented at a later stage.

18. What are the identification codes as prescribed by SEBI?

- **Brokers:** SEBI registration number (until MAPIN ID is available for every broker).
- **Mutual Funds and schemes of Mutual Funds:** SEBI registration number for Mutual Funds and Unique client code issued by the exchanges for schemes (until MAPIN ID is available for each scheme of a mutual fund).
- **FIIs and sub-accounts:** SEBI registration number for FII and Unique client code issued by the exchanges for sub-account (until MAPIN ID is available for each FII and their sub-accounts).
- **Custodians:** SEBI registration number (until MAPIN ID is available for every custodian).
- **STP service providers and STP centralised hub:** MAPIN ID.
- **Depositories and exchanges/clearing house/clearing corporation:** MAPIN ID.
- **Other Institutional Investors like financial institutions, banks etc.:** Unique client code issued by the exchanges (until MAPIN ID is available for each Institutional Investor).

19. Which are the four STP Service Providers currently recognized to execute STP in India?

- BSE
- NSE
- NSDL
- FTIL

Glossary of Capital Market Terms

Glossary of Capital Market Terms

A

Accounts Payable: A current liability showing the amounts due to others within a period of one year when such liability resulted from the purchase or manufacturing of inventory.

Accounts Receivable: Any money due to a business for merchandise or securities that it has sold or for services it has rendered. This is a key determinant in analyzing a company's liquidity.

Accreting: A description applicable to a range of instruments, e.g. caps, swaps, collars and swaptions, where the notional amount on which the instrument is based increases successively during its life.

Accrued Interest: The interest accruing on a security since the previous coupon date. If a security is sold between two payment dates, the buyer usually compensates the seller for the interest accrued, either within the price or as a separate payment.

Acid Test Ratio: The value of cash equivalents and accounts receivable (the quick assets) divided by current liabilities. Also known as quick asset ratio or liquidity ratio, it is a measurement of corporate liquidity.

Acquirer: Any individual/company/any other legal entity, which intends to acquire or acquires substantial quantity of shares or voting rights of target company or acquires or agrees to acquire control over the target company along with the persons acting in concert.

Active Portfolio Strategy: A strategy that uses available information and forecasting techniques to seek a better performance than a portfolio that is simply diversified broadly.

Ad hoc Margin: Margin collected by the Stock Exchange from the members having unduly large outstanding position or the margin levied on volatile scrips based on ad hoc basis keeping in view the risk perspective.

Adjustable Peg: Term for an exchange rate regime where a country's exchange rate is pegged (i.e. fixed) in relation to another currency (normally the dollar), but where the rate may be changed from time to time.

Adjusted Beta: The estimation of a security's future beta, which is derived from historical date, but is modified assuming that the security's real beta has tendency to move towards the market average of one.

Admission to Dealing: The process of granting permission to the securities of a company to be listed in a Stock Exchange and to provide trading facilities for the securities in the market.

Advance/Decline Line: A technical analysis tool representing the total of differences between advances and declines of security prices. The advance/decline line is considered the best indicator of market movement as a whole. Stock indices such as Dow-Jones Industrial Average only tell us the strength of 30 stocks where as the Advance/Decline line provides much more insight.

Adviser: A financial planner or financial intermediary who offers advice on personal financial matters. Advisers may be paid an upfront or an ongoing commission for the investments that they recommend.

Agency Orders: Orders that a broker dealer executes for the account of a customer with another professional or retail investor.

Allotment Advice: A letter sent to the successful applicant by the company stating allotment of shares or debentures or other securities against his application. The advice is not negotiable in the market.

Allotment Letter: Document of title issued to investors by companies stating allotment of shares/debentures /other securities to applicants subscribing for such securities or in pursuance of certain contracts entered into in that behalf. These letters are negotiable in the market.

Alpha: In a Jensen Index, a factor to represent the portfolio's performance that diverges from its beta, representing a measure of the manager's performance.

American Depository Receipts (ADR): A certificate issued in the United States in lieu of a foreign security. The original securities are lodged in Bank/Custodian abroad, and the American Depository Receipts (ADRs) are traded in the US for all intents and purposes as if they were a domestic stock. An ADR dividend is paid in US dollars, so it provides a way for American investors to buy foreign securities without having to go abroad, and without having to switch in and out of foreign currencies.

Analyst: A firm/company/an individual who is engaged either on his own behalf or on behalf of any other firm or organization that is regularly publishing securities recommendations based on research either through print media and/or electronic media.

Appreciation: A rise in the price of a security or in the value of one currency in terms of another.

Approved Intermediary: A person duly registered by the SEBI Board under the Securities Lending Scheme, 1997 through whom the lender of securities will deposit the securities and the borrower will borrow the securities.

Arbitrage: Technically, arbitrage consists of purchasing a commodity or security in one market for immediate sale in another market (deterministic arbitrage).

Arbitration: An alternative dispute resolution mechanism provided by a stock exchange for resolving disputes between the trading members and their clients in respect of trades done on the exchange.

Asset-backed Securities: Securities backed by assets that are not mortgage loans. Examples include assets backed by automobile loans, credit card receivables and others.

Asset Management Company: The company which handles the day to day operations and investment decisions of a unit trust.

Asymmetric Information: A situation where access to information by one party (or parties) to a transaction is better than access by another party (or parties). Asymmetric information can be used as a source of power in determining the outcome of the transaction.

Auditor: A person who is professionally qualified to examine and scrutinize accounts. He/she inspects records and reports on the profitability and financial position of the company.

Authorized Assistants: Assistants or clerks of members who are authorized by them to do business on their behalf in the market. The member has to take responsibility of fulfilling all the transactions and business commitments of the authorized assistants entered into on behalf of the members.

Authorized Capital: The amount of capital that a company has been authorized to raise by way of equity and preference shares, as mentioned in the Articles of Association/Memorandum of Association of the company.

Automatic Reinvestment: A fund service giving unit holders/ shareholders the option to purchase additional units/ shares using dividend and capital gain distributions.

Average Annual Growth Rate: The average increase in the value of a portfolio over the period of a year.

Averaging: The process of gradually buying more and more securities in a declining market (or selling in a rising market) in order to level out the purchase (or sale) price.

B

Badla: Carrying forward of transactions from one settlement period to another without effective delivery. This is permitted only in specified securities and is done at the making up price which is usually the closing price of the last day of settlement.

Badla Charge/Contango: Consideration or interest paid to the seller by the buyer for carrying over a transaction from one settlement period to another.

Bail out of Issue: When the public issue do not get good response from the public or fails to garner minimum subscription, the issuer or promoters approaches the financiers or some persons to arrange subscription to bail out the issue for consideration of buy-back shares subsequent from the financiers at higher price or compensating the financier by payment of interest on the amount of the subscription money paid in the public issue.

Balance Sheet: An accounting statement of a company's assets and liabilities, provided for the benefit of shareholders and regulators. It gives a snapshot, at a specific point of time, of the assets that the company holds and how the assets have been financed.

Balanced Fund: Funds which aim to provide both growth and regular income as such schemes invest both in equities and fixed income securities in the proportion indicated in their offer documents.

Bancassurance: The phenomenon whereby a financial institution combines the selling of banking products and insurance products through the same distribution channel. Popular in the early 1990s bancassurance rested on the premise that it is easy to cross-sell banking and insurance services because customers feel confident buying insurance from the same institution where they keep their savings.

Banker to an Issue: A scheduled bank carrying on all or any of the issue related activities namely acceptance of application and application monies; acceptance of allotment or call monies; refund of application monies; and payment of dividend or interest warrants.

Basis: In a futures market, basis is defined as the cash price (or spot price) of whatever is being traded minus its futures price for the contract in question. It is important because changes in the relationship between cash and futures prices affect the values of using futures as a hedge. A hedge, however, will always reduce risk as long as the volatility of the basis is less than the volatility of the price of whatever is being hedged.

Bear: A pessimist market operator who expects the market price of shares to decline. The term also refers to the one who has sold shares which he does not possess, in the hope of buying them back at a lower price, when the market price of the shares come down in the near future.

Bear Hug: A variety of takeover strategy that seeks to hurry target company managements to recommend acceptance of a tender offer in a short period of time.

Bear Market: A weak or falling market characterized by the dominance of sellers.

Bear Trap: A false signal indicating that the rising trend of a stock or index has reversed when in fact it has not. This can occur during a bear market reversal when short sellers believe the markets will sink back to its declining ways. If the market continues to rise, the shorters get trapped and are forced to cover their position at higher prices.

Bench Mark: Security used as the basis for interest rate calculations and for pricing other securities. Also denotes the most heavily traded and liquid security of a particular class.

Bid: An offer of a price to buy as in an auction. Business on the Stock Exchange is done through bids. Bid also refers to the price one is willing to pay for a security.

Bid Spread: The difference between the stated and /or displayed price at which a market maker is willing to sell a security and the price at which he is willing to buy it.

Bilateral Netting: An arrangement between two parties in which they exchange only the net difference in their obligations to each other. The primary purpose of netting is to reduce exposure to credit/settlement risk.

Blank Transfer: Where the name of the transferee is left blank on share transfer form, it constitutes a blank transfer. A person depositing shares with a stock broker for immediate or eventual sale has to sign a blank transfer form. It is also done when shares are mortgaged, so that in the event of non payment the mortgager can fill in his own name in the transferee column and sell the share.

Block Trading: Buying and selling a block of securities usually takes place when restructuring or liquidating a large portfolio.

Blue Chip: The best rated shares with the highest status as investment based on return, yield, safety, marketability and liquidity.

Bond: A negotiable certificate evidencing indebtedness - a debt security or IOU, issued by a company, municipality or government agency. A bond investor lends money to the issuer and, in exchange, the issuer promises to repay the loan amount on a specified maturity date. The issuer usually pays the bondholder periodic interest payments over the life of the loan.

Book Building Process: A process undertaken by which a demand for the securities proposed to be issued by a corporate body is elicited and built up and the price for such securities is assessed for the determination of the quantum of such securities to be issued by means of a notice, circular, advertisement, document or information memoranda or offer document

Book Closure: The periodic closure of the Register of Members and Transfer Books of the company, to take a record of the shareholders to determine their entitlement to dividends or to bonus or right shares or any other rights pertaining to shares.

Book Runner: A Lead Merchant Banker who has been

appointed by the issuer company for maintaining the book. The name of the Book Running Lead Manager will be mentioned in the offer document of the Issuer Company.

Book Value: The net amount shown in the books or in the accounts for any asset, liability or owners' equity item. In the case of a fixed asset, it is equal to the cost or revalued amount of the asset less accumulated depreciation. Also called carrying value. The book value of a firm is its total net assets, i.e. the excess of total assets over total liabilities.

Boom: A condition of the market denoting increased activity with rising prices and higher volume of business resulting from greater demand of securities. It is a state where enlarged business, both investment and speculative, has been taking place for a sufficiently reasonable period of time.

Break Even Point: The stock price (or price) at which a particular strategy of transaction neither makes nor loses money. In options, the result is at the expiration date in the strategy. A dynamic break-even point changes as time passes.

Broker: A member of a Stock Exchange who acts as an agent for clients and buys and sells shares on their behalf in the market. Though strictly a stock broker is an agent, yet for the performance of his part of the contract both in the market and with the client, he is deemed as a principal, a peculiar position of dual responsibility.

Brokerage: Commission payable to the stockbroker for arranging sale or purchase of securities. Scale of brokerage is officially fixed by the Stock Exchange. Brokerage scales fixed in India are the maximum chargeable commission.

Broker Dealer: Any person, other than a bank engaged in the business of buying or selling securities on its own behalf or for others.

Bubble: A speculative sharp rise in share prices which like the bubble is expected to suddenly burst.

Bull: A market player who believes prices will rise and would, therefore, purchase a financial instrument with a view to selling it at a higher price. Opposite of a bear.

Bull Market: A rising market with abundance of buyers and relatively few sellers.

Bulldog Bond: A bond denominated in sterling but issued by a non British borrower.

Buoyancy: A rising trend in prices.

Business Day: A day on which the Stock Exchange is open for business and trading in securities.

Butterfly Spread: An option strategy involving the simultaneous sale of an at the money straddle and purchase of an out of the money strangle. Potential gains will be seen if the underlying remains stable while the risk is limited should the underlying move dramatically. It's also the simultaneous buying and selling of call options at different exercise prices or at different expiry dates.

Buy Back: The repurchase by a company of its own stock or bonds.

C

Call Money: The unpaid instalment of the share capital of a company, which a shareholder is called upon to pay.

Call Option: An agreement that gives an investor the right, but not the obligation, to buy an instrument at a known price by a specified date. For this privilege, the investor pays a premium, usually a fraction of the price of the underlying security.

Capital Gain Distribution: Profits distributed to unit holders/shareholders resulting from the sale of securities held in the fund's portfolio for more than one year.

Cash Market: A market for sale of security against immediate delivery, as opposed to the futures market.

Certificate of Deposit: A negotiable certificate issued by a bank, usually for a period of one month to a year, as evidence of an interest bearing time deposit. This may also be offered at a discount.

Circuit Breaker: A system to curb excessive speculation in the stock market, applied by the Stock Exchange authorities, when the index spurts or plunges by more than a specified per cent. Trading is then suspended for some time to let the market cool down.

Circular Trading: A fraudulent trading scheme where sell or buy orders are entered by a person who knows that the same number of shares at the same time and for the same price either have been or will be entered. These trades do not represent a real change in the beneficial ownership of the security. These trades are entered with the intention of raising or depressing the prices of securities.

Clean Float: Where there is no official intervention – the price is permitted to vary in line with the market forces.

Clearing: Settlement or clearance of accounts, for a fixed period in a Stock Exchange.

Clearing House: A department of an exchange or a separate legal entity that provides a range of services related to the clearance and settlement of trades and the management of risks associated with the resulting contracts. A clearing house is often central counterparty to all trades, that is, the buyer to every seller and the seller to every buyer.

Clearing Member: A member of a clearing corporation or clearing house of the derivatives exchange or derivatives segment of an exchange, who may clear and settle transactions in securities.

Closing Price: The rate at which the last transaction in a security is struck before the close of the trading hours.

Commercial Paper: A short term promise to repay a fixed amount that is placed on the market either directly or through a specialized intermediary. It is usually issued by companies with a high credit standing in form of a promissory note redeemable at par to the holder on maturity and therefore does not require any guarantee.

Common Stock: Units of ownership of a public corporation. Holders of common stock typically have voting rights and receive dividends, but there is no guarantee of dividend payment.

Competitive Bid: An offer made by a person other than the acquirer who has made the first public announcement.

Composite Issues: An issue of securities by a listed company on a public-cum rights basis offered through a single offer document wherein the allotment for both public and rights component of the issue is proposed to be made simultaneously.

Compulsory Delisting: Permanent removal of securities of a listed company from a stock exchange as a penalizing measure at the behest of the stock exchange for not making submissions/complying with various requirements set out in the Listing agreement within the time frames prescribed.

Convergence: Narrowing of the difference between the futures contract and the value of the underlying asset during the final days of the contract.

Conversion Price: The price at which a convertible instrument is converted into shares of the company.

Conversion Ratio: The number of shares which may be acquired upon the conversion of a convertible instrument. The ratio is calculated as instrument's principal amount divided by conversion price.

Convertible Bond: A bond giving the investor the option to convert the bond into equity at a fixed conversion price or as per a pre-determined pricing formula.

Corporate Governance: The way in which companies run themselves, in particular the way in which they are accountable to those who have a vested interest in their performance, especially their shareholders.

Coupon: The interest paid on a bond expressed as a percentage of the face value. If a bond carries a fixed coupon, the interest is paid on an annual or semi-annual basis. The term also describes the detachable certificate entitling the bearer to payment of the interest.

Coupon Rate: The interest rate stated on the face of coupon.

Credit Rating: Credit ratings measure a borrower's creditworthiness and provide an international framework for comparing the credit quality of issuers and rated debt securities. Rating agencies allocate three kinds of ratings: issuer credit ratings, long-term debt, and short-term debt. Issuer credit ratings are amongst the most widely watched. They measure the creditworthiness of the borrower including its capacity and willingness to meet financial needs. The top credit rating issued by the main agencies – Standard & Poor's, Moody's and Fitch IBCA - is AAA or Aaa. This is reserved for a few sovereign and corporate issuers. Ratings are divided into two broad groups - investment grade and speculative (junk) grade.

Credit Rating Agency: Credit rating agency means a body corporate which is engaged in, or proposes to be engaged in, the business of rating of securities offered by way of public or rights issue.

Credit Risk: The risk that a counterparty will not settle an obligation for full value, either when due or at any time thereafter. Credit risk includes pre-settlement risk (replacement cost risk) and settlement risk (Principal risk).

Current Asset: Cash or an item of value expected to be converted into cash within one year or one operating cycle, whichever is longer.

Current Liability: Accounting term for money payable within the current accounting year, on account of trade creditors, taxation, dividends, etc. To these are often added provisions, i.e. any charges or liabilities (various government duties, disputed claims, etc.) which the company may have to settle within the accounting year.

D

Daily Margin: The amount that has to be deposited at the Stock Exchange on a daily basis for the purchase or sale of a security. This amount is decided by the stock exchange.

Dalal Street: Street on which The Stock Exchange, Mumbai is situated. Used synonymously for The Stock Exchange, Mumbai.

Dealer: A firm that enters into transactions as a counterparty on both sides of the market in one or more products.

Debentures: Bonds issued by a company bearing a fixed rate of interest usually payable half yearly on specific dates and principal amount repayable on a particular date on redemption of the debentures.

Delisting Exchange: The exchange from which securities of a company are proposed to be delisted in accordance with SEBI Delisting Guidelines.

Delisting of Securities: Permanent removal of securities of a listed company from a stock exchange. As a consequence of delisting, the securities of that company would no longer be traded at that stock exchange.

Delivery: Presentation of securities with transfer deeds in fulfilment of a transaction.

Delivery Price: The price fixed by the Stock Exchange at which deliveries on futures are invoiced. Also the price at which the future contract is settled when deliveries are made.

Dematerialise: The process of transforming securities holdings in physical form to those in electronic form through a Depository Participant.

Depository: A system of organisation, which keeps records of securities, deposited by its depositors. The records may be physical or simply electronic records.

Depository Participant (DP): An agent of the depository through which it interfaces with the investor. A DP can offer depository services only after it gets proper registration from SEBI.

Depreciation: A fall in value of a security or security index or a currency in terms of others or its purchasing power.

Depth of Market: The number of shares of a security that can be bought or sold at the best bid or offer price.

Derivative Market: Markets such as futures and option markets that are developed to satisfy specific needs arising in traditional markets. These markets provide the same basic functions as forward markets, but trading usually takes place on standardized contracts.

Derivative: (1) A security derived from a debt instrument, share, loan whether secured or unsecured, risk instrument or contract for differences or any other form of security; (2) A contract which derives its value from the prices, or index or prices, of underlying securities.

Direct Quotation: The quotation of variable units of domestic currency in terms of fixed units of foreign currency.

Dirty Float: A floating security whose value is not solely determined by free market supply and demand pressures but also by interventions of the concerned authorities.

Dirty Price: A price for a bond which includes the amount of interest that has accrued on the bond since the date of the last interest payment.

Disclosure: Full and material information given by a company that may allow an investor to take an informed investment decision.

Discount: When a security is quoted at a price below its nominal or face value, it is said to be at a discount.

Disintermediation: A situation where some intervention usually by government agencies for the purpose of controlling or regulating the growth of financial intermediaries lessens their advantage in the provision of financial services and drives financial transfers and businesses into other channels.

Dividend: Payment made to shareholders, usually once or twice a year out of a company's profit after tax. Dividend payments do not distribute the entire net profit of a company, a part or substantial part of which is held back as reserves for the company's expansion. Dividend is declared on the face value or par value of a share, and not on its market price.

Dumping: In the securities market the offering of large amounts of stock without regard for the effect on prices on the market. In the international trade, the selling of goods overseas below cost to get rid of a surplus or to gain a competitive edge over the foreign firms.

E

Electronic fund transfer (EFT): System which utilizes computer and electronic components in order to transfer money or financial assets. EFT is information based and intangible.

Employee Stock Option: "Employee stock option" means the option given to the whole-time directors, officers or employees of a company which gives such directors, officers or employees, the benefit or right to purchase or subscribe at a future date, the securities offered by the company at a predetermined price.

Employee Stock Purchase Scheme (ESPS): "Employee stock purchase scheme (ESPS)" means a scheme under which the company offers shares to employees as part of a public issue or otherwise.

Emerging Markets: Term used to describe the financial markets of developing countries. Definitions vary of which countries are emerging and which are not. However, the emerging market indices compiled by the IFC and Morgan Stanley are often used as benchmarks.

Entry Fee: Fee paid by an investor when purchasing units in a trust or managed fund. The fee is included in the price that new investors pay.

Equity: The ownership interest in a company of holders of its common and preferred stock.

Equity premium: The difference between the expected return from holding stock and from holding riskless bonds.

Equity Trust: Unit Trust which invests mainly in equity shares with a component in cash and in fixed interest investment.

Ex: Means 'Without'. A price so quoted excludes recently declared dividends (xd) rights (xr) or bonus shares (xb).

Exchange: Regulated market place where capital market products are bought and sold through intermediaries.

Exchange Rate Risk: The risk that adverse movements in exchange rates lead to capital losses in assets or revaluation of liabilities.

Exchange-traded Derivative: A derivative which is listed and traded at an organised market-place. Derivatives exchanges generally provide standardised contracts and central clearing facilities for participants.

Exchange Traded Funds (ETF): A security that tracks an index but has the flexibility of trading like a stock.

Ex-Dividend Date: The date on or after which the buyer of a security is not entitled to the dividend already declared.

Ex-Right Date: The date on which the official quotation for a share is marked XR i.e. ex rights, in the daily official list.

F

Face Value: The value that appears on the face of the scrip, same as nominal or par value of share/debentures.

Firewall: A barrier designed to prevent losses or risks taken in one part of a financial institution from weakening other parts of institution.

Firm Allotment: Allotment on a firm basis in public issues by an issuing company made to Indian and multilateral development financial institutions ,Indian mutual funds, foreign institutional investors including non-resident Indians and overseas corporate bodies and permanent/regular employees of the issuer company.

Float: The number of shares issued and outstanding of a company's stock.

Floating Rate Coupon: Coupon rate that varies with ("floats against") a standard market benchmark or index.

Floating Stock: The fraction of the paid up equity capital of a company which normally participates in day to day trading.

Floor: Trading hall of the Stock Exchange where transactions in securities take place. The trading ring where members and their assistants assemble with their order books for executing the order of their constituents.

Floor Price: The minimum offer price below which bids cannot be entered. The Issuer Company in consultation with the lead book runner fixes the floor price.

Flow Back: Securities recently placed in the markets that are resold on the issuers' national market. It is one of the major risks in an equity placement because it may frustrate the objective of internationalization of the equity market and cause downward pressure on its market price.

Foreign Institutional Investor: An institution established or incorporated outside India which proposes to make investment in India in securities; provided that a domestic asset management company or domestic portfolio manager who manages funds raised or collected or brought from outside India for investment in India on behalf of a sub-account, shall be deemed to be a Foreign Institutional Investor.

Forward Contract: An agreement for the future delivery of the underlying commodity or security at a specified price at the end of a designated period of time. Unlike a future contract, a forward contract is traded over the counter and its terms are negotiated individually. There is no clearing house for forward contracts, and the secondary market may be non-existent or thin.

Forward Rate Agreement: A forward contract on interest rates in which the rate to be paid or received on a specific obligation for a set period of time, beginning at some time in the future, is determined at contract initiation.

Futures Contract: An exchange traded contract generally calling for delivery of a specified amount of a particular financial instrument at a fixed date in the future. Contracts are highly standardized and traders need only agree on the price and number of contracts traded.

G

Gilt Edged: A term used to describe a bond, generally issued by the Government or issued with a Government Guarantee so much so that there are no doubts about the ability of the issuer to pay regular interest and the principal amount to the bond holders.

Global Depository Receipts: Any instrument in the form of a depository receipt or certificate (by whatever name it is called) created by the Overseas Depository Bank outside India and issued to non-resident investors against the issue of ordinary shares or Foreign Currency Convertible Bonds of issuing company.

Golden Share: A share with special voting rights that give it peculiar power vis-à-vis other share. The term applies particularly to share retained by a government after privatisation. If a government wishes to sell off a company in a sensitive industry (defence, say) and yet retain control, it can hold on to a golden share. This might give it the right to veto any takeover bid.

Good Delivery: Proper delivery by a seller to the buyer of the securities without any defect so that they can be transferred without any additional documentation.

Goodwill: The part of value of a business that is based on good customer relations, high employee morale and other factors.

Growth Fund: Unit trusts or Mutual Funds which invest with the objective of achieving mostly capital growth rather than income. Growth funds are mostly more volatile than conservative income or money market funds because managers invest on shares or property that are subject to larger price movements.

Guaranteed Coupon: Bonds issued by a subsidiary corporation and guaranteed as to principal and /or interest by the parent corporation.

H

Hand Delivery: Delivery and payment on the date stipulated by the Stock Exchange.

Hedge: An asset, liability or financial commitment that protects against adverse changes in the value of or cash flows from another investment or liability. An unhedged investment or liability is called an "exposure". A perfectly matched hedge will gain in value what the underlying exposure loses or lose what the underlying exposure gains.

Hedge Funds: Private investment pools that invest aggressively in all types of markets, with managers of the fund receiving a percentage of the investment profits. The name is something of a misnomer since a hedge fund's raison d'etre is quite the opposite of hedging.

Hedge Ratio: The proportion of one asset required to hedge against movements in the price of another.

Hot Issue: A security that is expected to trade in the after market at a premium over the public offering price.

Hot Money: Short term international capital movements, motivated by interest rate differential or revaluation hopes/devaluation fears.

Hypothecation: Pledging assets against a loan. The ownership of the asset or the income from the asset is not transferred, except that in default of repayment of loan the asset may be sold to realize its value. Brokers will accept shares as collateral for loans to finance purchase of shares or to cover short sales.

I

Implied Volatility: The value of the price or rate volatility variable that would equate current option price and fair value. Alternatively, the value of the volatility variable that buyers and sellers appear to accept when the market price of an option is determined. Implied volatility is calculated by using the market price of an option as the fair value in an option model and calculating (by iteration) the volatility level consistent with that option price.

Income Distribution: Distribution of income of a mutual fund to its unit holders, in proportion to the number of units held.

Indexed Asset: An indexed asset has coupon and principal payments that are adjusted upward in response to increase in price level. This adjustment is intended to compensate lenders for the decline in purchasing power of loan repayments.

Indian Depository Receipt: A receipt, evidencing an underlying foreign security, issued in India by a foreign company which has entered into an agreement with the issuer and depository, custodian and depository or underwriters and depository, in accordance with the terms of prospectus or letter of offer, as may be prescribed.

Initial Public Offering (IPO): The first public issue by a public limited company.

Insider: Any person who, is or was connected with the company or is deemed to have been connected with the company, and who is reasonably expected to have access, connection, to unpublished price sensitive information in respect of securities of a company, or who has received or has had access to such unpublished price sensitive information.

Insider Trading: Practice of corporate agents buying or selling their corporation's securities without disclosing to the public significant information which is known to them but which has not yet affected the price.

Interim Dividend: A dividend payment made during the course of a company's financial year. Interim dividend, unlike the final dividend, does not have to be agreed in a general meeting.

Investment Banker: Financial conglomerate which conducts a full range of investment related activities from advising clients on securities issues, acquisitions and disposal of businesses, arranging and underwriting new securities, distributing the securities etc.

Investment Company: A corporation, trust or partnership that invests pooled unit holder/shareholder money in securities appropriate to the organization's objective. Mutual funds, close–ended funds and unit investment trusts are the three types of investment companies.

Investment Profit: Profit which results from the difference between the purchase and selling prices of a security. Trading profit is short term while investment profit is medium or long term.

Issuer: An entity which is in the process of issuing its securities. Also known as the "Originator".

J

Jobber: Member brokers of a stock exchange who specialize, by giving two way quotations, in buying and selling of securities from and to fellow members. Jobbers do not have any direct contact with the public but they serve the useful function of imparting liquidity to the market.

Jobbers Spread: The difference between the price at which a jobber is prepared to sell and the price at which he is prepared to buy. A large difference reflects an imbalance between supply and demand.

Junk Bond: High yield bond issued by low rated companies.

K

Kapli: A standard form used by the broker to inform the Stock Exchange of his transactions for the purpose of matching a settlement.

Killer Bees: Law firms, proxy solicitors and public relations firm employed to help a company management fight off an unfriendly takeover.

Kiss Principle: Advice given by old pros to neophyte brokers on how they should explain to investors such sophisticated investment concepts as options and arbitrage. Keep it simple, stupid.

L

Lagging Indicators: Market indicators showing the general direction of the economy and confirming or denying the trend implied by the leading indicators or concurrent indicators.

Lame Duck: A defaulter on a Stock Exchange who is not able to meet his market commitment and financial obligations of his business.

Law of One Price: An economic rule stating that a given security must have the same price regardless of the means by which one goes about creating that security. This implies that if the payoff of a security can be synthetically created by a package of other securities, the price of the package and the price of the security whose payoff it replicates must be equal.

Lay Off: The sell off by an issuer of any or all unsubscribed shares in a rights offering to the underwriters at the subscription price.

Leading Indicators: Market indicators that signal the state of the economy for the coming months.

Lead Manager: The merchant banker(s) associated with the issue and responsible for due diligence and other associated issue related activities.

Legal Risk: The risk of loss because a law or regulation is applied in an unexpected way or because a contract cannot be enforced.

Letter of Offer: A letter of offer is a document addressed to the shareholders of the target company containing disclosures of the acquirer/ (Persons Acting in Concert) PACs, target company, their financials, justification of the offer price, the offer price, number of shares to be acquired from the public, purpose of acquisition, future plans of acquirer etc.

Liquid Assets: Proportion of listed unit trust's or mutual fund portfolio that is kept in cash or easily encashable assets to meet any request for redemption.

Liquidity Risk: The risk that a solvent institution is temporarily unable to meet its monetary obligations.

Listed Company: A company which has any of its securities offered through an offer document listed on a recognized stock exchange and also includes Public Sector Undertakings whose securities are listed on a recognised stock exchange.

Listing: Formal admission of a security into a public trading system.

Lock in Trade: A securities transactions in which all the terms and conditions to the transactions are irrevocably accepted by the buyer and seller.

Long Position: A position showing a purchase or a greater number of purchases than sales in anticipation of a rise in prices. A long position can be closed out through the sale of an equivalent amount.

Loss on Security Provisions: The risk that changes in security prices may lead to capital losses.

M

Maintenance Margin: The minimum margin that must be maintained on a futures contract.

Manipulation of Financial Markets: Activities whose objective is to alter prices in financial markets through the use of techniques that result in unnatural market prices, often through the use of wash sales or reporting of fictional or apparent market prices.

Maple Leaf: Debt warrants entitling the holder to purchase a Government of Canada Bond.

Margin: An advance payment of a portion of the value of a stock transaction. The amount of credit a broker or lender extends to a customer for stock purchase.

Markdown: A charge levied by a broker when buying securities on its own account from a customer. (These purchases as principals from customer take place at the best bid prices minus a commission equivalent to markdown).

Market Maker: A member firm who give two way quotation for particular security(ies) and who is under an obligation to buy and sell them subject to certain conditions such as overall exposure, spread etc.

Market Model: This relationship is sometimes called the single-index model. The market model says that the return on a security depends on the return on the market portfolio and the extent of the security's responsiveness as measured by beta (b). In addition, the return will also depend on conditions that are unique to the firm. Graphically, the market model can be depicted as a line fitted to a plot of asset returns against returns on the market portfolio.

Market Price: The last reported sale price for an exchange traded security.

Marking Up Prices: Prices fixed by the Stock Exchange to facilitate settlement of bargains in the specified securities, particularly at the end of the settlement period.

Mark-up: A charge levied by a broker when selling securities from its own account to a customer. These sales as principals to a customer take place at the best ask price plus a commission equivalent to mark-up.

Maturity Value: The amount an investor receives when a

security is redeemed at maturity not including any periodic interest payments. The value usually equals the par value although on zero coupon, compound interest and multiplier bonds, the principal amount of the security at issuance plus the accumulated investment return on the security is included.

Merchant Banker: Any person who is engaged in the business of issue management either by making arrangement regarding selling, buying or subscribing to securities or acting as manager, consultant, adviser or rendering corporate advisory service in relation to such issue management.

Money Laundering: Process of converting the proceeds of illegal activities – disclosure of which would trigger financial losses or criminal prosecution – into real or financial assets whose origins remain effectively hidden from law enforcement officials and from society in general.

Money Market: The market encompassing the trading and issuance of short-term non-equity debt instruments, including treasury bills, commercial paper, bankers' acceptance, certificates of deposits etc. The market may be local or international.

Money Market Mutual Funds: Schemes investing exclusively in safer short-term instruments such as treasury bills, certificates of deposit, commercial paper and inter-bank call money, government securities, etc.

Mortgage-backed Securities: Securities backed by mortgage loans, including pass-through securities, modified pass-through securities, mortgage-backed bonds, and mortgage pay-through securities.

Mortgage Trust: Unit trust which invests in mortgage loans. Effectively the unit trust invests money in real estate and receives an interest return with security over the property which has been purchased. The interest which is charged on mortgage trust loans is normally higher than that other sources of finance like banks so that the investor usually receives a very competitive rate or return.

Moral Hazard: The risk that a party to a transaction has not entered into a contract in good faith has provided misleading information about its assets, liabilities or credit capacity or has an incentive to take unusual risks in a desperate attempt to avoid losses.

Mutual Funds /Unit Trusts: Mutual Fund is a mechanism for pooling the resources by issuing units to the investors and investing funds in securities in accordance with objectives as disclosed in offer document. A fund established in the form of a trust to raise monies through the sale of units to the public or a section of the public under one or more schemes for investing in securities, including money market instruments.

N

NASDAQ: Acronym for the National Association of Security Dealers Automated Quotations. This is an organization that does exactly what its name stands for. The system provides a computerized information network through which brokers, banks and other investment professionals can obtain up to the minute price quotations on securities traded over the counter.

Narrowing the Spread: The action taken by broker/dealer to narrow the spread between bids and offers by bidding higher or offering lower than the previous bid or offer. Also called closing the market.

Negotiated Dealing System (NDS): Electronic platform for facilitating dealing in Government Securities and Money Market Instruments, introduced by RBI.

Net Dividend: Dividend after deduction of tax payable from gross dividend.

Net Liquid Assets: Cash and readily marketable securities minus current liabilities of a company. This is the strictest test of a company's ability to meet current debt obligations.

Net Working Capital: The excess of current assets over current liabilities.

Net Worth: The aggregate value of the paid up equity capital and free reserves (excluding reserves created out of revaluation), reduced by the aggregate value of accumulated losses and deferred expenditure not written off, including miscellaneous expenses not written of.

New Issue: Shares of a company offered to the public, through a public issue, for the first time to be listed on the Stock Exchange.

Net Asset Value (NAV): The current market worth of a mutual fund's share. A fund's net asset value is calculated by taking the fund's total assets, securities, cash and any accrued earnings, deducting liabilities, and dividing the remainder by the number of units outstanding.

Non-deliverable Swap: Similar to a non deliverable forward, the only difference being that settlement for both parties is done through a major currency.

O

Off Balance Sheet Risk: Risk relative to operations that are not reflected in variation of the institutions assets or liabilities, when undertaken, but are reflected when profit or loss occurs.

Offer Document: As per SEBI DIP guidelines, offer

document means Prospectus in case of a public issue or offer for sale and Letter of Offer in case of a rights issue.

Offer Period: The period between the date of entering into Memorandum of Understanding or the public announcement, as the case may be and the date of completion of offer formalities relating to the offer.

Offer Price: Price at which units in trust can be bought. It often includes an entry fee. It also refers to the price at which securities are offered to the public.

Ombudsman: An independent person appointed to hear and act upon citizen's complaint about government services. Invented in Sweden, the idea has been widely adopted. For example, groups of banks, mortgage lenders and insurance companies in various countries have appointed ombudsmen to attend to the complaints of their customers. Customers who use the ombudsman's (free) service retain their full right to take legal action should they not agree with the ombudsman's decision.

Open-ended Scheme: An open-ended fund or scheme is one that is available for subscription and repurchase on a continuous basis.

Open Market Operation: Purchase or sale of government securities by the monetary authorities (RBI in India) to increase or decrease the domestic money supply.

Open Order: An order to buy and sell a security that remains in effect until it is either cancelled by the customer or executed.

Opening Price: The rate at which the first transaction in a security is struck after the opening of the market.

Operating Income: Net Sales less cost of sales, selling expenses, administrative expenses and depreciation. The pre-tax income from normal operations.

Operational Risk: The risk that deficiencies in information systems or internal controls could result in unexpected losses.

Order Book: It is an 'electronic book' that shows the demand for the shares of the company at various prices.

OTC (Over the Counter): A financial transaction that is not made on an organised exchange. Generally the parties must negotiate all the details of each transaction or agree to use simplifying market conventions.

Overtrading: A broker/dealer overpays a customer for a security to enable the customer to subscribe to another security offered by that broker/dealer at a higher mark-up than the loss to be sustained when the firm sells the customer's first security at prevailing market prices.

P

Paid in Capital: The difference between par or book-keeping, value of a security and the amount realized from the sale or distribution of those shares by the company.

Paid up Capital: The amount of capital, both equity and preference, paid up by the shareholders against the capital subscribed to by them.

Par Value: Means the face value of securities.

Pari Passu: A term used to describe new issue of securities which have same rights as similar issues already in existence.

Partial Tender Offer: A tender offer for less than all target shares; specifies a maximum number of shares to be accepted, but does not announce bidder's plans with respect to the remaining shares.

Participating Preference Shares: The right of certain preference shareholders to participate in profits after a specified fixed dividend contracted for is paid. Participation right is linked with the quantum of dividend paid on the equity shares over and above a particular specified level.

Partly Paid: Shares on which full nominal value has not been called up.

Pig: Operators who get killed by the speculators.

Pink Sheets: Listing of Over the Counter Stocks, the dealers who trade them and the prices at which these dealers are willing to buy and sell. Printed daily on loud pink newsprint and found in brokerage house and many banks.

Placing Power: The ability of the financial institutions to place securities with the investor.

Players: A diverse range of intermediaries and institutional investors active in the capital market. This includes securities firms, broker dealers, commercial banks, merchant banks, unit trust/mutual fund etc.

Pooling: The basic concept behind mutual funds in which a fund aggregates the assets of investors who share common financial goals. A fund uses the investment pool to buy a diversified portfolio of investments and each mutual fund share purchased represents ownership in all the funds underlying securities.

Portfolio: A collection of securities owned by an individual or an institution (such as a mutual fund) that may include stocks, bonds and money market securities.

Preferential Allotment: Further issue of shares/securities convertible into equity shares at a later date, to a select group of persons in preference to all the existing shareholders of the company.

Premium: If an investor buys a security for a price above its eventual value at maturity he has paid a premium for it.

Profit Taking: Realizing profits by closing out an existing position.

Prospectus: Any document described or issued as a prospectus and includes any notice, circular, advertisement or other document inviting deposits from the public or inviting offers from the public for the subscription or purchase of any shares in, or debentures of, a body corporate.

Proxy: One who votes for and on behalf of a shareholder at a company meeting.

Public Issue: An invitation by a company to public to subscribe to the securities offered through a prospectus.

Put Option: An option that gives the right to sell a fixed number of securities at a specified price (the strike price) within a specified period of time.

Q

Quotation: The NASD requirement that a market maker who receives order from another broker dealer executes the order at its displayed price on NASDAQ for the normal unit of trading or its displayed size, whichever is greater.

R

Random Walk Theory: Claims that a stock's past price action is no guide to future prices because prices move randomly, not in a pattern. Random walk theoreticians would sneer at the idea that because a stock has been moving up during the last few weeks it is likely to continue moving up.

Real Time Gross Settlement (RTGS): Concept designed to achieve sound risk management in the settlement of inter-bank payments. Transactions are settled across accounts held at the Central Bank on a continuous gross basis where settlement is immediate, final and irrevocable.

Record Date: A date on which the records of a company are closed for the purpose of determining the stockholders to whom dividends, proxies rights etc. are to be sent.

Registrar to an Issue: The person appointed by a body corporate or any person or group of persons to carry on the activities of collecting applications from investors in respect of an issue; keeping a proper record of applications and monies received from investors or paid to the seller of the securities and assisting body corporate or person or group of persons in-determining the basis of allotment of securities in consultation with the stock exchange; finalising of the list of persons entitled to allotment of securities; processing and despatching allotment letters, refund orders or certificates and other related documents in respect of the issue.

Rematerialisation: The process of converting electronic holdings into physical securities through a Depository Participant.

Reverse Book Building: Reverse book building is similar to the process of book building, which is aimed at securing the optimum price for a company's share. In reverse book building the investors' aim is to sell the shares to exit the company.

Rigged Market: Manipulation of share price to attract buyers and sellers to the riggers advantage.

Rights Issue/ Rights Shares: The issue of new securities to existing shareholders in a fixed ratio to those already held.

Rolling Settlement: The practice on many stock markets of settling a transaction a fixed number of days after the trade is agreed.

Ruling Price: The current market price of a security.

Run: A run involves a person creating activity in a security by successively buying or selling that security. The intention is that the increased activity would, in case where the person is buying, attract others to buy and push up the price. At that point, those organizing the run would then attempt to sell out at a financial gain. This is sometimes known as "pumping and dumping."

S

Sauda Book: Members and authorized assistants are given a book called "Sauda Book" to record transactions of sales and purchases.

Screen-based Trading: Form of trading that uses modern telecommunication and computer technology to combine information transmission with trading in financial markets.

Secondary Market: The market for previously issued securities or financial instruments.

Securitization: The process of homogenizing and packaging financial instruments into a new fungible one. Acquisition, classification, collateralization, composition, pooling and distribution are functions within this process.

Self-clearing Member: A member of a clearing corporation or clearing house of the derivatives exchange or derivatives segment of a stock exchange who may clear and settle transactions on its own account or on account of its clients only and shall not clear or settle transactions in securities for any other trading members.

Selling Short: A manner in which an investor sells securities he does not posses in the hope of buying them back later at a lower price.

Sensitive Index: A share price index based on 30 active scrips developed by the Bombay Stock Exchange with 1978-79 as the base year.

Share Transfer Agent: Any person, who on behalf of any body corporate maintains the record of holders of securities issued by such body corporate and deals with all matters connected with the transfer and redemption of its securities. It can also be a department or division (by whatever name called) of a body corporate performing the above activities if, at any time the total number of the holders of securities issued exceed one lakh.

Short Covering: Buying of stocks by a seller to complete his previous commitments.

Short Position: In futures, the short has sold the commodity or security for future delivery; in options, the short has sold the call or the put and is obligated to take a futures position if he or she is assigned for exercise.

Spot Delivery Contract: A contract which provides for (a) actual delivery of securities and the payment of a price therefore either on the same day as the date of the contract or on the next day, the actual period taken for the despatch of the securities or the remittance of money therefore through the post being excluded from the computation of the period aforesaid if the parties to the contract do not reside in the same town or locality; (b) transfer of the securities by the depository from the account of a beneficial owner to the account of another beneficial owner when such securities are dealt with by a depository.

Stakeholder: Any individual or group who has an interest in a firm; in addition to shareholders and bondholders, includes labour, consumers, suppliers, the local community and so on.

Stamp Duty: The ad valorem duty payable by buyer for transfer of shares in his name. Also payable on contracts issued by a stock-broker.

Standard Price: The standard price of a security is generally worked out as a weighted average price of all recorded transactions for that security adjusted to the nearest rupee.

Stock Dividend: A dividend paid to stockholders in shares of stock of the issuing corporation, issued to stockholders or record out of the unissued stock of the corporation, involving no payment of cash, and used to reflect positive interest in the security.

Stock Exchange: Any body of individuals, whether incorporated or not, constituted for the purpose of assisting, regulating or controlling the business of buying, selling or dealing in securities.

Stock Option: The right to purchase shares of common stock in accordance with an agreement, upon payment of a specified amount; a compensation scheme under which executives are granted options to purchase common stock over an extended option period at a stated price.

Swap Reversal: An Interest rate swap designed to end counterparty's role in another Interest rate swap, accomplished by counterbalancing the original swap in maturity, reference rate, and notional amount.

Sweat Equity: A sweat equity share is an equity share issued by the company to employees or directors at a discount or for consideration other than cash for providing know-how or making available rights in the nature of intellectual property rights or value additions.

Systemic Risk: Risk that affects an entire financial market or system, and not just specific participants. It is not possible to avoid systemic risk through diversification.

T

Takeover Panel: An acquirer who proposes to acquire shares through a mode which is not specifically covered under takeover regulations may seek exemption from the applicability of the provisions of the offer process by making an application. SEBI has constituted a panel consisting of independent persons to examine such applications which is called the Takeover Panel.

Target Company: A Target company is a listed company i.e. whose shares are listed on any stock exchange and whose shares or voting rights are acquired/ being acquired or whose control is taken over/being taken over by an acquirer.

Technical Position: Condition of the market created by various internal factors and opposed to external forces.

Tender Offer: Tender offer means an offer by a company to buy back its specified securities through a letter of offer from the holders of the specified securities of the company.

Thin Markets: Characterized by relatively few transactions per unit of time and where price fluctuations are high relative to the volume of trade.

Tracking Error: When using an indexing or any other benchmarking strategy, the amount by which the performance of the portfolio differed from that of the benchmark.

Trading Member: A member of the derivatives exchange or derivatives segment of a stock exchange who settles the trade in the clearing corporation or clearing house through a clearing member.

Transaction Statement: The depository participant gives a Transaction Statement periodically, which will detail current balances and various transactions made through the depository account. If so desired, DP may provide the Transaction Statement at intervals shorter than the stipulated ones, probably at a cost.

Transfer Agents: An agent designated by the company to carry out the function of transfer of shares.

Transferee: The buyer of the securities in whose favour the securities are bought to be registered is known as the Transferee.

Transferor: The seller of the security is the transferor of the security.

Treasury Bills: A short term bearer discount security issued by governments as a means of financing their cash requirements. Treasury Bills play an important role in the local money market because most banks are required to hold them as part of their reserve requirements and because central bank open market operations undertaken in the process of implementing monetary policy are usually conducted in the treasury bill market.

U

Underlying: The designated financial instrument which must be delivered in completion of an option or futures contract.

Underwriter: One who does underwriting. A financial organization that handles sales of new securities which a company or municipality wishes to sell in order to raise money. Typically the underwriters will guarantee subscription to securities say, an issue of equity from the company at a stated price, and are under an obligation to purchase securities up to the amount they have underwritten, should the public not subscribe for the issue.

Underwriting: An agreement with or without conditions to subscribe to the securities of a body corporate when the existing shareholders of such body corporate or the public do not subscribe to the securities offered to them.

V

Value Investing: The investment style of attempting to buy under-priced stocks that have the potential to perform well and appreciate in terms of price.

Value at Risk (VAR): VAR is the maximum loss over a target horizon such that there is a low, pre-specified probability that the actual loss will be larger.

Vanilla Issue: A straight fixed rate issue which has terms and conditions usually accepted as being conventional to a particular securities market.

Vanishing Companies: Companies which have not complied with specific provisions of the listing agreement and regulations of the stock exchanges, and are not physically traceable at the registered address mentioned in the offer document.

Venture Capital: Professional moneys co-invested with the entrepreneur usually to fund an early stage, more risky venture. Offsetting the high risk is the promise of higher return that the investor takes. A venture capitalist not only brings in moneys as "equity capital" (i.e. without security/charge on assets) but also brings on to the table extremely valuable domain knowledge ,business contacts, brand equity, strategic advice, etc. He is a fixed interval investor, whom the entrepreneurs approach without the risk of "takeover".

Vertical Spread: Buying and selling puts or calls of the same expiration month but with different strike prices.

Vesting: The process by which the employee is given the right to apply for shares of the company against the option granted to him in pursuance of Employee Stock Option Scheme.

Volatility: Volatility equates to the variability of returns from an investment. It is an acceptable substitute for risk; the greater the volatility, the greater is the risk that an investment will not turn out as hoped because its market price happens to be on the downswing of a bounce at the time that it needs to be cashed in. The problem is that future volatility is hard to predict and measures of past volatility can, themselves, be variable, depending on how frequently returns are measured (weekly or monthly, for example) and for how long. Therefore, putting expectations of future volatility into predictive models is of limited use, but resorting to using past levels of volatility is equally limited.

Volume of Trading: The total number of shares which changes hands in a particular company's securities. This information is useful in explaining and interpreting fluctuation in share prices.

Voluntary Delisting: Delisting of securities of a body corporate voluntarily by a promoter or an acquirer or any other person other than the stock exchange.

W

Warrant: An options contract often sold with another security. For instance, corporate bonds may be sold with warrants to buy common stock of that corporation. Warrants are generally detachable.

Window Dressing: A manoeuvre often engaged in by companies, banks, mutual funds etc., at the end of the accounting period in order to impress stock holders who will be receiving the report showing that funds are better managed and invested than what might have been drawn up.

Wolf: Speculators who make a kill in the market.

Writer: A person who issues an option. The individual who at the end of the day has to buy or sell the asset on which the option is written, should the person who holds the option wish to exercise his rights.

X

X Dividend: A term meaning 'without dividend'. A stock bought on or after the X- dividend day will not pay the purchaser the dividend already declared.

Y

Yankee Bond: A bond offering in the U.S. domestic market by a non-U.S. entity registered with the SEC.

Yield to Maturity (YTM): The rate of return anticipated on a bond if it is held until the maturity date. YTM is considered a long term bond yield expressed as an annual rate.

Yuppie Scam: The name given to Wall Street insider trading scandal after a host of smart young lawyers, bankers and arbitrageurs were found to be in the dealing ring.

Z

Zero Coupon Bond: A bond that pays no interest while the investor holds it. It is sold originally at a substantial discount from its eventual maturity value, paying the investor its full face value when it comes due, with the difference between what he paid initially and what he finally collected representing the interest he would have received over the years it was held.

Zero Coupon Yield Curve

A yield curve of zero coupon bonds. Market practice is often to derive this curve theoretically from the par yield curve. Frequently used to derive discount factors. Also known as spot yield curve.

Bibliography

Bibliography

Alexander, S. S., 1961, "Price Movements in Speculative Markets: Trends or Random Walks", *Industrial Management Review* II, May, 7-26.

Alexander, S. S., 1964, "Price Movements in Speculative Markets: Trends or Random Walks, Number 2", *Industrial Management Review* V, Spring, 25-46.

Ali, Mukhtar M. and Giaccotto, Carmelo, 1982, "The Identical Distribution Hypothesis for Stock Market Prices-Location-and Scale-Shift Alternative", *Journal of the American Statistical Association,* March, Vol. 77, No. 377, 19-28.

Amihud, Yakov, and Mendelson, Haim, 1987, "Trading Mechanisms and Stock Returns: An Empirical Investigation", *The Journal of Finance*, July, Vol. XLII, 533-553.

Andersen, Torben G. and Bollerslev, Tim, 1998, "Deutsche Mark-Dollar Volatility: Intraday Activity Patterns, Macroeconomic Announcements, and Longer Run Dependencies", *The Journal of Finance,* February, Vol-LIII, No.-1, 219-265.

Ariel, R.A., 1987, "A Monthly Effect in Stock Returns", *Journal of Financial Economics*, 18, 161-174.

Asquith, P., 1983, "Merger bids, Uncertainty and Stockholder Returns", *Journal of Financial Economics,* 11, 51-83.

Asquith, P., and Mullins, David W., 1983, "The Impact of Initiating Dividend Payments on Shareholders' Wealth", *Journal of Business* 56, 77-96.

Asquith, P., and Mullins, David W., 1986, "Equity Issues and Offering Dilution", *Journal of Financial Economics* 15, 61-89.

Bachelier, L. J. B. A., 1900, "Theorie de la speculation", *Annales Scientifiques de l' Ecole Normale Superiente*, 3, No.1018 Paris: Gauthier- Villars. Translated in *The Random Character of Stock Market Prices*, edited by Paul H. Cootner. M.I.T. Press. Cambridge 1964.

Ball, Ray, 1989, "What Do We Know about the Stock Market Efficiency", A paper presented at *the Inaugural Conference on Ásia-Pacific Financial Markets*, Nov., Singapore.

Banz, R. W., 1981, "The Relationship between Return and Market Value of Common Stock", *Journal of Financial Economics*, 9,

3-18.

Barberis, N., Shleilfer, A. and Vishny, R., 1996, "A Model of Investor Sentiment", *Journal of Financial Economics* 49, 307-343.

Barua, S. K. and Raghunathan, V., 1986, "Inefficiency of the Indian Capital Market", *Vikalpa*, Vol. 11, No.3, 225-229.

Barua, S. K., Raghunathan, V and Varma, J.R., 1994, "Research on the Indian Capital Market: A Review", *Vikalpa*, January-March, Vol. 19, No. 1, 15-27.

Basu, S., 1977, "Investment Performance of Common Stocks in Relation to their Price-Earnings Ratios: A Test of the Efficient Market Hypothesis", *The Journal of Finance*, June 1977, Vol. XXXII, No.3, 663-681.

Bhattacharya, Kaushik and Samanta, G.P., 2003, "A Tale of Two Indices: The Story of the Nasdaq and the Sensex", *Journal of Quantitative Economics*, July, Vol. 1, No. 1, 89-102.

Biswal, Pratap Chandra and Kamaiah, B., 2001, "Stock Market Development in India: Is there any Trend Break?", *Economic and Political Weekly*, Jan 27, 377-2001

Blanchard, Oliver J. and Watson, Mark, "Bubbles, Rational Expectations and Financial Markets",*NBER Working Paper*, No.945,639-660.

Bombay Stock Exchange Website; *www.bseindia.com*

Broca Dilbagh S., 1994, "Volatility Shifts in Stock Market Returns: A Look at Emerging Markets", *Vikalpa*, Jan-March Vol. 19, No.1, 47-53

Broca, Dilbagh S., 1995, "Monitoring Volatility Changes on the Bombay Bourse: A Control Chart Approach", *Vikalpa*, July-Sep, Vol. -20, No.-3, 43-51.

Brown, P., Kleidon, A.W. and Marsh, T.A., 1983, "New Evidences on the Nature of Size Related Anomalies in Stock Prices", *Journal of Financial Economics*.

Byun, Jinho and Rozeff, Michael S., 2003, "Long-run Performance after Stock Splits: 1927 to 1996", *The Journal of Finance*, Vol. LVIII, No. 3, 1063-1085.

Campbell, John Y. and Shiller Robert J., 1988, "Stock Prices, Earnings, and Expected Dividends", *The Journal of Finance,* July, Vol. XLIII, No. 3, 661.

Campbell, John Y., Lettau, Martin, Malkiel, Burton G. and XU, Yexiao, 2001, "Have Individual Stocks Become More

Volatile? An Empirical Exploration of Idiosyncratic Risk", *Journal of Finance,* February, Vol.-LVI, No.-1,1-43.

Campbell, John Y., Lo, A. W., and Mackinlay, A. C., 1997, *The Econometrics of Financial Market*, Princeton University Press, Princeton, New Jersey.

Chakrabarti, B.B., 2003, "State of the Equity Market", *Portfolio Organizer,* March, 16-19.

Chan, K.C., Chen, N., and Hsieh, D., 1983, "An Exploratory Investigation of the Firm Size Effect", *Manuscript, University of Chicago*, Cited in Dimsom, 1988.

Charest, Guy, 1978, "Dividend Information, Stock Returns, and Market Efficiency-II", *Journal of Financial Economics* 6,297-330.

Chaudhuri, S. K., 1991a, "Short-run Share Price Behaviour: New Evidences on Weak Form of Market Efficiency", *Vikalpa*, Vol. 16, No. 4, 17-21.

Chaudhuri, S. K., 1991b, "Seasonality in Share Returns: Preliminary Evidences on Day-of-the-Week Effect", *Chartered Accountant*, November, Vol. 40, No. 4, 407.

Cheng, Pao L. and Deets, M. King, 1970, "Portfolio Returns and the Random Walk Theory", *Journal of Finance,* 11-30.

Chowdhury, S.S.H., Sadique, M.S. and Akhter, M.S., 2002, "The Size Effect on the Speed of Stock Price Adjustment to Information in the Indian Stock Market", *Asian Economic Review*, 111-123.

Christie, A., Hertzel, M., 1981, "Capital Asset Pricing Anomalies", *University of Rochester, Working Paper*, Cited in Dimson, 1988.

Cochrane, John H., 1991, "Volatility Tests and Efficient Markets: A Review Essay", *Journal of Monetary Economics*-27,463-485.

Cochrane, John H., 1991a, "A Critique of the Application of Unit Root Tests", *Journal of Economic Dynamics and Control*, 15, 275-284.

Conrad, J. and Kaul, G., 1988, "Time-Variance in Expected Returns", *Journal of Business*, 61(4), 409-425.

Cooke, T.J., and Rozeff, M.S., 1984, "Size and Earnings/ Price Ratio Anomalies: One Effect or Two?", *Journal of Financial and Quantitative Analysis*.

Cooper, M., Gutierrez, Roberto C. and Marcum, Bill, 2005, "On the Predictability of Stock Returns in Real Time", *Journal of Business*, Vol. 78, No. 2, 469-499.

Cootner, Paul H., ed., 1964, *The Random Character of Stock- Market Prices*, Cambridge, Massachusetts, The M.I.T. Press.

Cox, John C. and Stephen, A. Ross, 1976, "The Valuation of Options for Alternative Stochastic Finance," *Journal of Financial Economics* 3, 145-166.

Damodaran, Aswath, 1993, "A Simple Measure of Price Adjustment Coefficients", *The Journal of Finance*, March, Vol. XLVIII, No. 1, 387-400.

Daniel, Kent, Hirshleifer, David, and Subrahmanyam, Avanidhar, 1997, "A Theory of Overconfidence, Self-attribution, and Security Market Under-and Over Reactions", *Unpublished Working Paper*, University of Michigan.

Dann, Larry V., 1981, "Common Stock Repurchases: An Analysis of Returns to Bondholders and Stockholders", *Journal of Financial Economics* 9, 113-138.

DeBondt, Werner F.M. and Thaler, Richard H., 1985, "Does the Stock Market Overreact?" *The Journal of Finance,* July, Vol-XL, No. 3, 793-805.

Dennis, Patrick J. and Strickland, Deon, 2002, "Who Blinks in Volatile Markets, Individuals or Institutions?", *The Journal of Finance*, October,Vol..LVII, No.5, 1923-1949.

Desai, Hemang, and Jain, Prem C., 1997, "Long-run Common Stock Returns Following Stock Splits and Reverse Splits", *Journal of Business,* Vol.70, 409-433.

Diba, Behzad T. and Grossman, Herschel I., 1987, "On the Inception of Rational Bubbles", *Quarterly Journal of Economics*, Aug 697-700.

Dickey, D. A. and Fuller, W. A., 1979, "Distribution of the Estimators in Autoregressive Time Series with a Unit Root", *Journal of the American Statistical Association*, Vol. 74, 427-431.

Dimson, Elroy (Ed.), 1988, *Stock Market Anomalies*, Cambridge University Press.

Dodd, Peter, 1980, "Merger Proposals, Management Discretion and Stockholder Wealth", *Journal of Financial Economics* 8, 105-137.

Edwards, Sebastian, Biscarri J.G. and Gracia F.P., 2003, "Stock Market Cycles, Financial Liberalisation and Volatility", published in *www.nber.org.*

Elton, E.J. and Gruber, M. J., 1975, *International Capital Market,*

Amsterdam: North Holland Publishing Co.

Fama, Eugene F. and French, Kenneth R., 1988(a), "Permanent and Temporary Components of Stock Prices", *Journal of Political Economy*, Vol. 96, No.2, 246-273.

Fama, Eugene F. and French, Kenneth R., 1988(b), "Dividends Yields and Expected Stock Returns", *The Journal of Financial Economics*, 22, 3-25.

Fama, Eugene F., 1965, "The Behaviour of Stock-Market Prices", *The Journal of Business*, January, Vol. XXXVIII, 34-105.

Fama, Eugene F., 1970, "Efficient Capital Markets: A Review of Theory and Empirical Work", *The Journal of Finance*, May, Vol. 25, 383-417.

Fama, Eugene F., 1976, *Foundations of Finance*, New York: Basic Books.

Fama, Eugene F., 1990, "Stock Returns, Expected Returns, and Real Activity", *The Journal of Finance,* Vol-45, 1089-1108.

Fama, Eugene F., 1991, "Efficient Capital Market: II", *The Journal of Finance*, December, Vol. 46(5), 1575-1617.

Fama, Eugene F., 1998, "Market Efficiency, Long-Term Returns, and Behavioural Finance, *Journal of Financial Economics*, 49, 283-306.

Fama, Eugene F., Fisher, Lawrence, Jensen, Michael C., and Roll, Richard, 1969, "The Adjustment of Stock Prices to New Information", *International Economic Review*, Vol. 10, No. 1, 1-21.

Feinstone, Lauren J., 1987, "Minute By Minute: Efficiency, Normality, and Randomness in Inta-Daily Asset Prices", *Journal of Applied Econometrics*, Vol. 2, 193-214.

Figlewski, Stephen, 1978, "Market 'Efficiency' in a Market with Heterogeneous Information", *Journal of Political Economy*, Vol.86, No. 4, 581-597.

Finnerty, Joseph E., 1976 b, "Insiders and Market Efficiency", *The Journal of Finance,* Vol-XXXI, No-4, September 1976, 1141-1148.

Fisher, Lawrence, 1996, "Some New Stock Market Indexes", *Journal of Business*, 39(2), 191-225.

Flavin, Marjorie, 1983, "Excess Volatility in the Financial Market: A Reassessment of the Empirical Evidence", *Journal of Political Economy,* Oct, 929-956.

Flood, Robert P. and Hodrick, Robert J., 1986, "Asset Price

Volatility, Bubbles and Process Switching", *Journal of Finance*, Vol-41, 831-842.

Fogler, H. Russell, 1978, *Analyzing the Stock Market: Statistical Evidence and Methodology*, Grid Inc., Columbus, Ohio.

Gaba, Prakash, 2003, "Reasons for Volatility in the Market", *Portfolio Organizer*, February, 51-52.

Givoly, Dan and Palmon, Dan, 1985, "Insider Trading and the Exploitation of Inside Information: Some Empirical Evidence", *The Journal of Business* 58(January), 69-87.

Godfrey, Michael D., Granger, Clive W. J. and Morgenstern, Oskar, 1964, "The Random-Walk Hypothesis of Stock Market Behavior", *Kyklos,* January, Vol. XVII, 1-30.

Goyal, M.M.,1992, "Security Returns in an Inefficient Market", *Indian Journal of Finance and Research*, July 1992, Vol. 2, No. 2, 61-67.

Graham, Benjamin, 1959, *The Intelligent Investor*, Harper and Row Brothers Publishing, New York.

Granger, Clive W. J. and Morgenstern, Oskar, 1963, "Spectral Analysis of New York Stock Market Prices", *Kyklos*, XVI, January, 1-27.

Gupta, L.C., 1992, *Stock Exchange Trading in India: Agenda for Reform*, Society for Capital Market Research and Development, Delhi.

Gupta, O.P., ed, 1989, *Stock Market Efficiency and Price Behaviour: The Indian Experience*, Anmol Publication, N. Delhi.

Gupta, O.P., 1985, *Behaviour of Share Prices in India- a Test of Market Efficiency*, National Publishing House, New Delhi.

Hariss, Lawerence, "Intra-Day Stock Return Patterns", *Cited in Dimson*, 1988.

Haugen, Robert A., 2002, *The Inefficient Stock Market*, Prentice-Hall, Upper Saddle River, NJ.

Haugen, Robert A., Talmor, Eli, and Torous, Waltmor N., 1991, "The Effect of Volatility Changes on the Level of Stock Prices and Subsequent Expected Returns", *Journal of Finance*, July, Vol-XLVI, No.-3, 985-1007.

Hausman, W. H., West, R.R. and Largay J. A., 1972, "Stock Splits, Price Changes, and Trading Profits: A Synthesis", *The Journal of Business*, 69-77.

Jaffe, Jeffrey F., 1974, "Special Information and Insider Trading", *The Journal of Business*, July, 410-428.

Jegadeesh, Narasimhan and Titman, Sheridan, 1993, "Returns to Buying Winners and Selling Losers: Implications for Stock Market Efficiency", *The Journal of Finance*, March, Vol. XLVIII, No. 1, 65-91.

Jensen, Michael C., 1968, "The performance of Mutual Funds in the Period 1945-1964", *The Journal of Finance*, 389-416.

Johnson, Keith B., 1966, "Stock Splits and Price Change", *The Journal of Finance*, December, Vol. XXI, 675-686.

Kaur, Harvinder, 2002, *Stock Market Volatility in India,* Deep & Deep Publication, Pvt. Ltd.

Keane, Simon M., 1983, *Stock Market Efficiency: Theory, Evidence and Implications*, Heritage Publishers.

Keim, D. W., 1982, "Size-Related Anomalies and Stock Returns Seasonality", *Journal of Financial Economics*, 12, 13-32.

Keim, Donald B., and Stambaugh, Robert F., 1984, "A Further Investigation of the Weekend Effect in Stock Returns", *Journal of Finance*.

Kendall, M. G., 1953, "The Analysis of Economics Time Series", *Journal of the Royal Statistical Society* (Series A), XCVI, 11-25.

Keynes, John M., 1936, *The General Theory of Employment, Interest, and Money,* Harcourt, Brace, and Company, New York.

Kuhn, F.S., 1970, *The Structure of Scientific Revolutions*, The University of Chicago Press. Chicago.

Laeven, Luc, 2003, "Does Financial Liberalisation Reduce Financing Constraints?", *Financial Management,* Spring, Vol. 32, Issue-1, 16-20.

Lai, E., Brooks, Robert and Faff, Robert, 2003, "Persistence and Predictability of Skewness in Country Equity Market Returns", *Journal of Quantitative Economics*, July, Vol. 1, No. 1, 36-51.

LeRoy, Stephen F., 1989, "Efficient Capital Markets and Martingales", *Journal of Economics Literature* 27, 1583-1621.

Lo, A. and Mackinlay, C., 1988, "Stock Market Prices Do Not Follow Random Walks: Evidence from a Simple Specification Test", *Review of Financial Studies* 1, 41-66.

Lo, A. and Mackinlay, C., 1989, "The Size and Power of the Variance Ratio Test in Finite Samples: A Monte Carlo Investigation", *The Journal of Econometrics*, Vol. 40, 203-238.

Ma, Shiguang, 2004, *The Efficiency of China's Stock Market*, Ashgate Publishing Ltd., England.

Madhusoodanan, T. P., 1995, "Overreaction Hypothesis and Winner-Loser Effect in Indian Stock Market Returns", *Indian Journal of Finance and Research*, July, Vol. VII, No. 2, 1-10.

Madhusoodanan, T. P., 1998, "Persistence in the Indian Stock Market Returns: An Application of Variance Ratio Test", *Viklpa,* Vol. 23, No. 4, 61-66.

Mahajan, Vinay, 2003, "Volatility Temptation: Everyone is Invited", *Portfolio Organizer,* April, 55-58.

Mahapatra, R. P., 1995, "Relative Strength in Performance of Share Prices in India: A Weak Form Test of Capital Market Efficiency", *Decision*, 22(3), 177-185.

Malik, N.S., 2006, "Active Portfolio Management: A Study of Country Funds of Developed and Emerging Markets of the World", ed. by O.P. Gupta and others.

Mandelbrot, Benito, 1966, "Forecast of Future Prices, Unbiased Markets and Martingale Models", *Journal of Business*, 39, Special Supplement (January), 242-255.

Masulis, Ronald W. and Korwar, Ashok W., 1986, "Seasoned Equity Offerings: An Empirical Investigation", *Journal of Financial Economics* 15, 91-118.

Mcqueen, Grant and Thorley, Steven, 1991, "Are Stock Returns Predictable? A Test Using Markov Chains", *The Journal of Finance*, March, Vol. XLVI, No. 1, 239-263.

Merville, Larry J. and Pieptea, Dan R., 1989, "Stock-Price Volatility, Mean-Reverting Diffusion, and Noise", *Journal of Financial Economics*, Vol. 24, 193-214.

Mohanty, Prabir Kumar and Kamaiah, B., 1997, "Volatility and its Persistence in the Indian Stock Market: A Case Study of 30 Scrips", *Journal of Foreign Exchange and International Finance*, Vol. XIII, No.4, 289-303.

National Stock Exchange Website; *www.nse-india.com*

Osborne, M. F., 1959, "Brownian Motion in the Stock Market, *Operations Research* 7, 145-173.

Pandey, I.M. and Bhat, Ramesh 1987, "Efficient Market Hypothesis: Understanding and Accepting in India, *Working Paper* No. 691, July-September, Indian Institute of Management, Ahmedabad.

Poterba, James M. and Summers, Lawrence H., 1988, "Mean Reversion in Stock Prices", *The Journal of Financial Economics*, 22, 27-59.

Poterba, James M. and Summers, Lawrence H.,1986, "The

Persistence of Volatility and Stock Market Fluctuations", *American Economic Review*, Vol 76 ,No-5, 1142-1151.

Ramasastri, A.S., 2001, "Stock Market Efficiency- Spectral Analysis", *Finance India*, September, Vol. XV, No. 3, 885-890.

Ranganatham, M. and Subramanian V., 1993, "Weak Form of Efficient Markets Hypothesis: A Spectral Analytic Investigation", *Vikalpa,* April-June, Vol. 18, No. 2, 25-30

Rao, Krishna N and Mukherjee, K., 1971, "Random-Walk Hypothesis: An Empirical Study", *Arthaniti,* Vol. 14, No. 1&2, 53-60.

Rao, Roshni, 2003, "Two-Day Delivery", *Capital Market*, March 3-16, 4-9.

Ray, D., 1976, Cited in *Stock Market Efficiency and Price Behaviour: The Indian Experience*, Anmol Publications, ed. by O.P. Gupta.

Reinganum, M.R., 1981 "Misspecification of Capital Asset Pricing: Empirical Anomalies Based on Earnings' Yields and Market Values", *Journal of Financial Economics* 9, March, 19-46.

Reinganum, M.R., 1982 "A Direct Test of Roll's Conjecture on the Firm Size Effect", *Journal of Finance.*

Reserve Bank of India Website; *www.rbi.org.in*

Roberts, H., 1959, "Stock-Market 'Patterns' and Financial Analysis: Methodological Suggestions", *Journal of Finance*, 14.1-10.

Roll, R., 1983, "Vas Is Das? The Turn of the Year Effect and the Return Premium of Small Firms", Journal of Portfolio Management, 9, 18-28.

Roll, Richard, 1981, "A Possible Explanation of the Small Firm Effect", *Journal of Finance.*

Roll, Richard, 1988, "R^2", *Journal of Finance, July*, Vol-XLII, No-3, 541-566.

Rosenberg, B. and Rudd, A., 1982, "Factor Related and Specific Returns of Common Stocks: Serial Correlation and Market Efficiency", Journal of Finance, May.

Roy, Malay K. and Karmakar, Madhusudan , 1995, "Stock Market Volatility: Root and Results", *Vikalpa,* Jan-Mar, Vol. 20, No. 1, 37-48.

Sahadevan, K. G. and Thiripalraju, M., 1995, "Money and Stock Prices: Some Empirical Evidences on Their Lead-Lag Relationship", *Indian Journal of Finance and Research*, January, Vol. VI, No. 1, 11-29.

Samanta, G. P., 2002, "Evolving Weak-Form Informational Efficiency of Indian Stock Market", *Journal of Quantitative Economics*, 66-75.

Samuelson, Paul A., 1965, "Proof That Properly Anticipated Prices Fluctuate Randomly", *Industrial Management Review*, 6, Spring, 41-49.

Santhapparaj, A. Solucis and Reddy, R. Sunayana, 2000, "Secondary Financial Market Efficiency in India: An Empirical Testing of Weak Form of Efficiency", *The Indian Journal of Commerce*, Jan-June 2000, Vol.53, Nos 1&2, 40-47.

Saxena, Anand and Gupta, O.P., 1992, "Stock Market Efficiency: Anomalous Price Behaviour-A Survey", *Indian Journal of Finance and Research*, July, Vol. 2, No. 2, 69-87.

Scholes, Myron S., 1972, "The Market for Securities: Substitution versus Price Pressure and the Effects of Information on Share Prices", *The Journal of Business*, April 1972, 179-212.

Schwert, G. William, 1989, "Why Does Stock Market Volatility Change Over Time?", *The Journal of Finance*, December, Vol. XLIV, No 5, 1115-1147.

Securities Exchange Board of India Website; *www.sebi.gov.in*

Seth, A. K., and Gupta, Saloni, 2005, "Understanding Volatility at BSE: A Quality Control Approach (Implications for Investors), *Decision*, Vol. 32, No.1, Jan-June.

Sharma, J.C., 2002, "Do Indian Stock Prices Follow Random Walk? An Enquiry", *Asian Economic Review*, 86-102.

Sharma, J.L. and Kennedy, E., 1977, "A Comparative Analysis of Stock Price Behaviour on the Bombay, London, and New York Stock Exchanges", *Journal of Financial and Quantitative Analysis*, September

Sharma, J.L., 1983, "Efficient Capital Markets and Random Character of Stock Price Behaviour in a Developing Economy", *The Indian Economic Journal*, Vol. 31, No. 2, October-December, 53-69.

Shiller, Robert J., 1981, "The Use of Volatility Measures in Assessing Market Efficiency", *The Journal of Finance*, May, Vol. XXXVI, No.2, 291-310.

Summers, Lawrence H., 1986, "Does the Stock Market Rationally Reflect Fundamental Values?", *The Journal of Finance*, July, Vol. 41, No. 3, 591-601.

Vaidynathan, R. and Gali, Kantikumar, 1994, "Efficiency of the

Indian Capital Market", *Indian Journal of Finance and Research* Vol V, No.-2, 27-40.

Vermaelen, Theo, 1981, "Common Stock Repurchases and Market Signalling: An Empirical Study", *Journal of Financial Economics* 9, 139-183.

Wallis, W. and Roberts, H., 1956, *Statistics: A New Approach*, Glencoe, III, Free Press.

West, Kenneth D., 1988, "Bubbles, Fads and Stock Market Volatility Tests: A Partial Evaluation, 1986", *The Journal of Finance*, July, Vol XLIII, No. 3,639-660.

Yalawar, Y.B., 1985, "Bombay Stock Exchange-Rate of Return and Efficiency", *Indian Economic Journal*, Vol-35, No-4, 68-121.

Index

Index